CONRAD'S POLISH
BACKGROUND

CONRAD'S POLISH BACKGROUND

LETTERS TO AND FROM POLISH FRIENDS

EDITED BY

ZDZISŁAW NAJDER

AND TRANSLATED BY

HALINA CARROLL

LONDON
OXFORD UNIVERSITY PRESS
NEW YORK   TORONTO
1964

Oxford University Press, Amen House, London E.C.4

GLASGOW NEW YORK TORONTO MELBOURNE WELLINGTON
BOMBAY CALCUTTA MADRAS KARACHI LAHORE DACCA
CAPE TOWN SALISBURY NAIROBI IBADAN ACCRA
KUALA LUMPUR HONG KONG

PRINTED IN GREAT BRITAIN

ACKNOWLEDGEMENTS

I WISH to express my deepest gratitude to all those who in various ways have helped me in preparing this book: they are too numerous to make a full list possible. My first thanks must go to Professor Sir Isaiah Berlin, who proposed the idea of this work. The Warden and the Fellows of St. Antony's College in Oxford, in offering me a research scholarship in philosophy and sympathetically tolerating my other activities, made the fulfilment of this project possible. And, above all, I enjoyed throughout the encouragement and unfaltering friendly assistance of Jocelyn Baines.

I am indebted to Miss Barbara Kocówna of the Department of Manuscripts of the National Library in Warsaw and to Miss Marjorie G. Wynne of the Rare Book Room in the Yale University Library for their help in making the Bobrowski and Conrad manuscripts, preserved in these libraries, easily available; and to the editorial staff of the Oxford University Press.

The translator of the texts, Mrs. Halina Carroll, wishes to express her gratitude to Mr. Jocelyn Baines and Mr. Norman Leggett for their patient help.

A NOTE ON THE TEXTS

THE present collection of letters and documents is in two parts. One consists of all hitherto discovered letters from Conrad to Polish addressees. Most were originally written in Polish, some in French, and a few in English; all have been specially translated for this edition and nearly all appear in English for the first time. Whenever possible, I checked the text, before translation, against the original, but unfortunately most of the original manuscripts were destroyed during the Second World War; the whereabouts of many others are unknown and therefore in most cases I had to rely on copies, published or unpublished. The source of the text is in every case given in a footnote.

The other part of the book consists of letters to and about Conrad, written by his uncles Tadeusz and Kazimierz Bobrowski, and of a 'Memorial' prepared for his nephew by Tadeusz Bobrowski. All texts in this part are based on original manuscripts. Their translation, however, presented certain difficulties. Tadeusz Bobrowski wrote in principle quite correctly, but not always with care; the translator had from time to time to make changes to make the author's idea comprehensible. Bobrowski's punctuation was highly idiosyncratic, and we have tried to preserve this peculiarity, within sensible limits. Writing about his life as a Polish nobleman in the Ukraine, Bobrowski used many words and notions which do not have their exact counterparts in English. The translator has aimed at preserving, at least partly, this exoticism of language and expression. An example of the attempts to preserve the authentic flavour of these letters is that we follow the old Polish custom of writing the pronouns referring to the members of the family with capital letters. Diminutives of first names, commonly used in Polish, are also preserved throughout.

CONTENTS

CONTENTS

INTRODUCTION

I

THE 'biographical' approach to literature and, more generally, the 'intentional fallacy' (which presupposes some knowledge of an author's mind) have been severely criticized in modern discussions on the theory of literary criticism. There are, however, cases where I think even the most ardent supporters of 'formalistic' schools of criticism would agree that knowledge of a writer's life, family background, &c., is important not only for a reconstruction, as far as this is possible, of his intentions, but for the understanding of his work not just in a personal but in a broader cultural sense.

Without dwelling on this complicated theoretical problem, I shall say that Joseph Conrad seems to present such a case. To understand what his work means, not in the sense of its reception nor in the terms of his presumed intentions, but in terms of what is the full implied cultural context of this work (its linguistic resources, literary forms and symbols, themes and motifs, &c.), we have to learn something about his national and social background.

Perhaps a few examples will help to elucidate my point. To understand (in the above sense of interpreting within a certain cultural context) Jane Austen or Hardy we do not need to know very much about their lives: dates of the particular books are almost sufficient. The rest will be supplied by our knowledge of English history and of other works of nineteenth-century English literature. It is impossible, however, to understand Conrad fully within any such uniform cultural framework. He seems to be a sort of self-translating author: a writer who conveys the experiences and conventions of one culture in the language of another. But even this suggests an over-simplification: Maupassant when translated presents an easily identifiable block of 'Frenchness' rendered in the English; Conrad presents a mixture of different and remote traditions. To call him a 'cosmopolitan of French culture', as Dr. Leavis does, is to describe him in much too crude and imprecise terms.

The difference between explaining a work of literature in personal and in generally cultural terms can be clearly shown by *Lord Jim*. The sense and—what follows—the literary value of this novel do not depend on whether it is or is not an expression of Conrad's personal feeling of guilt; they depend on the knowledge

of the literary and ideological origins of the general problems involved—on whether, for instance, we understand properly the way
in which the word 'romantic' (one of the key words of the book) is
used. And we cannot obtain this knowledge without learning about
Conrad's Polish background.

II

Joseph Conrad was born on 3 December 1857 at Berdyczów
(Ukrainian Berdichev) in Podolia,[1] son of Apollo Korzeniowski,
a writer and journalist, and Ewa Bobrowska, both members of the
Polish landowning nobility. The Korzeniowskis' record goes back
to the beginnings of the seventeenth century, when they were
already an established noble family of medium wealth and social
importance. They lost practically all their estates (by confiscation)
in the insurrections of 1794 and 1830. The Bobrowskis' background was similar but, thanks to their avoiding involvement in
uprisings, they preserved a handsome property.

On the occasion of Conrad's birth Apollo Korzeniowski wrote
a poem 'To My Son born in the 85th year of Muscovite oppression'.
In 1772 occurred the first partition of Poland by the neighbouring
states of Russia, Prussia, and Austria. In 1793 followed the second
and in 1795 the third and total partition. The once biggest and
most powerful continental European state ceased to exist; and its
downfall meant an end of the most liberal (Switzerland excepted)
governing system in Europe.

The most important part of Polish society was the landowning
nobility—the *szlachta*,[2] which formed, incidentally, a much larger
part of the whole population than did the French, German, or
English nobility and gentry. The nobility was the reigning cultural
force; the *bourgeois* element was to become more active only in the
eighteen-seventies. The life of the nation was therefore dominated
by the values now commonly called 'soldierly' and 'aristocratic',

[1] Podolia, Volhynia, and the Ukraine were the old provinces of what was then called
Ruthenia and is now commonly called the Ukraine. Until 1793 Ruthenia formed a part
of the United Kingdom of Poland and Lithuania. Her inhabitants were mainly Ukrainians
(or Ruthenians), but most of the landowners were Polish and Polish was the language
used by the educated classes.

[2] The term cannot be adequately rendered in English because there was no difference
in Poland between nobility and gentry: every member of the *szlachta* was legally equal
to any other member, however rich; there were no titles (apart from that of prince—
książę—given to royal cousins); any member of the *szlachta* could theoretically become
a member of the *Sejm* (Polish parliament, established in 1493) or even be elected a king.
Belonging to the *szlachta* was marked by possessing a coat of arms; every coat of arms had
a name and names of coats of arms were frequently used along with family names to
indicate belonging to a sort of a 'clan'. In this book the word 'nobility' is generally used as
a counterpart of *szlachta*, as etymologically analogous and closer in reference.

descending from the medieval ideals of chivalry. The material values of wealth and economic progress were pursued, if at all, rather shamefacedly and disregarded for the sake of more lofty and adventurous ideals of honour and duty; not a merchant or an industrialist but a soldier was held to be an example to follow. Such at least was the typical attitude. Money, of course, played its part as was the case everywhere—but it was never 'knighted', as for example in England. During the long years of foreign suppression, interrupted at least once in a generation by violent outbursts of patriotic insurrections and interwoven with an almost continuous thread of conspiracies and plots, that attitude was markedly strengthened and radicalized. At the same time Polish literature, and particularly poetry, came to play the role of a guide to the nation and a substitute for its normal political life. From the moment the Polish state fell in 1795 the function of preserving the national culture alive and united was taken over by literature. Small volumes of forbidden poetry and prose circulated in hand-written copies, with prison and hard labour threatening those who possessed them; they awakened national feelings and strengthened resistance. It was at that time that the notion of a *wieszcz*—a prophetic bard, a poet and spiritual and political leader of the nation—was born. In the years of a slackening in the oppressors' rule great political discussions, so disguised as to pass the censors' notice, took place in dramas and verse tales; elsewhere they would have found their place at the forum of a parliament or in inter-party debates. Literature, above all else, was *magister vitae*.

The Polish nobility in the Ukraine was very active in the anti-Russian insurrections of 1794 and 1830, and the feelings for independence were no less strong here than in ethnic Poland. The Poles were, however, divided both as to the methods of achieving independence and the degree hoped for. In general, three major groups may be distinguished. First, the appeasers, who wanted to preserve Polish national identity but within the scope of the Russian Empire (their most prominent representative was Count Aleksander Wielopolski, 1803–77). Secondly, the 'Whites' who thought about rebuilding the Polish Kingdom of the pre-partition time without basically changing its internal structure and preserving its feudal outlook; they relied heavily on the hope of foreign, mostly French and British, support of the Polish cause. Thirdly, there were the 'Reds' of various shades, who linked the fight for national independence with programmes for social reforms (particularly land reform and the abolishment of serfdom) and counted rather on a successful armed uprising than on the results of international political manœuvring. The appeasers were, of course, dead against the two other groups. However, even the two 'patriotic' groups, the Whites and the Reds, opposed each other violently, especially just before and in the early stages of the January 1863 insurrection.

The family tradition of the young Conrad was politically divided. The Korzeniowskis were ardent patriots and soldiers to a man, and Apollo was an outspoken left-wing member of the Reds. The attitude traditionally prevailing in the Bobrowski family was one of appeasement. Not that they were indifferent to the fate of the nation and to the social problems facing the nobility in the last years of feudal rule over the serfs, but they would put 'reason' and economic considerations before 'romantic follies'. Such at least was the attitude of Józef Bobrowski, Ewa's father, and of Tadeusz Bobrowski, her eldest brother, a judicious and stubborn man who dominated the whole family after his father's death. Both Józef and Tadeusz Bobrowski strongly opposed the marriage of Ewa to Apollo Korzeniowski, and it was only after old Bobrowski's death, and thanks to some help rendered to Tadeusz in his own marital plans, that the pair was allowed to be united. The relations between the two families however were never very cordial. The fact that Stefan Bobrowski (1840–63), Ewa's youngest brother and a man of quite exceptional abilities, became a prominent member of the Reds and a brave and skilful organizer of the underground Polish National Government, helped only to sharpen the division of opinions and attitudes.

The young Conrad, whose full name was Józef Teodor Konrad Korzeniowski, coat of arms Nałęcz, grew up in a tense emotional atmosphere. The political and moral traditions he was born into are well symbolized by his three Christian names: with his first name, given after his maternal grandfather, was connected a legacy of anti-romanticism, political opportunism, and enlightened conservatism in social opinions. The second name the boy received after his paternal grandfather, ex-captain of the Polish Army and a fervent patriot. But the most heavily loaded with meaning was his third name, which had been made popular in Poland by two heroes of Adam Mickiewicz's poems. The first one, the title-hero of a romantic tale in verse, *Konrad Wallenrod* (1827), is a Lithuanian who, captured as a boy by the German Knights of the Teutonic Order, stealthily becomes the Grand Master of the Order with the sole purpose of destroying it. The other and more important is the main character in Mickiewicz's great poetic drama 'The Fore-fathers' Eve' (*Dziady*, 1832). At the beginning of the action he bears the name of Gustaw and is a typical young romantic poet of Western

4

Introduction

European brand: a lonely egocentric, desperately in love, highly
self-conscious and endowed with fantastic imagination. Later,
under the impact of severe political persecutions to which he and his
friends are exposed, his personality and his poetry change abruptly.
Becoming aware of his national responsibilities he turns into a
romantic patriot, who is no longer isolated and self-centred: 'My
name is Million, because I suffer and am tortured for millions.'
He is still exceptional—but now not only because of an exceptional
sensibility, but primarily because of exceptional duties, imposed on
him by the fact that he is to represent his whole oppressed nation.

Apollo Korzeniowski and Ewa Bobrowska were married on
8 May 1856. For the first three years Apollo tried to continue to
work as an estate manager and leaseholder. However, his literary
activities and political interests were not compatible with that
earthbound occupation, and after losing almost all his money,
Ewa's dowry included, he moved with his family to Żytomierz,
then a centre of the intellectual life of the province. He was by that
time an established, if only *minorum gentium*, writer: he was the
author of two quite good satirical comedies and a number of poems,
mostly patriotic and some of burning social radicalism; and he
translated extensively from the French, concentrating especially on
Victor Hugo.

In the poem written to commemorate his son's baptism, Korzeniowski wrote:

My child, my son, if the enemy calls you a nobleman and a Christian
—tell yourself that you are a pagan and that your nobility is rot. . . . My
child, my son—tell yourself that you are without land, without love, without Fatherland, without humanity—as long as Poland, our Mother, is
enslaved.

Indeed, Conrad's early years can be looked on as almost symbolic in
the combination of national and personal tragedy.

On settling down in Żytomierz, Korzeniowski became directly
involved in underground political work. Massive patriotic demon-
strations in Warsaw in November 1860 and in April 1861, bloodily
suppressed, increased tension throughout the whole country. In
May 1861 Korzeniowski moved to Warsaw, apparently to establish a new literary fortnightly on the pattern of the *Revue des Deux
Mondes* but in fact to become one of the leaders of the Reds. His
wife, left behind in the Ukraine on her grandmother's estate,
Terechowa, wrote to him every few days. She did not suspect that
her letters, containing frequent mentions of Polish patriotic feelings
and Russian reprisals, would be additional evidence in the court case
against herself. These letters, tender and well written, confirm

what we know about Ewa Korzeniowska from other sources: they show her as an intelligent person of deep affections and a strong will. She enjoyed the reputation of a beautiful woman, exceptionally well educated, demanding much from herself, highly strung and self-sacrificing.

The little Conrad is frequently mentioned in his mother's letters: 'I am tired: I have spent the whole day sewing a mourning dress for Konradek [national mourning was being held for the demonstrators killed in Warsaw]. It is so black here—children too—that the boy asks for the mourning himself. . . . Love him and me . . .' (20 June 1861). 'Konrad grows up beautifully. He has a heart of gold, and with his conscience and intellect there won't be any difficulty with you working for his future' (5 July 1861). 'I feel that our dear Konradzio is going to be an exceptional man of heart' (8 July 1861).

Ewa and Conrad joined Apollo Korzeniowski in Warsaw at the beginning of October 1861. On the 17th of that month the underground City Committee—the kernel of the future National Government—was formed on Apollo's initiative, and four days later Korzeniowski was arrested and imprisoned in the Warsaw citadel.

He spent seven months in prison, suffering from scurvy and rheumatism. It is not clear whether Ewa was imprisoned as well; it is certain, however, that she was co-accused in the trial before a military tribunal and sentenced to exile together with her husband (not accompanying him voluntarily, as Conrad thought).[1] Indicted for several patriotic activities (fortunately the court did not know about many of more of them), Apollo and Ewa were sentenced to settlement in a distant province of the Empire.

With an escort of two policemen the Korzeniowskis left for their exile on 8 May 1862. First they were supposed to settle in the Perm province. General Lashkarev, however, the governor of Perm and a former schoolmate of Apollo, asked for a change of destination. From Nizhni Novgorod the exiles were therefore sent back to Vologda, famous for its bad climate; they arrived there on 16 June. On the way Ewa and Conrad became seriously ill. Apollo wrote to his cousins, Karol and Aniela Zagórski, upon arrival at Vologda:

---

[1] Record of the Permanent Investigating Commission, Part II, No. 4091, now in the Central Archives of Ancient Records (A.G.A.D.) in Warsaw. Mr. Jocelyn Baines (*Joseph Conrad*, p. 12) is mistaken in assuming that 'the court record is not conclusive evidence because the Russians had no desire to draw attention to people ready to become martyrs' —in fact, both investigation and court records were secret under martial law then in force. On the contrary, it was in the interest of the family to pretend that Ewa went into exile at her own wish.

Introduction

In Moscow the boy gets pneumonia; the doctor applies leeches and calomel. Better. Just then they start harnessing the horses. Naturally I protest against leaving, particularly as the doctor says openly that the child may die if we do so. My passive resistance postpones the departure but causes my guard to refer to the local authorities. The civilized oracle, after hearing the report, pronounces that we have to go at once—as children are born to die (*sic*). . . . In Nizhni Novgorod Ewusia fell ill. When they started to telegraph there and back asking if she could stay to be cured, a few days passed and, although they refused the permission, we learned in the meantime about the change in our destination.

During the journey the Korzeniowskis were helped on occasions by accidentally-met Russian regular army officers, friends of Ewa's late brother Stanisław, who had served in the Guards. In Vologda —where they met some twenty other Polish exiles—they were treated reasonably well, thanks to the humaneness of the governor, a White Ruthenian, Stanisław Chomiński. However, the climate was deadly—and deadly was the news from Poland. The insurrection began on 22 January 1863; after considerable success in the first days, the four-to-one numerical superiority of the Russian regular troops over the partisans, a lack of sufficient military training and of artillery, internal quarrels, and the indifference of Western powers, checked the successful progress of the uprising. The Russians fought back brutally and mercilessly, and after two years of bloodshed suppressed the movement. A long period of ruthless reprisals followed; however, the achievement of the 1863 insurrection was by no means negligible. The underground National Government acquired amazingly powerful authority, reviving the traditions of administrative independence; and the decree abolishing serfdom, proclaimed by this Government, marks a milestone on the road to the formation of the modern Polish nation. The importance of the uprising for subsequent Polish social, cultural, and political history can be compared only to the impact of the Civil War on the history of the United States.

In the bleak months of 1863 the exiles did not look at events from an historical point of view: what they saw was simply the ruin of their dearest hopes. Moreover, both families suffered heavy losses: Stefan Bobrowski was murdered by his right-wing political opponents in a staged duel; his brother Kazimierz was imprisoned; Apollo's father Teodor died on his way to join the partisans; one of Apollo's brothers, Robert, was killed in battle; another, Hilary, was sent into exile. A tone of despair (muffled, because of the censorship of the mail) is in Apollo's letters to his friends and the family. From that period is preserved[1] an affecting memento in the form of

[1] Now in Yale University Library.

7

Conrad's oldest existing autograph, inscribed on the back of a photograph: 'To my beloved Grandma who helped me send cakes to my poor Daddy in prison—grandson, Pole, Catholic, nobleman—6 July 1863—Konrad.'

Ewa's health deteriorated visibly: she had tuberculosis and required special attention and medical care. Fortunately the Korzeniowskis succeeded, again thanks to the help of the late Stanisław Bobrowski's friends, in obtaining permission to move to Chernikhov, much farther south. Ewa and her son were even allowed to visit their family in Nowofastów, Tadeusz Bobrowski's estate between Berdichev and Kiev: Bobrowski enjoyed a good political reputation with the authorities. After three months, however, in spite of an attack of illness, Ewa was ordered to go back to Chernikhov. The visit to his uncle's home provided Conrad with his earliest recorded reminiscences, told in *A Personal Record*. It was there that he met his great-uncle Mikołaj Bobrowski, an ex-Napoleonic soldier, whose misfortunes he describes so vividly.

In Chernikhov Apollo occupied himself with translating Victor Hugo's *Les Travailleurs de la mer*, Dickens's *Hard Times*, and Shakespeare's *The Comedy of Errors*; he was also writing bitterly anti-Russian memoirs, entitled *Poland and Muscovy*, where he argues that while the history of mankind is a history of the struggle between barbarism and civilization, Tsarist Russia is the contemporary embodiment of the former.

After the return to Chernikhov, Ewa's health declined rapidly. 'For several years', wrote Apollo on 26 February 1865 to his friend Kazimierz Kaszewski, 'nostalgia and the repeated blows falling on our families have been slowly killing my wife. For the last few months critically ill, confined to her bed—she is barely strong enough to glance at me, to speak with muted voice. Only today has she been permitted to go to Kiev for a cure, but lack of strength does not allow her to . . . . Konradek is inevitably neglected.'

Conrad's mother died on 18 April 1865, at the age of thirty-two. She was the only member of his whole family who seems to have been unanimously and consistently praised. Conrad did not remember her well, although he was seven and a half at the time she died. Probably his reminiscences of those years were obscured in a mist of grief and poverty. Apollo, who was consumptive himself, collapsed after the death of his wife, and for some time only the thought of his son seemed to keep him alive. He continued to work on his translations and tried to give Conrad some rudiments of education. In letters to Kaszewski he asks frequently for school manuals and pedagogical advice. '. . . my dear little boy looks after me—there are only two of us here. I shall not be ashamed of his heart; he has his Mother's talents—but a head not to be envied: mine' (31 Oct. 1865). They both read a lot. Conrad remembered in an interview given in 1914: 'My father read me *Pan Tadeusz*[1] and asked me to read it aloud too. More than once. I preferred *Konrad Wallenrod* and *Grażyna*.[2] Later I preferred Słowacki. Do you know why Słowacki? Il est l'âme de toute la Pologne, lui.'

Apollo turned to sombre religiosity; even his patriotism, practical and socially conscious before, now became permeated with mysticism: he saw no hope in this world and desperately sought for it in the idea of divine purpose. He realized only too well that the atmosphere at home was too morbid for his son: the child had no friends of his age and 'grew up as though in a monastic cell'. So in May 1866 he sent the boy with his grandmother, Teofila Bobrowska, to Nowofastów, Tadeusz Bobrowski's estate. Conrad met there Tadeusz's daughter Józefa (Józia, Józieczka), a year older than himself; and it was probably during this visit that he saw Prince Roman Sanguszko, the hero of his *Prince Roman*. Accompanied by his grandmother he went back to Chernikhov in the autumn, but only for a short time: because of poor health he was taken first to Kiev for a medical consultation, and then to Nowofastów for treatment at home. Apollo later described his ailment as 'an illness very rare with children: gravel forms in his bladder and causes gripes' (letter to Kaszewski, summer 1868). This is the first time we hear about the mysterious afflictions suffered by Conrad for several years. His complaints, differently and vaguely described by various witnesses, often prevented him from participating in a normal child's life, and particularly from learning and attending schools. (In the letter just quoted, Apollo writes that Conrad 'has not studied for almost two years' for reasons of health.) However, the conjectural evidence suggests that Conrad's ailment was of the epilepsy type. He grew out of it at the age of fourteen, or possibly later.[3]

---

[1] Adam Mickiewicz's greatest work, an epic in twelve parts (1834). English prose translation by A. R. Noyes, Everyman's Library.

[2] Mickiewicz's historical tale in verse (1823); the heroine prevents her husband, a medieval Lithuanian prince, from making a fratricidal alliance with the Teutonic Order and is killed in a battle against the Germans.

[3] This new and interesting possibility requires a more detailed discussion. Conrad's excessive nervousness is invariably mentioned in the reminiscences of people who knew him as a child. Tadeusz Bobrowski, writing to Conrad about his health in the first preserved letter to him, says significantly: '. . . you may become completely well—not giving way to feelings and thoughts which are not really proper to your age' (8/20 Sept. 1869; p. 36). Mrs. Halina Carroll, working on the translation of Bobrowski's letters, directed my attention to the information they contained about the illness of Bobrowski's other nephew, his brother Kazimierz's youngest son Michaś. This illness is plainly described as epilepsy, and the whole family was worried that the boy would be mentally

Apparently Conrad missed his father intensely, in spite of a much gayer life in Nowofastów. They were reunited only after a year, in the autumn of 1867, when Apollo, already ill beyond hope of recovery, obtained permission to leave Chernikhov and go abroad. The doctors advised Madeira, but he had neither money nor strength to go there and settled with Conrad in Lvov, then under the Austrian (infinitely more liberal than the Russian) occupation. The cautious, pedestrian, and at the same time complacent mood prevailing in Galicia[1] was hateful to the tortured exile, but Apollo's very bitterness was a sign of spiritual recovery. He became socially active, met many people, established new contacts, and planned to launch a new democratic daily, *Kraj* ('The Country'), in Cracow. His letters of this period, and the reminiscences of his closest friends, present a quite different picture from the brooding melancholiac, consumed by despair and religious mania, described in Tadeusz Bobrowski's *Memoirs*. Conrad's own recollections of his father's last months are strangely one-sided and blurred; no wonder, however, that the sickly boy remembered better his father's gloom than his feverish activities.

Conrad did not attend classes, as Apollo was horrified by the Germanization of the Polish schools in Lvov. He studied at home, irregularly because of poor health. 'He is fairly able', reported Apollo to Kaszewski, 'but so far does not show a liking for study, and there is nothing definite in him yet' (24 Dec. 1868). To this time, according to four independent witnesses,[2] belong Conrad's first literary efforts: he started writing plays, invariably of patriotic content, which were performed by his friends. Apollo wrote to Stefan Buszczyński: 'Konradek is going to write to you. He writes without my encouragement, and writes well' (10 May 1868). He liked to recite poems, particularly Mickiewicz, and had the reputation of an exceptionally sensitive child and a book-devourer.

retarded (letter of 26 Dec./7 Jan. 1892; p. 160). Now Bobrowski states openly that Conrad's case was similar: 'The youngest, Michaś, may be suffering from the same illness as you were—anyway he had a similar fit to yours in the autumn. The only difference is that the symptoms appeared much later than in your case and this makes one wonder if he will grow out of it by the age of fourteen, as you did?' (20 Nov./2 Dec. 1891; p. 158). Michaś was at that time eleven. About Conrad's illness we hear first when he is less than nine; there are, however, reliable indications that he was unwell after the age of fourteen (e.g., in a letter of his tutor Marek Pulman, of 3 March [1874], now in Yale University Library).

Lastly, we find a confirmation of Bobrowski's allusions in the recollections (otherwise not always trustworthy) of Mrs. Tekla Wojakowska. She remembered that in 1873 Conrad would have 'frequent attacks of migraine and nervous fits'; S. Czosnowski, 'Conradiana', *Epoka*, 1929, No. 136.

[1] The official name of the southern part of Poland occupied by Austria.

[2] Mrs. Jadwiga Kałuska, Zygmunt Radzimiński, Leon Syroczyński, and Mrs. Tekla Wojakowska (cf. Bibliography). It is, however, difficult to assess whether these recollections do not refer rather to Conrad's second stay in Lvov, in 1873–4.

In February 1869 Apollo fulfilled his long-held desire and moved, together with Conrad, to Cracow—then the cultural capital of Galicia. He was busy with the newly born *Kraj*, but not for long. His health deteriorated during the spring and soon he was confined to bed. Conrad was apparently attending school. Many years later he recalled these months in *A Personal Record*—but his reminiscences are not wholly reliable. Apollo did not in fact destroy all his manuscripts a fortnight before he died; they were entrusted to Stefan Buszczyński, the poet's closest friend, and Conrad himself had an opportunity of seeing them in 1914, preserved in the Jagiellonian Library in Cracow.

Apollo Korzeniowski died on 23 May 1869. He did not die a broken man, although his son might well have thought so later. The funeral took the form of an enormous patriotic manifestation: a silent tribute to the man who had burned himself out in the service of his nation. Conrad walked at the head of the cortège. According to his grandmother he was in utter, inconsolable despair.

It is doubtful if he ever understood his father: he was too young at the time Apollo died, and soon afterwards he came under the powerful influence of a man whose political opinions and emotional attitude were the exact opposite: his uncle Tadeusz Bobrowski. To sympathize with Apollo's desperate determination to subordinate his whole life to a common cause one had to understand his reasons and to share, at least partly, his beliefs. Bobrowski did not share them and hardly ever tried to discover what had led Apollo to his extreme political views. His idea of his brother-in-law as a woolly-headed sentimentalist, who pitied the poor but was not in fact a true democrat or a man who understood politics, is plainly belied by many of Korzeniowski's manuscripts. But if Apollo's beliefs were seen as nonsensical or capricious, then his whole life, into which he had drawn his wife, must have appeared one of cruel folly.

Thus his father's heritage was for Conrad a cause of strong internal conflict. On the one hand he could not escape the powerful appeal of Apollo's fascinating personality and of the heroic fidelity with which he had served to the tragic end the ideals of patriotism as he had conceived them. On the other hand he was by no means sure if these ideals had had any reasonable basis. Conrad's father must have seemed to him at once awe-inspiring and absurd; his attitude towards him was a mixture of admiration and contemptuous pity. And he could never forgive his father the death of his mother.

Conrad's first guardian was Stefan Buszczyński but, probably under Tadeusz Bobrowski's influence, his family soon designated as his legal guardians Mrs. Teofila Bobrowska and Count Władysław

Mniszek. He was placed in a boarding-house run by Ludwik Georgeon in Floriańska Street in Cracow. It was not possible to send him to a gymnasium [i.e. high school] as he lacked the necessary knowledge of German and Latin. His grandmother, who stayed in Cracow till December, was worried by his poor health. A certain Adam Marek Pulman (born in 1846), a medical student at the Jagiellonian University, was chosen to be his private tutor. They went together for a summer holiday to Krynica, a well-known spa in the Carpathian Mountains. In the autumn of 1870 Conrad apparently passed an examination to the fourth form of St. Anne's Gymnasium, but he never attended it.[1] It is possible that he was sent to the other secondary school for boys in Cracow, St. Jacek's Gymnasium, which was nearer his home. However, nothing definite is known about his studies, and it may be that he did not at that time attend any school at all. We read in Bobrowski's 'Document' that both in 1871 and 1872 Conrad went to Krynica as early as May; we can assume, therefore, that his studies must have been, at best, irregular. In fact, the three years spent in Cracow are the period in Conrad's life about which we know least. Almost the only certainty is that his uncle's attempts to secure Austrian citizenship for him failed in 1872. This refusal was probably the turning point in Conrad's life: it meant that he could not stay indefinitely in ethnic Poland without risking possibly as many as 25 years of military service in the Russian army, to which he was liable as the son of a convict.

His grandmother returned to Cracow in December 1870 to take better care of the boy, and remained there till the summer of 1873. That summer Conrad went for his first trip abroad and stayed, again with Pulman, for three months in Switzerland. On coming back in August he was sent to Lvov, to a boarding-house for orphans of the 1863 insurrection, directed by Conrad's distant cousin Antoni Syroczyński ('Uncle Antoni'). The reasons for this decision were probably not financial (as Baines suspects) but disciplinary: Conrad was becoming a troublesome child and seemed to require a hand stronger than his grandmother's.

On the basis of various reminiscences—unfortunately those who knew Conrad best did not leave any—it is possible to construct a fairly reliable picture of Conrad in his teens. He was a solitary boy, rather capricious and certainly egocentric. Intelligent and well-read,

---

1 There is no mention of Conrad's name in the fully preserved archives of the school; nor do we find there the names of Konstanty Buszczyński and the Taube boys, known to have been Conrad's friends. However, Tadeusz Żuk-Skarszewski (cf. Bibliography) has apparently seen a document (now lost) stating that Conrad passed the examination to the fourth form.

hypersensitive, accustomed to the company of grown-ups and to being confided in by his father, well aware of his unusual past— he was at the same time retarded in his school studies, and treated as a child. All that, taken together, must have developed in him a feeling of being underestimated and misunderstood. The tension between him and his environment was probably very high: the son of Apollo Korzeniowski must have regarded himself as different from and superior to the tame Galician Philistines. He felt like a high-flying bird kept among the fowls.

Mrs. Tekla Wojakowska (née Syroczyńska) remembered: 'Intellectually well developed, he hated the rigours of school, which tired and bored him; he used to say that he had a great talent and would become a great writer. This, coupled with a sarcastic smile on his face and frequent critical remarks on everything, provoked surprise in his teachers and ridicule among his colleagues. He liked always to be untrammelled and at school, at home, or on a visit preferred to lounge rather than sit.' He had very few friends: Stefan Buszczyński's son Konstanty ('Kocio') and perhaps some of the numerous family of the Taubes, who lived in the same building to which Mr. Georgeon's boarding-house moved in 1871, in Franciszkańska Street. It has been frequently assumed that he was in love with one of the Taube sisters, Janina, later Baroness de Brunnow, but there is no evidence to support this hypothesis. Apparently he had some flirtation with Antoni Syroczyński's daughter Tekla in Lvov and was severely reprimanded by her father.[1] The only documentary evidence concerning the young Conrad's emotional attachments in Poland is, however, to be found in his own confessions in the Author's Note to *Nostromo* and in a cancelled opening to *The Arrow of Gold*.

After a few months spent in Lvov Conrad was again compelled to interrupt his studies because of severe attacks of migraine, and perhaps because of some other ailment. The summer of 1874 he spent with Pulman somewhere in the country. Then he went back to Cracow, whence his uncle Tadeusz, yielding to a two-years' pestering and to doctors' advice, dispatched him to Marseilles, to become a sailor.

Conrad's biographers have discussed at length what his reasons may have been for deciding to leave Poland and go to sea. It would be a waste of time to dwell on the various far-fetched and anachronistic hypotheses proposed, as it is possible to explain the whole problem in simple terms, without resorting to speculation. Going

---

[1] From information provided by Mr. Tadeusz Garczyński, a cousin of the Syroczyńskis.

abroad was a rather obvious thing to do for a young exile, a Russian subject eligible for military service in the army of the hated oppressor. Dreaming about adventures and a life out of the ordinary is, again, quite normal among young men of all nations and times. In Conrad's case the dreams must have been reinforced by his feeling of being misunderstood and superior, and out of tune with his environment. It is obvious that he wanted to say good-bye to it all— to free himself from restrictions and constant surveillance, to be independent in his actions as he felt himself to be independent in his thoughts and emotions. That he decided to go to sea was perhaps a matter of chance rather than a deliberate choice of profession. Had Conrad felt a vocation to become a seaman, he would not have mentioned so often in his letters to his uncle various other projects and possibilities; indeed, frequently it was Bobrowski himself who reminded Conrad that he should spend less time on shore and more under sail. Only much later does Conrad seem to have acquired a stronger passion for his profession.

His uncle's reasons for granting him, very reluctantly, permission to go abroad even before finishing his secondary education were of course quite different. The most important one was Conrad's health: the doctors seem to have been convinced that the sea air and plenty of physical exercise were going to restore the boy's nervous balance and put an end to the recurring attacks of migraine. It is now impossible to ascertain to what extent Conrad's laziness and egocentricity made the situation worse, but the fact was that he did not make much progress in his school work. The year in Lvov was supposed to be his last but one in a gymnasium, but he did not pass to the next form and in the summer of 1874 was still facing two years of study. Thus there was little choice but to let him go.

There were other reasons as well. Bobrowski could not look after his nephew himself without taking the risk of bringing him back into Russia. Cracow was evidently no good, Grandma Bobrowska too lenient, and in Lvov Mr. Syroczyński had had enough of Conrad. To let the troublesome boy go was obviously the simplest way of dealing with him. Bobrowski probably thought that faced with the difficulties of adult life, Conrad would become more responsible, would even perhaps return, chastened and meek, after a few months of 'adventures'. And so in October 1874 Conrad, not yet seventeen, found himself in Marseilles, alone and free, and reasonably well equipped with money.

Introduction

III

What was his cultural equipment for this journey, from which he was never to return for good? Nothing definite is known about the programme of his school studies but he did not take them very seriously, and anyway the reading of Livy or Klopstock could not have had much influence on him. It is more important to describe the type of literature which he must have read, living in Poland at that particular time and with his particular family background. The reflections of his reading are easily visible in his works to an 'armed vision'; we have only to understand precisely what it is that is being reflected.

'Polonism I have taken into my works from Mickiewicz and Słowacki', confessed Conrad in 1914. They were the leaders of Polish romantic literature, and romanticism was still very much alive in Poland in the late 'sixties and early 'seventies: not only as a source of inspiration for legions of epigones, but primarily as providing a paradigm of the social role of literature and standards for the evaluation of all future achievements.

Ideas of moral and national responsibility pervaded this literature: it would be difficult to find a major work in which the two types of duty were not closely linked. It meant that the moral problems of an individual were posed in terms of the social results of his actions; and ethical principles were based on the idea that an individual, however exceptional he might be, is always a member of a group, responsible for its welfare. A poet was a typical example of such an exceptional individual, burdened with special duties to his nation.

Thus, for example, the main character of Mickiewicz's greatest work *Pan Tadeusz*, Jacek Soplica, alias Father Robak, is shown as trying to atone, by many years of heroic service to Poland, for a moment of weakness in his youth when his private feelings made him forget his national obligations: a perfect forerunner of Conrad's Jim. The hero of Juliusz Słowacki's drama *Kordian* wanders forlornly around Europe, a typical romantic 'lost soul', till he realizes that he can find his moral identity only in fighting for his country's freedom. Słowacki, whom Conrad particularly liked, was an exquisite stylist, combining an exuberant, baroque imagery with a sharp and relentless eye for the problems of individual responsibility, power, and social justice. His broad descriptions of nature (particularly of the limitless and wild Ukrainian landscape) are usually a part of the psychological action of a poem; the fury of the elements—tempests or fires—is for him a magnificent background for the human drama.

Słowacki was a radical democrat and an anti-clerical, and in that strongly opposed to another great Polish romanticist, Zygmunt Krasiński (1812–59). This unhappy and disillusioned aristocrat gave in his best work, a poetic drama in prose, *The Un-Divine Comedy* (1835), a bitter and devastating criticism of the old feudal order and of the new forces which were bringing this order down. The old world of class privileges and economic inequality, frequently so charming on the surface, is totally rotten and evil beyond any possibility of improvement; but the emerging vengeful masses bring, according to Krasiński, only destruction and chaos. The only hope lies in the idea of Christianity—but Krasiński himself did not give any indication how this idea could be implemented in a world torn by hate and greed. He saw with rare lucidity the cruel injustice of the feudal order, but at the same time had no illusions about the prospects of 'progress', conceived in purely economic terms. He prophesied the destruction of the beauties of the old world and the coming of the kingdom of 'material interests' (to use Conrad's expression).

It is certain that Conrad knew the works of Mickiewicz, Słowacki, and Krasiński: they formed the basic reading of every educated Pole. But it is obvious that he must have read much more of Polish literature. For instance, in a letter to Edward Garnett (20 Jan. 1900) he comments on Jan Kochanowski (1530–84), a great Renaissance poet, and on his namesake Józef Korzeniowski (1797–1863), a novelist. But it is not his knowledge of one writer or another which is important: it is the fact that when leaving Poland Conrad was undoubtedly well acquainted with a rich and lively literary tradition, to a marked extent unified by distinctive characteristics in its moral and political attitudes. It was a serious literature, obsessed by the idea of responsibility—but by no means shrinking from artistic experiments and variety of form.

About the middle of the century one of the more popular genres was the *gawęda* (tale). It was a story told—in prose or in verse—by some clearly defined person, whose point of view usually played an important role. Most of these tales were 'reminiscences' of old soldiers, friars, or travellers; they provided splendid opportunities for stylistic *tours de force*, particularly interesting, as in the case of Henryk Rzewuski's (1791–1866) famous *Pamiątki Soplicy* ('Soplica's Memories', 1839), when the author's own opinions were skilfully suggested by the enunciations of his narrator. In some cases a 'tale' inserted in a larger work was used as a vehicle to convey the moral or political significance of the whole: such a role is played by 'Robak's confession' in *Pan Tadeusz* or by 'Halban's song' in

Konrad Wallenrod. To whatever extent, therefore, Marlow may owe his existence to his creator's theoretical considerations or to the example of the narrative structure in some of Henry James's novels, he had his way well prepared by Conrad's early Polish readings.

IV

For nineteen years, from 1874, Conrad's main link with Poland was his correspondence with his uncle and guardian, Tadeusz Bobrowski. The story of their relationship is told in Bobrowski's letters; Conrad's letters perished in the revolution of 1917. In the first years the relations were, to say the least, strained; only later the two lonely men (Bobrowski was very early widowed and lost his only child in 1870) were drawn together—probably more by the fact of their respective isolation than by any psychological affinities. It was characteristic of Bobrowski that he had no close friends, but many acquaintances who knew that they could rely on this rigorous and honest lawyer (he graduated in law at St. Petersburg University but had to give up his promising career to become the head of the family after his father's death). His *Memoirs*, published in 1900, created an uproar: they are full of malicious gossip and scornful opinions about most of the people he knew. The frustration of a clever man, self-confident to the point of conceit, who never achieved anything 'great' and was never sufficiently appreciated by his contemporaries, is clearly seen. He himself has written a pithy self-portrait: 'a doctrinaire pur sang, absolutely convinced of the unshakeable laws and duties of reason, criticism and free will . . . and rejecting all external influences of feeling, passions, and one's environment, possessing for every problem of life a ready formula obtained by abstract reasoning'.[1] We have to bear this confession in mind when reading his letters to his nephew: Bobrowski could be very tendentious.

This is most clearly seen in the case of two related issues: politics and family tradition. Bobrowski was a convinced opponent of the 1863 insurrection and generally of all projects for regaining the independence of Poland by force. He was equally strongly opposed to all socially radical movements. This opposition—strangely violent in an apostle of reason—led him not only to considering all people who thought differently to be either mad or dishonest, but sometimes also to altering, in his memoirs or letters, facts which did not suit his own views. I have already mentioned that his reports on Conrad's father are tendentious and frequently false. He never told Conrad the truth about his mother's clandestine activities.

[1] T. Bobrowski, *Pamiętniki*, Lvov, 1900, ii. 27.

Moreover, in his *Memoirs* Bobrowski 'rectifies' the political attitude of his brother Stefan (who at the time of the murderous 'duel' was head of the underground National Government), maintaining that he was an 'anti-Jacobin' leader—while in fact Stefan Bobrowski was the chief of the underground Left.

These examples (which can be multiplied) show not only the strength of Bobrowski's political prejudices but also the extent to which he was ready to sacrifice truth for the sake of a family mythology. Drawing a comparison between the families of the Bobrowskis and the Korzeniowskis (or 'the Nałęczs', from their coat of arms) is a recurrent motif in Bobrowski's letters to Conrad. The result is always to the Korzeniowskis' disadvantage: they are shown to be irresponsible visionaries with little strength of will or sense of duty, impulsive, and capricious; the Bobrowskis, on the contrary, are supposed to be reasonable, cool-headed, hard-working, and generally reliable. The facts, however, are far from being so simple. On the one hand, the Korzeniowskis' 'irresponsibility' manifested itself mainly in their taking part in the consecutive national insurrections, in which they lost most of their estates. They might have been capricious and inclined to dreaming, but their personal misfortunes were due mainly to the fact that they spent time, energy, and money trying to serve their country as well as they could. On the other hand, the maternal side of Conrad's family was by no means free of the characteristics allotted by Bobrowski solely to the Korzeniowskis. Two of his own brothers, Kazimierz and Stefan, were moulded rather according to the 'Nałęcz' pattern; and one of his maternal uncles, Seweryn Pilchowski, was a notorious adventurer—pseudo-mystic, liar, and embezzler. We do not hear anything about him from the garrulous author of the *Memoirs*.

Conrad's knowledge of his family background was, of course, to a large extent based on whatever Bobrowski told him. And his uncle was particularly indignant about Conrad's father. It is impossible to say whether it was a difference of views and temperaments, or subconscious envy, or yet something else, that caused Bobrowski to be so set against Apollo, who was in fact a much worthier, more sensible and distinguished man than Bobrowski showed him to be.

Bobrowski's didactic endeavours were not limited to politics and family tradition; sermonizing Conrad on the vices of the Korzeniowskis was an element in Bobrowski's general 'educational' pattern. In spite of his frequent protestations that he does not want to influence Conrad's way of life, it is obvious that he had a definite idea of what he wanted his nephew to be like. He did not at all object to Conrad's 'cosmopolitan career' (p. 51), nor even to his project of 'becoming a Yankee' (p. 65): on the contrary, he urged him constantly to obtain some foreign citizenship, mainly to enable Conrad to enter Russia safely. The career he wanted Conrad to pursue was to combine being a sailor and a salesman (p. 59). He wished his nephew to be sober-minded, 'realistic', and stable in his plans, and not to indulge in thoughts about 'things you cannot change'.

We find the fullest exposition of Bobrowski's view of life in his letter of 9 November 1891, written in reply to Conrad's 'pessimistic' meditations. The letter is very well worth reading, because it presents an interesting parallel to the memorable conversation between Stein and Marlow in *Lord Jim*. The analogy suggests itself by the motto *usque ad finem*, which both Bobrowski and Stein think ought to be the guiding principle in life.[1] But the ideals worth pursuing *usque ad finem* are for them very different: for Bobrowski it is resignation and duty; for Stein, following one's romantic 'dream', which may never come true but which still gives our life its sense. What Bobrowski tries to persuade Conrad to do in this letter is to take reality as it is, without complaining too much and without wanting to change it radically. It is by no means a gospel of optimism or even courage: it is a gospel of resignation; he does not attempt seriously to convince his nephew that the world is better than he thinks, but only that he cannot help it being as it is. In one word, Bobrowski contrasts his 'realism' with Conrad's 'romanticism'.

This Stoic sermon was not very successful: Conrad remained a romantic. But Bobrowski was not quite right when he blamed Conrad's innate disposition for his pessimism: he had contributed to it himself—first by his sarcastic criticism of Conrad's tragic family background, and secondly by mercilessly attacking all 'illusions' about the world and hopes for a possibility of basic improvements. Mickiewicz taught 'let our aims be the measure of our strength'; for Bobrowski nothing could have been more horrifying than this brave motto. It is likely that from Bobrowski's exhortations originated what was to become the curse of Conrad's inner life and the bitter inspiration of his art: his deep scepticism, frequently tinged with pessimism. Believing in the necessity for 'dreams' and ideals, and knowing them to be illusions, Conrad seems to have listened both to Mickiewicz and to Bobrowski. Whatever may have been the other merits and faults of Bobrowski's influence these two seem to have been by far the most important.

[1] Cf. Baines, *Joseph Conrad*, p. 126.

Apart from being a fascinating source for studying the formation of Conrad's personality and his *Weltanschauung*, Bobrowski's letters are a mine of factual information about Conrad's earlier years. In fact, most of what we know of Conrad's life between 1874 and 1894 comes from his uncle's letters to him and to Stefan Buszczyński. Two letters to Buszczyński contain invaluable and first-hand information about Conrad's stay in Marseilles and his beginnings as a sailor; we find in them the first full-scale report on Conrad's character, and it is these letters which prove beyond any doubt that the 'duel' described by Conrad in the pseudo-autobiographical *The Arrow of Gold* was in fact an attempted suicide.

Naturally, Bobrowski's letters to Conrad contain little direct information about their addressee. Still, from allusions, discussions, answers to questions, and quotations from Conrad's own letters we can learn or deduce a lot, as the case of Conrad's epilepsy bears witness. We read, for instance, about the constant changes in Conrad's plans for his future—which demonstrates that he did not treat his sea-going career as the only possible one, and was constantly on the look-out for something more stable. We get valuable information on the autobiographical background of *Youth* and *The Heart of Darkness* (as in Bobrowski's sardonic remark on Conrad's 'civilizing affair', p. 129). Conrad's romance with Mme Poradowska is warningly discussed by Bobrowski, who seldom spared his nephew admonitions, illustrating them, to our delight, with factual examples and essays in Conrad's psychology. True, these letters contain much uninteresting family gossip and complaints about the sender's health; 'the illusion of conversation makes my heart lighter', confessed Bobrowski. The value of the whole correspondence, however, seemed to be a sufficient excuse for publishing these letters in their entirety, as they have been preserved (with a few gaps, notably in 1883–5 and 1889–90).

V

Tadeusz Bobrowski died at Kazimierówka on 10 February 1894. However critically we may now, from a distance, assess his personality and views, it does not alter the fact that there had developed a deep and mutual affection between him and Conrad. Upon learning of his uncle's death Conrad wrote to Marguerite Poradowska: 'Il me semble que tout est mort en moi. Il semble emporter mon âme avec lui' (18 Feb. 1894), and six years later he told Garnett that he had stood to Tadeusz 'more in the relation of a son than of a nephew' (20 Jan. 1900). Conrad's first novel, *Almayer's Folly*, is dedicated to the memory of 'T. B.' Bobrowski left his nephew the considerable sum of 15,000 roubles, plus 1,200 roubles of interest on the capital, which Conrad received in February 1895—and lost, in shares in a gold mine, in the summer of 1896. The executors of Bobrowski's will asked him to come to the Ukraine but he refused, perhaps because he was busy placing *Almayer's Folly* with the publishers.

Bobrowski's death brought about a serious loosening of Conrad's links with Poland. Apart from their meetings abroad (in 1878 in Marseilles and in 1883 in Marienbad, today's Mariánské Lázně), Conrad visited his uncle twice, in 1890 and in 1893, both times restoring his contacts with members of the growing family, making new acquaintances, renewing his memories of Poland. During the first trip he even paid a flying visit to Warsaw, meeting some young people from literary circles. After 1894 the only permanent link, lasting for several years, was with the Zagórski family, his distant cousins.

However, the scarcity of Conrad's preserved correspondence with his Polish friends might suggest that he had even fewer contacts than was in fact the case. We know that there were more letters and more links: for instance, he was in touch with the Montresor family, to whom he sent a copy of *Almayer's Folly*;[1] in December 1902 he asked William Blackwood, his publisher, for a copy of *Youth* to be sent 'to Poland, for the very young lions of an extremely modern literary review in Warsaw, the *Chimera*' (22 Dec. 1900); in later years he became friendly with another famous Pole living in England, Bronisław Malinowski, whom he frequently met:[2] unfortunately I have been unable to discover any letters to or from him. Moreover, there was undoubtedly some correspondence with other members of the Bobrowski family after Tadeusz's death; but in Poland, which suffered heavy damage in both world wars, all traces of this family seem to have disappeared. One must realize, when reading this volume, that it contains only the sad relics of Conrad's Polish writings: probably no more than one-fourth of all his letters in Polish. Most of the others, like the letters to Bobrowski, are known to have been destroyed; the rest are lost.

It is not clear how much Polish literature Conrad read after he left Poland in 1874 and before he went to Cracow and Zakopane

---

[1] Letter to Conrad from Konstancja Montresor (*née* Lubowidzka) of 15 March 1897; National Library, Warsaw, sign. MS. 2889.

[2] In 1913 Malinowski presented Conrad with a copy of his *The Family among the Australian Aborigines* with an inscription in Polish (Catalogue of Second-hand Books, W. Heffer & Sons, Cambridge 1925, No. 251). Miss Wiktoria Karnicka told me that she had visited Conrad with Malinowski at Bishopsbourne in the summer of 1923; apparently they had known each other well and had been on very friendly terms.

in 1914. He took some Polish books with him to Marseilles but lost them in 1876, and we do not know whether he bought any replacements. The catalogue of a part of Conrad's library, sold in 1925 and 1926 by W. Heffer & Sons in Cambridge, contains several Polish items, but all of them published after 1914; it does not contain, however, Bobrowski's *Memoirs*, a copy of which[1] Conrad received immediately after publication in 1900. It seems unlikely that he read much Polish during those forty years, but we may fairly safely assume that first his uncle and later the Zagórskis and the editors of *Chimera* sent him books from Poland from time to time.

To supplement the story of Conrad's Polish connexions as reflected in his correspondence it is necessary to discuss two more events in his life: the attack on him by Maria Orzeszkowa in 1899, and the visit paid by the whole Conrad family to Poland from July to October 1914.

In a Polish weekly, *Kraj*, published in St. Petersburg, there appeared in March 1899 (No. 12) an article entitled 'Emigration of the Talents' ('Emigracja talentów') by Wincenty Lutosławski (1860–1947), then a leading authority on Plato, a Pole living mostly abroad. Lutosławski argued that people of ability—scientists, humanists, artists, and writers—have a right to emigrate and work abroad, if they find the atmosphere in Poland too stifling. As an example he cited the novels of Conrad (whom he mistakenly described as an ex-insurgent of 1863) and explained that the works of Poles, even if published in foreign languages, preserve 'the national spirit, different from the spirits of other nations'. *Kraj* was a weekly of conservatives and appeasers, but that apparently was too much even for them: in the same issue a reply was published by a well-known journalist Tadeusz Żuk-Skarszewski, who calmly but firmly opposed Lutosławski, concluding: 'I prefer a village school teacher in Przyszowa or Poniemóń [names of little villages in Poland] not only to a brilliant commentator on Plato, but to Plato himself—in Boston.'

Żuk-Skarszewski did not mention the case of Conrad; it was mentioned, however, a month later in a highly emotional article by Maria Orzeszkowa, a well-known Polish novelist. To understand her violent bitterness one must remember that Orzeszkowa (1842–1910), a woman of quite exceptional intelligence and knowledge, spent most of her life in self-imposed seclusion in the small provincial town of Grodno, subordinating all her own interests to what she

---

[1] Copy now in the library of the Polish Research Centre in London, with an explanatory inscription by Jessie Conrad.

conceived to be her 'national duties'. The main theme of Orzeszkowa's article was her idea of the supremacy of national duties:
'The doctrine absolving the individual of ability from participating
in works and sufferings common to the whole society, is obviously
unjust.' Then, referring to Lutosławski's remark that Conrad was
writing in English 'for bread', Orzeszkowa attacked the latter as a
shameless careerist, betraying for money his country and his language.
Orzeszkowa's article, expressing contempt mixed with horror, was
to a certain extent based on a misunderstanding—Conrad was at that
time far from any financial success; but the whole discussion reflected
the typical Polish attitude of those years, an attitude slightly
hysterical but, in the existing political circumstances, understandable:
it was dictated by the ethics of the 'besieged city', allowing for no
desertions. Conrad did almost certainly read this article, although
many years later he mentioned a 'letter' from Orzeszkowa when
explaining his hostility to her:[1] it seems unlikely that Orzeszkowa
would have written a letter of that kind.

It is commonly assumed that Conrad's words in *A Personal
Record* were written in answer to Orzeszkowa's accusations: 'No
charge of faithlessness ought to be lightly uttered. . . . It would take
too long to explain the intimate alliance of contradictions which
makes love itself wear at times the desperate shape of betrayal.'
Many critics and biographers think also that *Lord Jim* was written
under the influence of this controversy, as a detailed analysis of the
problems of failing to fulfil one's duty and of guilt. Similar motifs
appear, however, in Conrad's earlier works. For instance, is not
An Outcast of the Islands a dress rehearsal for *Lord Jim*, played
before a mirror, with the basic trend of the action reversed? It is
possible that Orzeszkowa's article simply made Conrad more
acutely aware of his personal and national predicament.

As soon as Conrad became financially more comfortable, after the
success of *Chance*, he accepted an invitation from Józef Retinger,
a Polish friend (to whom unfortunately one letter only has been
found), to spend a long holiday in Poland. The journey coincided with
the outbreak of the First World War: the Conrads left England on
25 July 1914 and arrived in Cracow probably on 30 July, the day
before Austrian mobilization was announced. They must have been
in touch with the Zagórski family because almost immediately they
proceeded to Zakopane, a well-known mountain resort, to stay in
the Zagórskis' villa 'Konstantynówka'. They remained there,
worried by lack of money and uncertainty as to their future as
citizens of a hostile power, till 8 October; then they succeeded,

[1] Aniela Zagórska, 'Kilka wspomnień', *Wiadomości Literackie*, 1929, No. 51.

thanks to the combined efforts of their Polish friends and of the American Ambassador in Vienna, in obtaining the necessary permits to go via Cracow and Vienna to Genoa and thence back to England.

About Conrad's stay in Zakopane we have numerous reports by his friends, and particularly by Miss Aniela Zagórska, his cousin and translator into Polish. During that time Conrad took part in many political discussions concerning the future of Poland (one result of which was his 'Political Memorandum', pp. 303–4), met many Polish personalities, notably the prominent novelist Stefan Żeromski, and read a great number of Polish books, mainly novels. Apparently he was particularly enthusiastic about the writings of Bolesław Prus, the pen-name of Aleksander Głowacki (1846–1912), which looks like an interesting case of attraction by hidden affinities: Prus, on the surface a realistic novelist, an enthusiast of science and an exponent of positivistic philosophy, was in fact a writer of strong romantic inclinations, damped by disillusionment and a self-defensive irony.

However, the case of Bruno Winawer, the only writer whose work Conrad ever translated (a comedy, *The Book of Job*; see his letters to Winawer), shows clearly how dangerous it is to draw any far-reaching conclusions from Conrad's literary likings. Winawer was a clever but rather superficial and showy writer of short stories and contemporary comedies, exploring in his works various themes from the borderland of life and science, such as the accidental discovery of a chemical formula; an engineer skilfully simulating a mental illness and so on. To watch Conrad showering him with compliments offers a rather puzzling spectacle.

VI

Conrad's attitude towards Poland, extensively discussed by many Polish critics, deserves a separate study; I must limit myself here to a broad outline of the problem. It was certainly a very complex attitude—highly emotional and by no means consistent.

Conrad's letter to Stefan Buszczyński written in 1883 shows that at least until then he regarded Poland as his homeland and thought of returning there. Whether he believed in the possibility of Poland regaining its independence, we do not know. His letters to Spiridion Kliszczewski[1] show that he did not so believe in 1885; moreover,

---

[1] Published by G. Jean-Aubry, *Joseph Conrad: Life and Letters*, London 1927, i. 79–86. Spiridion Kliszczewski was a son of Józef Kliszczewski who, after the failure of the Polish insurrection of 1830–1, emigrated to Britain and established himself as a watchmaker in Cardiff. Conrad met the Kliszczewskis in 1885 and for a time was very friendly with them. I have not included these well-known letters (the earliest preserved pieces of

he confesses there that 'When speaking, writing, or thinking in English, the word 'home' always means for me the hospitable shores of Great Britain' (13 Oct. 1885).

We may wonder to what extent this declaration was connected with Conrad's newly acquired British citizenship; the same letter, however, offers ample evidence of the causes of the shift in his spiritual allegiance. 'Events are casting shadows, more or less distorted, shadows deep enough to suggest the lurid light of battlefields somewhere in the near future, but all those portents of great and decisive doings leave me in a state of despairing indifference: for, whatever may be the changes in the fortunes of living nations, for the dead there is no hope and no salvation. We have passed through the gates where "lasciate ogni speranza" is written in letters of blood and fire, and nothing remains for us but the darkness of oblivion. . . . Yet, I agree with you that in a free and hospitable land even the most persecuted of our race may find relative peace and a certain amount of happiness, materially at least; consequently I understood and readily accepted your reference to "Home".'

Thus, the loss of hope for Poland's political rebirth was one motive for a change in Conrad's attitude; and a despairing resignation over the future of Poland remained for many years the chief element in his thinking about his country of origin. This resignation did not preclude a constant alertness to all international developments which could conceivably influence Poland's situation. His only political article written before 1914, 'Autocracy and War' (1905), not only represents a Polish point of view but contains many traditional Polish ideas on Russia.[1] The 'Polishness' of this article—which is tendentious almost to the point of incoherence—permeates its style: the whole piece reads like a literal translation from a late-romantic Polish writer; in a word, like a translation from Apollo Korzeniowski.

Admonishing Garnett for considering him 'a Slav', Conrad wrote: 'You seem to forget that I am a Pole. You forget that we have been used to go to battle without illusions. It's you Britishers that "go in to win" only. We have been "going in" these last hundred years repeatedly, to be knocked on the head only—as was visible to any calm intellect.'[2] And in 'Prince Roman' (written in 1911) we read about 'that country which demands to be loved as no other

Conrad's writing in English) as they were addressed to a person bound to Poland only by his father's origin, but they are not without relevance in a study of Conrad's Polish background.

[1] Julian Krzyżanowski, 'U źródeł publicystyki Józefa Conrada' (on the sources of J. Conrad's political journalism), *Ruch Literacki*, 1932.

[2] Undated letter of October 1907.

country has ever been loved, with the mournful affection one bears to the unforgotten dead and with the unextinguishable fire of a hopeless passion which only a living, breathing, warm ideal can kindle in our breasts for our pride, for our weariness, for our exultation, for our undoing'. The dark, desperate love, described in these sombre sentences, could not form a bridge to the living and fighting people in Poland. Hopeless fidelity was the essence of Conrad's feeling for Poland, but that made him not closer to but, on the contrary, more estranged from other Poles.

Hopeless, mourning fidelity to the memory of Poland was a recurrent motif in Conrad's correspondence with his friends, as his letters to R. B. Cunninghame Graham bear witness. But perhaps the most striking example of this attitude is contained in the interview he gave in 1914 to Marian Dąbrowski. Winding up, he said: 'I cannot think about Poland too frequently—it's painful, bitter, heart-breaking. I could not live, if I did. The English have an expression with which they part: "Good luck!" I cannot say that to you.'

Before 1914 Conrad mentioned Poland in his published work only three times: in 'Autocracy and War' (1905), in *A Personal Record* (1908–9) and in 'Prince Roman' (1911). Why did he not write about his home country more often? This problem was posed for the first time at the very beginning of his literary career. When he visited his Polish-British friends, the Kliszczewskis, for Christmas 1896, Spiridion Kliszczewski appealed to him to describe in his novels the miserable fate of Poland. Conrad is said to have retorted angrily: 'Ah, mon ami, que voulez vous? I would lose my public. . . .'[1] Even if faithfully told, the story is not to be taken at its face value. Trying to become popular was never a guiding principle in Conrad's work, although at the time of his literary apprenticeship he was, understandably, particularly anxious to secure readers for his books. In the following years, however, he changed his subjects several times without, apparently, any great concern for his public —and still he remained silent about Poland. At the same time he did not try to hide his Polishness and rejected, as in the letter to Waliszewski of 5 Dec. 1905, the idea that he had become 'an Englishman'. To Józef Korzeniowski he wrote in 1901: '. . . I have in no way disavowed either my nationality or the name we share for the sake of success. It is widely known that I am a Pole. . . .'

A sufficient reason for not writing about Poland may well have been that 'hopeless fidelity' is not among the feelings one is eager to show publicly; it seems rather to ask for a discreet silence.

---

[1] W. Chwalewik, 'Józef Conrad w Kardyfie'('Joseph Conrad at Cardiff'), *Ruch Literacki*, 1932, No. 8. The report is based on the Kliszczewskis' family reminiscences.

Moreover, Conrad probably had little to say about Poland itself: he did not even know it well. His home country constituted for him a difficult emotional and artistic problem; it could not, therefore, provide him—like the Malay Archipelago—with a comfortable background for significant human stories. Thus he became a victim of an internal conflict: on the one hand his national duties demanded that he should write about Poland (even if not in Poland and in Polish); on the other, his innermost feelings, sullen and proud, prevented him from doing so. It was perhaps this tragic conflict which he alluded to in *A Personal Record*: 'It would take too long to explain the intimate alliance of contradictions in human nature which makes love itself wear at times the desperate shape of betrayal.'

In 1914 the whole situation changed abruptly. During his visit to Poland Conrad became convinced that the political revival of the country was possible. He wanted to lend his hand, he drew up a political memorandum in Polish, and another in English (published later as 'A Note on the Polish Problem'), in which he attempted to influence responsible circles in England. Soon, however, he became bitterly disillusioned by the general indifference. In 1919 he wrote angrily to Sir Hugh Clifford: 'If the Alliances had been differently combined the Western Powers would have delivered Poland to the German learned pig with as little compunction as they were ready to give it up to the Russian mangy dog. It is a great relief to my feelings to think that no single life has been lost on any of the fronts for the sake of Poland. The load of obligation would have been too great. . . .' He develops the same idea, in more restrained tones, in the article 'The Crime of Partition', published in 1919. It is an outspoken piece of pro-Polish propaganda, describing briefly the parliamentarian traditions of Poland; the story of the partitions of the Polish State between Russia, Prussia, and Austria; and the long struggle for independence. The reborn Poland, reiterates Conrad with bitter pride, owes nothing to the Western Powers.

No longer hopeless, Conrad lost his reticence in writing about Poland. However, his attitude towards it remained a very complex one. The place of hopelessness was now taken by two other feelings: being proud of his home country (cf. his letter to J. Quinn of 24 March 1920) and being silently ashamed of himself for being so prematurely despondent. He begged his cousin, Miss Karola Zagórska, to forgive him that his sons did not understand Polish, and rejoiced at Stefan Żeromski's calling him an 'author-compatriot'. He shied at the proposals to become a Polish-British public figure, but at the same time took pains to have the covers of a collected edition of his works decorated with his family coat-of-arms, Nałęcz. (Incidentally, his refusal in 1924 to accept a knighthood is most easily explained by the fact that the Korzeniowskis had been noblemen for generations.)

To the end of his life he preserved towards Poland an unbalanced, uncomfortable attitude of mixed pride and shame, yearning and guilty conscience. It is very tempting to accept the suggestion of a Polish critic, Rafał Blüth, that *The Rover* expressed Conrad's deep-felt longing for a return to and a reconciliation with his homeland.[1]

VII

'The English critics—and indeed I am an English writer—when speaking of me always add that there is in my work something incomprehensible, unfathomable, elusive. Only you can grasp this elusiveness, understand the incomprehensible. It is Polishness.' So said Conrad in 1914 in the interview given to Marian Dąbrowski. It would be superfluous to quote the many prominent critics who have written about Conrad's exoticism, strangeness, and alien quality. Not once was he irritated with the identification of this exotic element with 'Slavonism'.[2] The question has been sometimes asked, particularly in Poland, whether Conrad was in fact an English writer? A German critic, Paul Wohlfahrt, produced a pedantic study enumerating various dissimilarities between the 'typically English' mental attitudes and those peculiar to Conrad. Taken separately, the problem 'English—or not?', even if less absurdly worded, is of little critical importance. Its relevance is based on the fact that the readers of Conrad find it difficult to understand and interpret him solely within the English cultural context; it is commonly felt that some additional clues are necessary.

The most popular way of 'explaining' the oddities and mysteries of Conrad's art, and particularly of his style, has recently been to point at his French linguistic and literary background. There is a tendency to identify everything un-English in Conrad with Frenchness; in this respect Baines's book is a rare example of critical sobriety. The influence of Flaubert and Maupassant, although undoubtedly strong and consciously absorbed by Conrad, was in fact doubly limited: it concerned mainly matters of literary technique, and affected almost exclusively his early and still immature books.

[1] Rafał Blüth, 'Powrót żeglarza' ('Sailor's Return'), *Ateneum*, 1936, No. 4. This suggestion finds support in Jessie Conrad's recollections (*Joseph Conrad and his Circle*, p. 363) of Conrad in his last years frequently talking about a return to Poland, although it was certainly no more than a vague idea.
[2] Cf. his letter to George T. Keating of 14 Dec. 1922.

Introduction

The case of Conrad's famous preface to *The Nigger of the 'Narcissus'* may serve as an instance of the limitations of this influence. George J. Worth pointed out[1] that the preface had been modelled on Maupassant's preface to *Pierre et Jean*; but if we compare both artistic declarations we notice, apart from obvious similarities, a striking and very Conradian innovation in the most important point of the programme: he introduces the notion of 'the highest king of justice', the attempt to render which 'to the visible universe' is the hallmark of art.

The critics who play with the idea that Conrad might have written not in his third, but in his second language, have probably never taken a closer look at his French: fluent but rather stiff and impersonal, and by no means faultless. The alleged 'gallicisms' of his English are in fact not gallicisms but simply polonisms; it is enough to set Conrad's original text side by side with a Polish translation to observe idiomatic borrowings and syntactical influences. Jessie Conrad complained that her husband, when in a fever, would always talk Polish; the subconscious pressure of that language on his mind must have been quite strong.

Unfortunately there exists only one serious study of this problem: A. P. Coleman's on 'Polonisms in the English of Conrad's "Chance" '.[2] It is impossible to make up here for this scarcity of published analytic evidence, and I must limit myself to generalized comments.

The difficulty in assessing the influence of Conrad's native Polish on his literary English is that we are inclined to notice this influence only in the cases of mistakes and irregularities. Thus, it is quite simple to observe that Conrad's use of prepositions is sometimes dictated by Polish linguistic customs, or that his use of tenses occasionally follows not English but Polish rules, &c.[3] And it is comparatively easy to demonstrate that the stylistic artificialities of *Almayer's Folly* or *The Rescue* are largely the result of the influence of Polish syntax and Polish literary conventions. I do not consider, however, that these aberrations are the only traces of Polish influence on Conrad's prose; nor do I think this influence, although frequently detrimental, was purely negative.

Polish is a highly inflected language, in which the relationship of words in a sentence is made clear by inflectional endings; therefore the sentence structure and word order depend not so much on grammatical rules as on the content of the sentence and the

---

[1] 'Conrad's Debt to Maupassant in the Preface to "The Nigger of the 'Narcissus' "', *The Journal of English and Germanic Philology*, Urbana, Ill., 1955, No. 4.
[2] *Modern Language Notes*, 1931, No. 9.   [3] Examples in Coleman, loc. cit.

accepted stylistic conventions. Here we have the roots of both Conrad's occasional looseness of sentence structure and the frequent rhetorical (not necessarily in the derogative sense) ring of his phrase. The influence of Polish syntax is most easily discernible in Conrad's descriptive pieces and, above all, in his journalistic writings (for example, 'The Censor of Plays'); at its worst, it produces an effect of artificial pomposity, but at its best it leads to an artistically successful subordination of the rules of grammar to the conveyed vision, as in some passages of *Heart of Darkness* and *Nostromo*.

Apart from linguistic influences, there are in Conrad's work numerous echoes of Polish literature, and notably of Polish romantic poetry. The list of evident or probable borrowings, discovered by Polish critics, even if not a long one, is quite impressive. The plot of 'Karain' is based on Mickiewicz's ballad *Czaty*; there are verbal echoes of *Konrad Wallenrod* in *Almayer's Folly* and in *An Outcast*; obvious borrowings from *The Forefathers' Eve* in *Under Western Eyes*[1] (which contains, incidentally, an anthology of traditional Polish conceptions and misconceptions about Russia;[2] 'Prince Roman' follows closely several Polish sources; *Lord Jim* seems to have been influenced by *Pan Tadeusz*, &c.

To the above list must be added the most obvious instance, so far overlooked: several fragments of Tadeusz Bobrowski's *Memoirs* directly translated or paraphrased in *A Personal Record*; e.g. pp. 27–29 are quoted almost literally from *Memoirs*, vol. ii, pp. 13–14; pages 49–53 are taken from vol. i, pp. 5–6; pp. 54–55 from i. 15; p. 56 from i. 9; &c.[3] Echoes of the *Memoirs* can also be found in *Under Western Eyes*.

The real importance of Conrad's Polish cultural background consists, however, in something more general and at the same time less tangible than these cases of direct influence on his books of some works of Polish literature. It consists, broadly speaking, in certain peculiarities of his imagination and his world outlook.

To begin with, in that age of the greatest cultural expansion of the *bourgeoisie* he was anything but a *bourgeois*: he hardly ever wrote

---

[1] For example, Mickiewicz on Russia: 'A land empty, white and open—like a page prepared to be written on—by history . . .'; Conrad: 'the snow . . . levelling everything under its uniform whiteness, like a monstrous blank page awaiting the record of an inconceivable history'.

[2] G. Herling-Grudziński, 'W oczach Conrada' ('In Conrad's eyes'), *Kultura*, Paris 1957, No. 10.

[3] Sometimes Conrad gives these passages the form of a story told by his uncle, but it is by no means a strictly observed rule. The number of fragments translated from Bobrowski's *Memoirs* belies F. M. Hueffer's claim that '*The Mirror of the Sea* and *A Personal Record* were mostly written by my hand from Conrad's dictation. Whilst he was dictating them, I would recall incidents to him—I mean incidents of his past life which he had told me . . .' (*Return to Yesterday*, London 1931, p. 194).

about this class (and if he did, he did so with irony and disdain), and he never represented its attitudes. His was the outlook of an uprooted nobleman, conscious of his chivalrous past, although now hard-working: an outlook very typical of Polish literature after 1863. The values he wanted to see cherished—honour, duty, fidelity, friendship—were typically romantic and typically chivalrous, and it is only too obvious that we have to look for their origin to Poland, where the life of the whole nation was, for better or for worse, dominated by these very values.

Politically he always remained an outsider. He did not understand the new, emerging social forces (he was almost hysterically afraid of the 'mob'), and at the same time he was outspokenly contemptuous of the contemporary socio-economic order of 'material interests'. His political attitude was very similar to one expressed by Count Zygmunt Krasiński who in *The Un-Divine Comedy* described a deadly struggle between the vengeful masses, led by 'converted Jews', and the defendants of the old, corrupt order—both sides being depicted with equally fierce scorn.

The influence of the peculiarly Polish romantic tradition can be clearly seen in Conrad's treatment of the problems of moral responsibility: his moral awareness is stated in social, not individual terms; in terms of duties and obligations, not in terms of conscience and self-perfection. However, his national background revealed itself not only in the characteristics he possessed but also in those he lacked. And he plainly lacked the feeling of belonging to some concrete social group, which is why he clung to the idea of being a 'British sailor'. Since he saw moral problems as being social in kind, he was sometimes compelled to cut his ideals down to the size of the MacWhirrs, not knowing any other social group he could trust, or at least fully understand.

He was an isolated man, but this very isolation, making him feel disturbed and insecure, at the same time made it possible for him to see problems which escaped many writers more tightly entangled in the prevailing social conditions: the problems of loneliness, responsibility, betrayal. Thus, his Polish background made Conrad a man disinherited, lonely, and (for a Western writer of that time) exceptionally conscious of the sinister brutalities hidden behind the richly ornate façade of *bourgeois* political optimism. And these characteristics are precisely what makes Conrad our contemporary.

TADEUSZ BOBROWSKI'S LETTERS
TO
CONRAD
[KONRAD KORZENIOWSKI]

I

My dear little Konrad,

It has pleased God to strike you with the greatest misfortune that can assail a child—the loss of its Parents. But in His goodness God has so graciously allowed your very good Grandmother and myself to look after you, your health, your studies and your future destiny. You know that the whole affection we felt for your Parents we now bestow upon you. You know too that your Parents were always worthy of that affection—so you as their son should be doubly worthy of being their son and become worthy of our love. Therefore you must try to take full advantage of all they taught you, and also of the instructions given to you by the friends chosen by your father and by us, such as Mr. Stefan B.[2] and Mr. A. Georgeon,[3] and in all things to follow their opinions and advice.

Without a thorough education you will be worth nothing in this world, you will never be self-sufficient, and a thorough education is gained only by thoroughly mastering the beginnings of every subject which is necessary for every cultivated man—which we hope you wish to become and we hope to see you become; therefore, my dear boy, apply yourself to mastering thoroughly their first principles. I know that all beginnings seem tiresome to a boy, but every effort must be made to master them by work and determination. If you want to become an engineer or a technician you must start with arithmetic and geometry—if you want to become a doctor or a lawyer you must start with languages, geography etc. In a word, one thing follows from another, one thing is built upon another. Therefore, not that which is easy and attractive must be the object of your studies but that which is useful, although sometimes difficult,

[1] Bobrowski's letters are preserved in the National Library (Biblioteka Narodowa) in Warsaw, sign. MS. 2889. Bobrowski usually gave his letters two dates: one according to the Julian calendar and the other according to the Gregorian calendar. The Julian calendar was used officially in Russia, but the Gregorian calendar used in the West has also been in use in ethnic Poland since the late sixteenth century. The difference in the nineteenth century was one of twelve days. Sometimes, when Bobrowski gives only a single date, it is impossible to know which calendar he has in mind.

[2] Stefan Buszczyński (1821–92), well-known patriot and political writer. Sentenced to death in his absence by a Russian military court for his activities in the 1863 Polish uprising (this is why Bobrowski does not write his name in full); Apollo Korzeniowski's close friend and biographer. His best known work, La Décadence de l'Europe (1867), was praised by Hugo and Michelet.

[3] Ludwik Georgeon (1832–79) took part in the 1863 rising; in 1867 opened a school for boys in Cracow.

for a man who knows nothing fundamentally, who has no strength of character and no endurance, who does not know how to work on his own and guide himself, ceases to be a man and becomes a useless puppet. Try therefore, my child, not to be or to become such a puppet, but to be useful, hard-working, capable and therefore a worthy human being—and thereby reward us for the cares and worries devoted to your upbringing.

Your education has been thought out by us, your needs supplied; it remains for you to learn and to be healthy and even in that matter (although it chiefly depends on God) if you take heed of the advice of your elders you may become completely well—not giving way to feelings and thoughts which are not really proper to your age.

Write to us, my boy, at least once a month; write what you think and feel. You know that news of you is always desired by us—it is particularly necessary for the peace of your dearest Grandmother—and will be eagerly awaited by me and Józia;[1] so please be punctilious about this.

You are starting your school studies with the wish to become a useful and worthy person—with the good advice of worthy people and with God's help. You start on this new road with my heartfelt blessing.

Your affectionate uncle,
T. BOBROWSKI.

Józieczka embraces you and also Emilija and Frania.[2]

2

27th September, old st., 1876
Kazimierówka

My dear boy,

Yesterday I received your letter written on the 10th September (new style), the second one from Martinique—and although I replied to your first letter hoping that it would reach you, I am writing again so that if by chance my first reply did not reach you, the second will reassure you, although I have nothing new to tell. Firstly, I am very well, so as to my health you have no need to worry. I saw no good reason to bombard you with letters, to a doubtful address, not being sure that they would reach you. There

---

[1] Bobrowski's daughter Józefa (1858–70).
[2] Miss Franciszka Dąbrowska ('Dąbrosia', 'Dąbrula'), from 1834 a servant (though of noble descent) at the Bobrowskis' home; virtually became a member of the family.

you have the whole secret of my silence. There was no anger on my part—and indeed it is a moot point whether my silence would be a punishment to you. Apparently, however, from your last letters I see that it could have been so understood. But, of course, I thought nothing of the kind! On the contrary I consider it my duty by advice and reminders to keep you on the right path: that is to say on the path of reason and of duty. Which I do and shall continue to do as often as is necessary. And if I ever had to remain silent 'in anger'—which in any case depends on you—then it would most likely be for ever. But that is a possibility which I do not even imagine.

The second piece of news I send you is this: on your return you will find 300 roubles of your allowance from the 3/15 October.[1] I shall send this money in a day or two; I haven't sent it yet but will certainly send it about the 5th October our style. You've thrown out my calculations with your requirements, so that my purse will be strained to meet all the obligations I promised, and as I was due to send money to Uncle Kazimierz[2] I gave him priority as he was not guilty of depleting my resources, and was the most in need. So that you, my dear Sir, must wait until the 5th of October. Besides, according to my reckoning, even if you returned from St. Thomas direct to Marseilles you could hardly be there before the end of November, and money sent to you on the 5/17 October will certainly be in Marseilles by the 17/29 of that month. In Marseilles you will find with Mr. Déléstang[3] my long letter in which I recapitulate your activities during the past two years, and give you my advice and wishes for the future—which advice and wishes I expect you to follow, not only in your thoughts and words but in your actions!

You always, my dear boy, made me impatient—and still make me impatient by your disorder and the easy way you take things—in which you remind me of the Korzeniowski family—spoiling and wasting everything—and not my dear Sister, your Mother, who was careful about everything. Last year you lost a trunk full of things—and tell me—what else had you to remember and look after if not

[1] This was supposed to form Conrad's allowance for half a year. Detailed accounts are to be found in the next letter and in Bobrowski's 'Memorial'.

[2] Kazimierz Bobrowski, Tadeusz's younger brother, was an officer in the Russian army in 1863. On receiving the news of the rising in Poland he voluntarily resigned his commission, but was prevented from joining the Polish forces and imprisoned for a few months. Having thus broken his career he worked till the end of his life as a minor official. Of poor health and burdened with a large family, he was a constant trouble for his brother, who had to support him.

[3] The owner of a shipping firm in Marseilles. Conrad was at this time serving in his ship the *Saint-Antoine*.

yourself and your things? Do you need a nanny—and am I cast in that role? Now again, you have lost a family photograph and some Polish books—and you ask me to replace them! Why? So that you should take the first opportunity of losing them again!? He who appreciates something looks after it. I have still today in my possession a small paper picture given me by my mother when I first went to school in 1839. It has been everywhere with me, and it is in the same condition as it was when it was given to me. And why? Because I looked after it with my heart. Ergo, apparently my young friend n'y met pas de cœur. So, if you do not look after intimate keepsakes (and that after all is a matter of your choice) why do you try to get replacements—and thereby cause somebody trouble? However, whatever family photographs I have got I shall send you this time—but if you lose them, please do not mention them to me again, I shall not believe that you really care about them. I can't send you the books—it is really too much trouble. It is much simpler for you to write to Cracow to the same bookseller from whom they were bought, and send 10 francs, or else write to Paris to the Librairie du Luxembourg, rue Tournon 16. That is Mr. Władysław Mickiewicz's bookshop.

Well, there's your reprimand for your carelessness about looking after your property. You deserve another one, for the carelessness with which you write your letters—I have told you that several times. Could you not possibly keep a supply of paper and write in an orderly fashion—as an orderly person I heartily wish my nephew to be and that is why I give him a dressing-down, which does not prevent me from loving you and blessing you, which I do with all my heart.

Embracing you from the depth of my heart,

Your uncle
T. BOBROWSKI

PS. When you lost your trunk did you not lose any of your documents? That would be a nice mess! Write the truth, and I can at least get you a birth certificate. Do not forget to write to me about it.

3

14/26 October, 1876
Kazimierówka

My dear Konrad!

Today, simultaneously with this letter which will await your
return to Marseilles, I am sending through the Bank of Galicia 300
roubles (at the present rate of exchange more or less 1,000 fr.) as
your allowance from the 1/13 October of this year—this being the
day from which our accounts have been kept for the last two
years. . . .

On that day two years will have passed since the moment when
I, with constricted heart, your Grandmother with tears, and both
of us with a blessing, let you go free into the world as you wished,
but with our advice and help—and by the time you read this letter
you will be 19 years old. That is an age at which one is a fully
fledged young man, often even earning one's own living and
occasionally even supporting a family, in any case an age when one
is completely responsible to God, to other people, and to one's self
for one's actions.

When we parted I took on myself the duty of supplying you with
the means of subsistence until you were able to earn them yourself;
means which are modest but sufficient, and which correspond to
my resources even though they may be somewhat stretched—but
which were fixed voluntarily by me after having secured Mr.
Chodźko's[1] opinion. You, for your part, have undertaken to make
prudent use of these means for your education, for your personal
benefit, and for your future. Let us after these two years go over the
past and ask ourselves to what extent each of us has fulfilled his
duties; for by answering this question, the recapitulation will enable
us to correct any shortcomings that we may find in our conduct and
will make each of us think of corrective measures to avoid them in
future.

You were to get 150 francs a month, that is an allowance of 1,800
francs a year, plus 200 francs for extra expenses—making 2,000
francs a year; together that makes, for two years, 4,000 francs, with
the reservation that this help is doubly limited: for exceeding it in
your favour either deprives me of some comforts or forces me to
diminish the help I give to your Uncle—my Brother—to whom
with his five children I can give barely one and a half times (i.e.
1,000 roubles annually) as much as to yourself.

[1] Wiktor Chodźko, a Pole living in Marseilles.

I don't know if you ever tried, with a pencil in your hand, to recapitulate what in the past two years you have received—at your request or unsolicited. I suspect that you have not looked deeply into these accounts—for if you have—what has happened would not have happened. To remind you, here you have our accounts for two years:

				Extra
in 1874	5/17	October on a/c of allowance	fr. 150	
	4/16	November ditto	fr. 150	
	6/18	December „	fr. 900	and fr. 300
in 1875	4/16	January—stolen		fr. 250
	3/15	June one payment	fr. 200	
	9/21	June on a/c of allowance	fr. 1,000	
	15/27	July to Mr. Chodźko		fr. 200
	19	November—to Havre		fr. 300
in 1876	2/14	January on a/c of allowance	fr. 1,200	
	12/24	April ditto	fr. 200	
	8	June		fr. 700
	4	July		fr. 400
	20	July		fr. 165
Telegrams and forwarding (16 roubles, 37 guldens)				fr. 104

Total on a/c of allowance   fr. 3,800 Extra fr. 2,419

Deducting 300 fr. for your initial equipment and 200 fr. additional for the second year   fr. 500

We get for 2 years, apart from your *allowance* fr. 4,000   Extra fr. 1,919

—in short, during 2 years you have by your transgressions used up your *maintenance for the whole third year!!!*

Here you have the bare facts, based on figures which I do not think you will deny—as each expenditure was made either for you or caused by you. And now, my dear Panie Bracie,[1] let us jointly consider if such expenditure on your behalf is and was possible, fair and worthy??? As regards possibility, perhaps it seems to you that I can bear such extraordinary expenditure out of love for my 'dearly beloved Nephew'? But this is not the case! My income is

[1] Literally 'Sir Brother', a mode of address used by one nobleman to another. All noblemen were addressed as 'Pan', i.e. 'Sir', and together they formed a 'brotherhood' of equal members.

around 5,000 roubles—I pay 500 roubles in taxes—by giving you 2,000 francs I am giving you approximately 700 roubles and to your Uncle 1,000 roubles yearly; so I give the two of you about one-third of my income. If therefore I were to give you 300 roubles more per year (as two years have used up the third one) I would have to cut down by half my expenditure on underwear, shoes, clothes, and my personal needs—since my budget for all these things is limited to 600 roubles a year for the very good reason that I cannot have more—there is no more to go round, if I am to fulfil my obligations towards my Brother and Nephew. Is it fair that I should repair your thoughtlessness at the expense of my personal comforts or, I should rather say, my essential needs? Would it be proper for me to reduce the help which I give to my Brother and his children whose right to my heart and help, if not greater (they are six), is certainly not less than yours? I am only too sure that the threefold reply to my threefold question could be only: impossible! and unfair! and unworthy![1] That will be the answer of your heart, but I wish for an answer of your will—not words, which I have had more than once—but deeds, i.e. the strictest adjustment of your expenditure to the allowance that I have allotted you, and if, in your opinion, this does not suffice, earn some money—and you will have it. If, however, you cannot earn it, then content yourself with what you get from the labour of others— until you are able to supplant it with your own earnings and gratify yourself. Apart from the fact of the expenditure itself, I must say frankly that I did not like the tone in which you refer to what has happened. Vous passez condamnation trop complaisante sur les sottises que vous avez faites! Certainly, there is no reason for one to take one's life or to go into a Carthusian monastery because of some folly one has committed—even if that folly causes acute pain to someone very close to you!—but a little more contrition would not be amiss and particularly a more thoughtful mode of behaviour, which would prove that after a temporary imprudence, reflection and common sense have prevailed! But these latter—my dear—in spite of my great wish to, I have not found—unfortunately! Thus, at first you keep a stubborn silence for two whole months, silence which you must know was disquieting to me! Then, you write me a long letter admitting your fault, but you do not say how much you need to repair your stupidities, when the plainest common sense would have made you connect one with the other, and not expose me to uncertainty and disquiet. Further, knowing how I detest telegrams and how much trouble and cost they entail (for I live

---

[1] In Conrad's hand on the margin, beside this paragraph: 'Je vs aime!!!'

41

7 miles[1] from the station) you telegraph for 700 fr. in June. Finally, having had a whole month in which to inform me of your need of 400 fr. more, you wait again and as late as the 4th July you telegraph again. To top everything, on your departure you tell me to pay a debt of 165 fr. this time, thank God, by letter! Where is here consideration, prudence, and reflection??? Where is here respect for others'—this time my own—peace of mind? Where is here any attempt to soften the impact of the absurdities committed, by prudent and tactful behaviour??? Having perpetrated stupidities, you lose your head and leave everything to chance. For, if your telegram had not found me at home, which could very well have happened; if, in the first case, I had had no money deposited in Cracow and in the second if a few days' credit had not been granted to me, what unpleasantness you would have caused yourself and what expense you would have caused me! Consider all that my dear —and you must admit that I am right—beat your breast—and swear to reform.

What is the conclusion to be drawn from this whole recapitulation of our actions? It is this: that you have committed absurdities— that in view of your youth and because it is the first time, all has to be forgiven you—and I, the victim of these absurdities, forgive you with all my heart, on condition, *that it is for the first and last time!!* And I myself, am I wholly innocent? Certainly, I am guilty, because I met your demands too promptly! I also beat my breast and swear to myself that this will be *the first and last* case of such giving way on my part! And I pledge myself to keep my word! And I ask you to remember this—both for yourself and for me. I would have refused my own son outright after so many warnings, but to you, the child of my Sister, grandson of my Mother, for once, but *only for once*, I forgive you—I save you so that it should not be said that I was too hard on you! May the shades of these two beings dear to us both protect you my dear boy in future from similar transgressions, *for believe me* I shall not give way a second time to any tenderness of heart. What practical means is there of patching up the holes you have made? You should be aware, then, that you had 500 Rhenish of your own, deposited in the Galician Bank, and you can easily reckon that this money has been exhausted by your demands; and as you spent 1,919 fr., which is approximately 1,000 guldens, it seems to me appropriate that you should pay for your own follies with your own money—and only appeal to my pocket for the balance! I take the balance then upon myself! Do you find this fair? Please let me have a plain answer in your next letter. I do

---

[1] A Polish mile is roughly 4⅔ English miles.

not find your proposition practical that your extraordinary expenses of the past should be covered out of your allowance;—for, first of all I do not want you to deny yourself food and modest but decent clothing; secondly, diminishing your allowance which is hardly sufficient would lead you back to incurring debts, which I do not want and which I forbid you under pain of forgoing my blessing; I ask as well that you should refrain from philanthropy until you are able to practise it at your own expense.

Thus you have 1,000 fr. deposited at your disposal, i.e. for the half year till the 1/13 April, 1877. It is my wish that if the health and trading circumstances of Mr. Déléstang permit, you should remain on land as little as possible, but try to return to sea as speedily as possible. If you have to stay on land, I ask you and recommend you not to take out of the Bank more than one or at most two months' allowance of 150 fr. and use it so that it suffices. As you hope again to have a free journey—*please do not count on it*, so that what has happened this time should not occur again—don't prematurely spend the money destined for it, and should your hope of a free journey be fulfilled, keep what you need as argent de poche, leaving the rest in the Bank—you will find it there on your return —and you will be able to use it sensibly for lessons, clothing, etc.,— this being your earned savings. In this way only you will give proof of your good sense. If I remember rightly, you were usually back in January and sailed in February to return in July—you will thus spend only one month on land, your health permitting—and in March I shall again send your half-yearly allowance, so that if you make in 1877 two free journeys, you will be able to save enough to spend a couple or more months on land by having lessons in science, and enjoy a slightly more comfortable life,—for only when the means are there is it fair to think of an easier way of existence. There you have a programme before you, and a way of utilizing the money I am putting at your disposal.

I had hoped and wished to see you in 1877 during the autumn, either in Switzerland or Cracow or even in Marseilles. My wish is certainly great, but shall I have the necessary means? That is the important question and according to all the probabilities I shall not have them, for part of my capital is invested in sugar refineries, which have been going through a great crisis for a year. The price of sugar has fallen a lot and the sugar refineries will most probably not yield any income this year—which will reduce my annual income from 5,000 to 4,000; and not wishing to withdraw my help to you or to your uncle—the expense of the journey to you would become impossible!—as impossible as it would be to cut down your allowance; so that according to all probability my plans will have to be postponed till the next year, that is till 1878. In any case the Kiev fair for 1877 will decide the question in July this year—that is by the time you return from your January trip—so I shall still have time to let you know if you should go, or should wait for me or meet me. At least a year and possibly two will elapse before we see each other.

Immediately after reading this letter, that is immediately after your return, please write to me about your health and further plans. Please give me also full details of *your studies*. What have you been working on during the voyage? You praise the present captain. So you have presumably profited from him? Did he give you lessons? If so, in what? What did you work on yourself? and what did you teach yourself? Are you also working on English or other languages? and so on. In short, write about everything regarding your moral and physical being. Did you recover your trunk which you so carelessly left in Havre? Your things and Polish books must have been in it? From a later letter I know what happened.[1]

Please inform me of the price of *une caisse de Liqueurs des Iles*—but it must be *des Iles*, that is from Marseilles; the Bordeaux brand is much inferior. Usually one caisse contains 40 bottles. What would be the price of such a caisse in Marseilles? and the cost of transport to Odessa? Many people here, knowing that you sail to Martinique, ask for it and are surprised that up till now I have not thought of getting it. Write to me also what the price is of 10,000 Havana cigars of medium strength and quality. Apparently cigars are traded in in lots of 10,000—at least so I have heard, but perhaps erroneously? But as in Cracow you had a talent for cigars, I imagine that while in Havana you looked with an experienced eye into the question, as an expert! Maybe there are some local price lists of these two articles; if so please send them to me, together with the information about the cost of transport from there to Marseilles and then on to Odessa. Maybe we could do some small business in these two articles if it should appear that tout frais compris they would still be much cheaper than here locally. Please answer all my questions—but not from memory but from my letter—as you are, my young man, very absent-minded and you frequently forget what I have asked you.

Finally I remind you to write to your uncle on your return, to Mr. Stefan and to Pulmann [*sic*];[2] it is unfair to forget about them

---

[1] The last sentence added later.

[2] Conrad's former tutor, Adam Marek Pulman, born 1846, studied medicine at the Jagiellonian University in Cracow and then lived in Czerniowce (Chernovtsy). Conrad did

and the letter apparently written to your uncle has never reached him, my dear. Oleś and Roman Taube[1] are in Riga; this summer they called on me and asked warmly after you.

Well, enough of this my boy, you have had a recapitulation of your wisdom, a lavasse which you deserved—and have advice and warnings for the future! Hoping that it is the first and last time that you cause me so much trouble, you have my embrace and my blessing. May they be effective!!!

Your Uncle
T. BOBROWSKI

4

10/22 June, 1877
Kazimierówka

My dearest boy!

Your letter of the 8th May (probably your style) reached me only a week ago, that is on the 3rd of this month (our style) and at last my mind is a little more at ease about you. I cannot really understand why my letters haven't reached you? For this is the third that I have written since the moment I got your communication about staying in Marseilles. I should be particularly upset if the letter of mine got lost in which I returned your captain's letter which you asked me to send back. This would not be my fault for I dispatched it most scrupulously. Do not forget to write to me if it has finally reached you. I remember having posted it on the 24th April (old style) from the Post Office in Bosy Bród on the way from Kazimierówka to Morozówka.

In your letter you say that now more than ever you would like news from us, since from the French newspapers you cannot learn anything.[2] However, I myself cannot tell you anything new as we know absolutely nothing but what our newspapers—which are even less well informed and less informative than yours—tell us, and then only 10 or 12 days after the event. Far away from the scene of the war, away from all question of participation in it, not expecting anything for ourselves either from victory or from defeat, we could only par amour du roi de Prusse take an interest in politics and war! What occupies our thoughts is the misery which is near to

not write either to him or to Stefan Buszczyński, as a letter from Pulman to Buszczyński of 10 March 1879 shows.

[1] Bobrowski's wards and Conrad's friends in Cracow.
[2] The Russo-Turkish war began on 24 April 1877.

us, which after two bad years weighs on us heavily—and we know full well that no one is thinking of us.

We had an exceptionally long winter which went on till the last days of March—then April was exceptionally cold and dry, then May dry and very hot; it is now the 6th week without rain and again it is cold and hailing. The rye and wheat are not too bad, I must admit, but other cereals are poor and so is the beet. The price of cereals has soared, but though there is a shortage of them, this rise of price is not so much caused by a sudden need for them as by the devaluation of our money. How long will the war last? it is impossible to foretell! but one thing which is certain is that whatever the outcome the economic effects will fall with a heavy burden on everyone and especially on us.

You inquire, my dear boy, if you may draw before the 3/15th August the 300 fr. deposited with the bank if you were to leave Marseilles before that date? *Certainly you may* and even earlier than that, for I see that having had expenses for your cure while only earning 60 fr. monthly it is hardly possible that you should not need it. Taking into account this need and not having anything myself to send you, particularly because of the terrible rate of exchange of our money, and wishing to protect myself as long as possible from a loss which would help nobody, and in the hope that the rate of exchange may improve, I am asking Uncle Antoni[1] to send you 200 fr. from the interest which has accumulated on the little capital of 1,000 gulden left for you in the Savings Bank by the late Katarzyna K.[2] I am writing to him today. This will be the interest which has accumulated during two years. You see now how long it takes to accumulate money and how quickly one can lose it. Obviously whatever may be the rate of exchange in September you must get your allowance, and you will get it! The question is by what means you will get it, since you are going to India for a whole year. Please think how it can be arranged? Perhaps one could arrange with Mr. Déléstang to instruct the captain to pay it out to you, and I would in turn arrange to pay it to him through the Galician Bank on appropriate dates; it's on the 1/13th September [*sic*] and 1/13th April. Or discuss it in the bank with Mr. Fressinet. It is essential that you should write about it to me, but discuss it prudently here and there to see which method is better? This year in particular it is difficult for me to send your whole yearly allowance in advance! So now you see, Panie Bracie, how a man always pays for his faults. If it had not been for your last year's escapade, which

---

[1] Antoni Syroczyński, living in Lvov.
[2] Katarzyna Korzeniowska, a distant cousin of Conrad.

swallowed up your whole allowance for half a year, you could get your whole annual allowance straight away as I could have arranged here for half a year's allowance always to be accumulated in advance. Discuss all this my dear fellow, and inform me how to arrange about this allowance while you are on the voyage to India, and think of it quickly, discuss it and write. Write to me also about your health and what sort of a job you have for the 60 fr. which you earn? Write frequently while you are in Marseilles.

I embrace you and bless you with all my heart.

Your Uncle
T. Bs.

5

28th July/8th August, 1877
Kazimierówka

My dearest boy!

You have evidently forgotten the national proverb that 'the humble calf sucks two mothers'. That must have been the cause of your losing your temper—which resulted in a breach with Mr. Délestang. I do not deny that, if things happened the way you describe them, the honourable épicier treated you too loftily, unmindful of having before him a descendant of the excellent family of Nałęcz—that's agreed. I see from your account of the talk with him that you have la repartie facile et suffisamment acérée in which I recognize your Nałęcz blood—in this tendency to fly into a passion I even detect a drop of Biberstejn[1] blood;—unfortunately I do not perceive in this whole affair any trace of that prudent common sense of which on the distaff side you have the right to be proud, deriving it from the House of Jastrzembczyk[2] to which I have the honour to belong. Now then, from the point of view of gloriola and wit your discourse with the épicier may satisfy you. I think that from the point of view of common sense and consideration of the circumstances—from the practical point of view—it can neither please me nor even yourself after a little sober deliberation. Let us consider this matter coolly. You write that you are looking for employment that would bring you some profit. Mr. Délestang in his majesty condescends to offer you such employment. Common

[1] Bobrowski's mother's maiden name was Biberstejn-Pilchowska; her brothers took part in the 1830–1 insurrection and their estate was confiscated.
[2] The Bobrowskis' coat of arms was 'Jastrzembiec', hence the family nickname 'Jastrzembczyk'.

sense should have made you accept this opportunity as he obviously trusted you in spite of your youth and of your being a foreigner; he showed a preference for you over his countrymen and trusted you; you could, when replying to him, have made him feel the unsuitable tone he used; but accepted it, while laying down your conditions, both as to present remuneration and as to his making your voyage to India free of charge. Had the épicier observed that you were tactful and could take advantage of your opportunities, que Vs avez de l'étoffe pour faire un homme de commerce, you would have profited in three ways: you would not have broken with a man who in one way or another might be useful to you; you would have raised yourself higher in his opinion; you would have earned something;—considerations not without importance!! Certainly I cannot expect of you in your 19th year to have the maturity of an old man, but I warn you that some day, perhaps soon, you will regret that conversation; for although Mr. d'Escarras[1] likes you and is maître à son bord, I feel that l'épicier likes being in that role himself; you will therefore do well to try and find yourself some employment till December. Thus there must be cabotage; perhaps you could, in the meanwhile, explore Algiers or the coast of Italy—at the same time relieving your pocket, which must be fairly empty. Possibly Mr. d'Escarras will not be able to take you—in any case to spend a whole year on land cannot be good either for your health or for practising and perfecting your profession??

I do not know to what extent your idea of transferring to the English merchant fleet may be practical? My first question is, do you speak English? As to that I am completely ignorant, since you never answered my question whether you are learning this language? I never wished you to become naturalized in France, mainly because of the compulsory military service which you would have to undergo, God knows for what and for whom. I thought, however, of your getting naturalized in Switzerland and I still think of it. Try then to find out what are the conditions and expense that Swiss naturalization would entail. Write about it to Mr. Izydor Sobański, apparently his residence is *Kinburn* somewhere near Pfäffikon where you were—but Mr. Orzechowski[2] has sold it already (and does not live there). I shall for my part discuss the matter with Mr. Jenny, my Swiss neighbour and friend, who has an estate here but who now lives in Dresden, but will be coming here in September,

[1] Captain d'Escarras was the master of the *Saint-Antoine* in which Conrad served for some time in 1876.

[2] Tadeusz Oksza-Orzechowski, a friend of Apollo Korzeniowski and in 1863 an envoy of the Polish National Government to Istanbul. Conrad visited him on his way to Marseilles in September 1874.

or to Kiev for the fair. Look after your papers well; your birth certificate and your father's passport, so as not to have any trouble later. I expect that next year, after your return from India, we shall finally settle this matter. I am very sorry about that good fellow Mr. Sallary[1] who was so kind to you—you have also not written whether the news that Mr. Chodźko perished with his ship was finally confirmed or not? I would mourn him as well, but I would be still more sorry for his poor parents. Write to me please about it. Write to me also how you are? What are you studying? and what will you do with yourself till December? Will you find employment and sail or remain on shore—whatever you do, go on studying and work on your character, my dear boy, for your whole future depends on work. In September I shall send you your allowance for half a year, but the rate of exchange for our money being so bad, I might have to withdraw 450 guldens of the 1,000 deposited in the Savings Bank. In that case I shall accumulate the equivalent sum of 300 roubles and will put them aside for you as I do not want the gift from your relative to be diminished;—only for the sake of naturalization might I possibly decide to sacrifice it. Hence you must think, Panie Bracie, how you can carry on with what you have until your departure, and get through the voyage on what you will have—and on your return speak to Mr. d'Escarras and let me know how it turns out? Whatever you do, do not send me telegrams for you must know how I dislike them, and generally it is impossible to find a solution immediately.

Your Uncle has found employment with the Nadwiślańska Railway as a station-master, 16 versts from Lublin, 600 roubles salary with accommodation en tout potage—how can he exist there with a wife and five children? He cannot survive without my help; and my income this year is damned uncertain—God grant that I shall be able to give each of you the same as before—but greater assistance cannot even be dreamed of; if I could give it, your Uncle would need it more than you—but that is a dream as I don't even know how I shall get through myself.

Well, I conclude by embracing you and send you my blessing, dear boy, with all my heart.

Your Uncle
TADEUSZ B.

Frania embraces you and thanks you for remembering her. Did you write to your Uncle—still: Nowolipki 7, Warsaw.

---

[1] Baptistin Solary (the spelling varies), a seaman and Conrad's friend in Marseilles.

6

2/14 September, 1877
Kazimierówka

My dearest boy!

Your letter of the 4/16 August has arrived. You defend your case eloquently, basing yourself even on the authority of the illustrious Mr. Salles, courtier-maritime, who is no great authority in my opinion. However, what has happened has happened and it is no use harping on it. I hope that you will not abuse the trust placed in you, and that you will tell no one of the activities of your ex-patron, not even the grand Mr. Salles, whose approval should in itself be sufficient for you. As I always repeat to you, however, do not count so much on Mr. d'Escarras, but consider what you would do if he, under pressure from his patron, should refuse to keep his promise? à l'impossible personne n'est obligé, and he surely does not love you so much that he would risk losing his own position for the sake of a promise given to you in different circumstances. Consider it well, so as not to be met with an unpleasant surprise—as an old player I warn you that this may easily happen! So think well about it. . . . You were absolutely within your rights to withdraw the last 300 fr. of your allowance of the 16th ultimo. So far as the next half-year is concerned, I have decided, out of the 1,000 gulden that you have in the Savings Bank from the late Miss Korzeniowska, to take 500 and send them to you. Thus I shall today ask Mrs. Justyna Syroczyńska to withdraw it from the Bank and to transfer it to the Galician Bank of Industry and Commerce with my instructions to the Bank to pay you monthly instalments or the whole sum on demand. In exchange for these 500 gulden I will buy for you now 400 roubles in securities of the Kiev Credit Society of Landowners, which will cost between 320 and 340 roubles and will earn $6\frac{1}{2}\%$. You will thus have 500 gulden, and 400 roubles for the other 500. This whole transaction is designed to avoid the terrible rate of exchange of our money, which now stands at 258 fr. for 100 roubles. At this rate your allowance would cost me 400 roubles, which sum is difficult for me to come by, so I save 60 to 80 roubles on the transaction, and if God permits our rate of exchange to improve something might be gained on the credit notes as well, as a coupon for a hundred, bought at 85, could stand at 95 as it used to before the war—and a rouble up to 154 [. . .][1], or even a rate of 340 centimes could come back as before. I am, therefore, writing today

---

[1] Word illegible.

to Mrs. Syroczyńska—as her husband has gone to Italy for reasons of health—to send you the gulden. Should there be a delay, let me know at once—by letter, for I am not suggesting that you telegraph me. I should tell you that Mr. Bekierski through whom you telegraphed me is no longer in Winnica, but a Mr. Padlewski—make a note of this name, which can come in useful in an emergency. You are right in what you say about Swiss naturalization;—if you could obtain it in the United States I would have nothing against it—if you have the possibility of arranging it there or in one of the more important Southern Republics. Who is the Baron Drużkowicz? The Austrian Consul? And this Japanese consul, who likes you, 'you do not know what for and why'—who may this individual be? Perhaps he could help you to find something in Japan after you get your Master's certificate? Perhaps you will become an Admiral in Japan? Indeed, once you have embarked on a cosmopolitan career such as yours is in the merchant navy—it is unimportant where one is. And I do not see that you are specially attached to the French, which I must say does not displease me—it would sadden me to know that you regarded France as your fatherland.

For the third time I ask whether Mr. Chodźko has perished? Is this news true? Because what you told me about Mr. Solary leaves no doubt that he certainly perished. Tell me the facts.

Of local news that may interest you I report having seen recently Mrs. Taube and her young gentlemen.[1] They all graciously asked after you. Artur still goes from place to place, not doing anything. Oleś and Romek suffer from the disease of being young noblemen and it seems they will also grow into idlers. Gucio holds out more hope; he is in Warsaw and his brothers in Riga. Lola is still a spinster. Kostuś B. has moved to Riga, but at least he is working. His sister is widowed and is left with four children; she is ill and is going to Algiers or Cairo with her father. About Pulman I know nothing. Uncle Kazimierz has a job on the K.Ż. Nadwiślańska, in Mińkowice.

I embrace you and bless you. Write frequently.

Your uncle,
T. Bobrowski.

---

[1] Bobrowski was the legal guardian of all the six young Taubes (Conrad's friends in Cracow): Artur, Aleksander (Oleś), Roman (Romek), Gustaw (Gucio), and the girls Karolina (Lola, who later married Bolesław Gnatowski) and Janina (later Baroness de Brunnow).

16/28 May, 1878
Śnieżna

My dear Konrad!

A few days after getting a letter from Mr. Richard Fecht[1] and sending him my reply—I was obliged to come here because of a fatal illness that befell the 11-year-old son of Mr. & Mrs. Zaleski. The boy died on the 12th instant leaving his parents in indescribable grief, so that I have had to remain here until now, and your letter asking me for 600 fr. reached me only yesterday after having been forwarded from home. So today I am replying to it.

I suppose that my reply to Mr. Fecht reached him long ago— so I see no reason to telegraph him as you ask me to—and which as you know I detest doing. My reply to Mr. Fecht was as follows: if it is really *indispensable* and if the premium cannot be paid after your return from the voyage,[2] as simple logic would indicate—(and which would coincide with sending you your allowance for the second half-year), I requested him to advance you the 500 fr. which he informed me that you needed—this to be deducted from your allowance for the second half-year which will be sent to him at the proper time—with the addition of interest for this advance—as with our rate of exchange and before the payment of funds into my account and considering the necessity of travelling to Kiev to get the money before the second half-year starts, it would be very tiresome for me!! I suppose, however, that Fecht, under the pressure of your letters and possibly your presence, has already sent you the desired sum—and giving you 500 he probably went as far as to give you 600—that is, as much as you are asking for. Whether, however, it will be possible to cover this advance out of your allowance remains to be seen; otherwise it would mean an increase of the burden on my pocket by a further 600 fr. and may God be my witness, you were not kind to it this year! When you calculate what you have had during the past three years, you will see that you have had between 3,000 fr. and 4,000 fr. per annum—which is twice as much as I had allocated—and than I can afford. However, I shall not desert you for the sake of 600 fr. if you need that to secure your future—but if it serves no purpose, as has been the case up till now—then you will answer for it to your own conscience and to God—for I have all my work cut out to supply you—ask yourself: per que? You will get this letter through Mr. Fecht, to whom

---

[1] A German from Wittenberg, Conrad's closest friend in Marseilles.
[2] As an apprentice Conrad was obliged to pay something for being articled to a ship.

16/28 *May* 1878

I am writing again authorizing the advance of up to 600 fr.—the whole of which sum, independently of the exchange, will have to be sent in September, which I will certainly do. I am writing this 'via Marseilles', you will easily guess why; firstly, Mr. Fecht is staying there permanently and is a reliable intermediary—secondly, at this moment all letters from and to England are liable to be suspected by the post and although we write about innocent matters (however burdensome for my pocket)—nevertheless we have no reason to admit confidants to our correspondence;—hence, I pray you to reply the same way. I am sending today a few words to the address I have indicated to you, so as to notify you here and there —and do not be surprised by any present or future delays that may occur as you are not the only person I have to think about—Mrs. Lub.,[1] Mr. & Mrs. Zaleska, the Montresor family—are all going abroad for cures and their affairs will be left in my care; hence this summer I shall have to travel about more than in the past.

This, however, does not release you from writing to me as if I were staying in one place, as I for my part will search for you with my letters all round the world according to your directions—only write to me where and when you will be! and I for my part shall write to you.

And now I embrace you and bless you.

Your Uncle
T. Bobrowski.

The deceased son of the Zaleskis' was not Staś, whom you know and who is at present 17 years old, but their other son Witold, who was next in age after the sister. They are the only two left now.

8

26 June/8 July, 1878
Kazimierówka

My good Konrad!

Yesterday your letter dated 9 June reached me via Richard—this being the third letter I have had from you since my return from Marseilles. Before you get this reply, you will certainly have already had the news from Richard about the 600 fr. sent him for you which you say are indispensable for paying the Captain's premium. Thus you have here again proof of my readiness to help you, and if you should wish to contemplate it in the proper light, I will tell you

---

[1] Mrs. Lubowidzka, Bobrowski's mother-in-law.

that if I did not go this year to Marienbad, in accordance with my doctor's orders, this was solely due to the lack of means;—after my journey to Marseilles, after paying off your debts, and now after the additional and unexpected expense of sending at a most inconvenient time 600 fr. (which in our money is 260 roubles)—expenses that I had to bear! I would not complain at all—I would not even mention it—if I knew that all my efforts and privations for you are in a good cause and that you appreciate them. But unfortunately this by no means seems to be the case! Reflect, I pray, if you are still capable of doing it, on what mischief you have done this year? and answer for yourself if even from your own father you could expect such patience and indulgence as you get from me,—and whether this should not have reached its limit?

You were idling for nearly a whole year—you fell into debt, you deliberately shot yourself—and as a result of it all, at the worst time of the year, tired out and in spite of the most terrible rate of exchange —I hasten to you, pay, spend about 2,000 roubles, I increase your allowance to meet your needs! All this is apparently not enough for you. And when I make a fresh sacrifice to save you from idleness and to ensure that you could stay on the English ship that you fancied, you leave the ship, giving me to understand that you did so because of the impossibility of paying the premium (for which they would certainly have waited, having in hand your 400 fr.)—you travel to London, God knows why, being fully aware that you could not manage by yourself, having nothing and knowing nobody—you then lose half the money you have left and you write to me as if to some school-chum 'send me 500 fr. which you can deduct from the allowance';—from which allowance, pray?—from the one you give yourself? and 'advise me what to do in these difficult circumstances'. In other words, you treat me like your banker: asking for advice so as to get money—assuming that if I give you advice— which you will or will not follow—I shall also give money for putting my advice into practice! Really, you have exceeded the limits of stupidity permitted to your age! and you pass beyond the limits of my patience! What possible advice can I—so far away—give, not knowing the conditions of your profession in general and the local conditions in particular? When you decided on this unfortunate profession, I told you: I don't want and am not going to chase after you to the ends of the world—for I do not intend nor do I wish to spoil all my life because of the fantasies of a hobbledehoy.

I shall help you, but I warn you that you must persevere in your decision, work, as upon this your whole future depends, I will not allow you to be idle at my expense—you will find help in me, but not for a lazy-bones and a spendthrift. I told you this when you set out to be a sailor. I repeated it in my letters and I repeated it again in Marseilles—you must think for yourself and fend for yourself, for you have chosen a career which keeps you far from your natural advisers. You wanted it—you did it—you voluntarily chose it. Submit to the results of your decision. You ask for advice in the 'present difficult situation'—this I shall not give, for I cannot—I did not send you where you are. I agreed that you should sail on an English ship but not to your staying in England, not to your travelling to London and wasting my money there! I can only give you one piece of advice—not a new one, for I have given it to you a hundred times already, and that is 'arrange your affairs within the limits of what I give you, for I will not give you more'—'commit no more stupidities, for I have no intention of making them good any more'. All the explanations of your actions, and of the circumstances; all insinuations designed to increase my trust in you (such as the last one, that you were returning to Marseilles, not mentioning it to me and that then you changed your mind) etcetera,—will only arouse my faith in you if they are confirmed by actions. You know that you have lost the trust I had in you—you must feel that you had it once and that my withdrawal of it was justified. Try to retrieve it, not by words but by deeds. You will retrieve it by working persistently in your chosen profession, by becoming serious and considerate, by telling the truth.

I repeat, it is all the same to me in which navy you work—the choice is your affair. If you decide to join the French Navy I have nothing against it, but until you are 21 do something; don't idle, learn, and don't pretend to be a rich young gentleman and wait for someone to pull your chestnuts out of the fire—for this will not happen. If you cannot get a ship, then be a commission agent for a time, but do something, earn something, for one cannot be a parasite. Many of your age are helping their families and work for them, while you, if you examine yourself scrupulously and impartially, will see that you are on the way to becoming a nuisance to your family. I am writing to Richard to pay you out 600 fr. after deducting what is due to him. Manage this sum as well as you can—if you cannot pay your premium to go on a ship, go as a simple sailor; if you learn what poverty is, it will teach you the value of money. If you wish to wait before signing on for the Navy, find yourself some occupation and earn some money, for you won't get a penny from me before it is due even if you write to me that you are certain of becoming an Admiral of the Fleet in the British Navy—I have had enough of these additional payments! And I repeat again, that if you have not secured yourself a position by the age of 24, do not count on the allowance, for I will stop it—I have no money for drones and I have no intention of working so that someone else may enjoy himself at my expense—I wonder if you ever considered how much you have cost me? To facilitate this problem for you I inform you that everything has been carefully noted by me here and that since your parents' death I have spent on you (apart from the 1,100 guldens squandered by you which you had from the late Mr. K.[1] and 500 roubles from Mme Korzeniowska) 9,119 roubles. It is a tidy sum, about 30,000 fr., and up till now what has it produced—nothing!!!

I now call on you to reflect! Think of your parents, of your grandmother, who sacrificed so much for you—remember my sacrifices, my fatherly indulgence and leniency—reform yourself—work—calculate—be prudent and doggedly pursue your aim and with deeds, not with words—prove that you deserve my blessing.

Your Uncle
T. BOBROWSKI.

Write what you are going to do.

9

2/14 September, 1878
Kazimierówka

My dear Konrad!

There is a shower of your letters pouring in every few days. However, I get them altogether once a week, for, as you know, I send for my mail once a week. So yesterday I got two of them—one of the 28th August and one of the 1st September. I observe that the growing proximity of the payment of your allowance puts you into a feverish state—which I would call a 'fever of receiving'. I confess frankly that I do not experience a similar 'fever of giving' and I calmly await the time of swallowing this pill, which in the present state of my pocket may cause a certain diarrhoea; which, however, will happen soon, so that the money may be sent to you in time. From your last letter but one, I see that you expect to get the whole 1,200 fr., as you explicitly show me with a great knowledge of arithmetic—sorry, I mean the art of addition—how you will use your 1,200 fr., forgetting that on account of this sum you have already had 600 fr., which proves to me that although exercising

[1] Onufry Korzeniowski (see Document, November 1870, p. 190).

yourself in one of the branches of arithmetic—*addition*—you have obviously neglected to practise another—*subtraction*—which while facilitating your accounts makes them devilishly complicated for me, at our present rate of exchange of 40 kop. to a franc. If my eyes do not deceive me, I read in your letter of the 15th July, in which you acknowledge the receipt of 600 fr. (forgetting the 200 fr. due to Richard) the following words: 'As for me, I shall have left on the 15th October 400 fr. which I ask you kindly to send me; not more than that, however, as my conscience would not permit me to take a greater sum, after what happened at the beginning of this year.' Apparently your conscience is now at rest as you reckon for certain on getting the whole 1,200 fr. If that is so, then it means that what you said in your letter of the 15th July was nothing but an empty phrase—what is the point of it?—whereas the matter in question was a serious one. But it is not words but deeds that count; hence why send a bill for 1,200 fr. to someone who has to give you only 600—a more natural and suitable way would have been to ask: 'Dear Uncle, give me this time more than you promised as otherwise I shall never be able to break out of this vicious circle in which I thoughtlessly got entangled.' That would be a straightforward way. However, in spite of my past statements to the contrary, once more I shall help you to get back on to the right road—but believe me that this is for the *third and last time*. I shall send you that total allowance of 1,200 fr. but believe me it is for the *last time*, and I shall not permit you to drag out of me a similar sum every 6 months, pretending that it is an advance on account of the next six months, for I do not manufacture money; I have to strive hard for it and must obtain it by certain dates—so manage on it as well you can—firstly pay Richard—for I swear in God's name that I shall give you no more under any pretence—either as an advance or in answer to a request—as I simply cannot. However, as you practise 'addition' condescend to add the following figures: Your debts and my journey 1,355, Allowance 15th March: 480, advance in July 240, Allowance 15th October 480—you will arrive at the sum of 2,675 roubles, that is 6,687 francs which is the equivalent of my personal maintenance for 4 years, for I have for myself only 600 roubles annually, which has to suffice me. I suspect that my nephew does not consider me so naïve that I should give him four times as much as I keep for myself. A bon entendeur salut.

I send you a letter in French as you requested and simultaneously with sending the money to Richard I shall write to him that he may send your money a bit earlier, possibly even on the 1st October. In the next few days I shall have to go to Kiev or Odessa to arrange to send it and when sending it I shall write both to you and to Richard.

Though you may be feverish now, before the wretched money reaches you, I shall also suffer from anxiety till I learn what use you have made of it. Therefore, Panie Bracie, write to me about your intentions and decisions and later on do not forget about your humble servant but fortify him with letters while he labours for your maintenance, for as I have told you in my last letter, I desire the reformation of the sinner and not the getting him out of my mind, thoughts, heart, and pocket; that would have been the easiest way and my concern is to be able to cherish him, love and, what is most important of all, respect him—which is all now up to you.

Embracing you a hundredfold and blessing you.

Your Uncle,
T. B.

10

26.10./7.11.1879
Kazimierówka

My dear boy!

May God be praised that you have returned safe and sound—at least I hope so as you do not report any damage, apart from great exhaustion and a need for rest. At your age—the first will quickly disappear and the second will quickly bore you.[1]

Your letter of the 20th (new style) reached me on the 20th (our style), that is in 12 days. I send to the post office once a week, each Friday, hence my reply to you may be sent only today, that is a week later, thus we need a minimum of 3 weeks to exchange letters —providing of course that I am at home, which usually, however, is the case in the autumn as I have no liking for bad roads. So, Panie Bracie, bear in mind this length of time. I hope that the messenger who will take this letter will on his return bring me your second promised one which I await eagerly—for the one I received, although full of details of your voyage, is at the same time rather lacking in news of yourself. In particular, how did you stand up to all these adventures? I cannot blame you for my expectation that on the first day after your return you should write me an exhaustive letter—so I thank you for what you have sent and ask for more later. Firstly personal news, and secondly, if I may, about what you have seen, as this is of more interest to me than the direction of the

---

[1] Conrad in the margin: 'répondu en detail le 12 9bre 1879.'

58

winds that brought you back and which I am ready to regard as favourable if they did not harm you and if you did not suffer from frost-bite.

I was greatly pleased with your assurance that you will be satisfied with part of the allowance now due to you for, as I have already written, I am an *absolute pauper* this year—500 fr. is all I have at my disposal—*I wait now for suggestions as to how, when, and to whom I should send it?* I think—I am not sure—that I could send it directly from Odessa to London. Having delighted your humble servant with your restraint, mind, Sir, not to cause him distress later by demanding all. You know well how a man gets used to good things and so I have got used already to the noble thought of giving you only 500 fr. and it would be an unpleasant surprise for me to have to say farewell to this idea. Recollecting, however, that staying on land has always had an inauspicious influence upon you, I tremble with fear lest you should cause me an unpleasant surprise and I therefore appeal to you—please bear in mind the bad effect land has on you and keep me constantly and steadily in your heart. As far as the idea of sailing the Mediterranean is concerned I answer as usual—do as you think! as you wish! I have no knowledge of it. I have read more than once that it is only 'a great lake', so a sailor enamoured as you are of your profession I suppose might like the ocean better? Besides, as I have mentioned before, I would like to see in you a sailor combined with a salesman, and as the roads around here are better trodden and known, I should have thought that the more distant and less known ones would be more appropriate for you. But you may know more about it all and therefore do what you think best. What happened to the captain and the ship that tempted you? Did you come across them? I should like to know. You plan to come to Odessa next year and to see me there. It is difficult to predict what will happen in a year's time—there might be a war—my old self might die. However, neither the one nor the other is in our power to prevent but it is our duty to foresee and avoid unnecessary trouble, and therefore I do not wish you to visit Russia until you are naturalized as an English subject;[1] but what you have not written to me about is whether after passing your examination for second mate you will obtain naturalization. So write to me and clear this up.

On the same day that I got your letter I sent to Mr. Déléstang a very lofty letter asking him for a testimonial for you—so I have done my part—now you must write to him giving him your address; I hope that he will do what we ask him to.

[1] Conrad was liable for Russian military service.

I am in good health, things are always the same, but I am growing old—only shaving keeps me in a state of relative youth. Uncle Kazim. is still on the Vistula Railway at the Mińkowice Station.[1] I very much doubt whether you have written, Good Sir, but if you should do so, you may be certain of getting the warmest reception. I take your letter to be an introduction to a longer chat and so I ask for the 'next instalment'; you can always be certain of getting a reply.

I embrace and bless you with all my heart.

Your uncle,
T. BOBROWSKI.

11

31 January/12 February, 1880
Kazimierówka

My dear boy!

I certainly did not get your letter from Patras, and remained in profound ignorance of your fate to my surprise and disquiet, from which I was delivered in an unpleasant way by your letter of the 2nd February from London, only to be plunged into fresh disquiet.

I was not so much upset by the troubles you had on the *Europa*, though I realize you must have felt them keenly, for these are inseparable from life and getting to know people. They pain you, because you feel that you did not deserve them and that you are being exploited. I understand this and partly agree with you. But in your position, in which everything you gain must be won by work and endurance, in a profession where the conditions are extremely hard, what has happened was to be foreseen—and was foreseen by me;—and probably now that you have had the first dose of experience they don't surprise you although they hurt—and hurt they must! I am much more affected by the news that you 'cough and sometimes have fever', for these are symptoms which, if prolonged, may endanger your health and even your life. I am deeply worried about this cough and fever. Undoubtedly the foggy London air will not help; more probably sailing on the Mediterranean, in a warm climate, would be beneficial if your duties did not involve too much exertion. Weigh the pros and cons from the point of view of your health, get the opinion of a good doctor, and write to me what he finds and advises, and what you yourself are thinking of doing so as to bring your health back to normal. I realize that a cure or a good

[1] Russian in the original: Привисленской Ж. Д. ст. Миньковицѣ.

rest cannot be had without money and if I only had any I would
advance it to you without delay; but as God is my witness, as usual
at this time of the year I am as poor as a church mouse and in a few
days' time I must travel to Kiev where only around the 15th
February I shall have money, as about that time the profits for the
year 1880 will start coming in, and in 1879 I had so many unexpected and extraordinary expenses that I myself have been living on
borrowed money for the past few months. From Kiev I shall send
via Odessa your 1,200 fr. allowance to Marseilles to that good
fellow Richard, although I must say truly that I cannot understand
how you can have only 3 pounds left after first having left in Marseilles 1,200 fr. on deposit and then having received 500 fr. Your
common sense should have told you—after having settled all your
essential requirements—to put aside a certain sum to be there for
your next stay in London where, as you have written yourself,
you would be returning every 9 weeks. I can understand that you
could spend more than you had, but I don't understand how you
could so arrange things after your experiences in the past.

I am going to Kiev in a few days, and today I am sending specially
to the post office to send this letter and see if your other, promised,
letter has arrived. But I am departing feeling very anxious about
you and should this letter find you in London, please write without
delay direct to Kiev: *Mr. Th. B., Grand Hotel*, informing me
about your health and plans. Particularly about your health as this
worries me—look after yourself Panie Bracie,—my letters, advice,
and complaints will serve no purpose without your taking care to
look after yourself and to preserve within the limits of possibility
and necessity your health,—something that should be treasured by
all, especially the young. Your letter from London reached me in 7
days; if this reaches you as quickly you should have it by the 7 February (our style) and I, in turn, should get your reply in Kiev by the
15th—I shall be staying there till our 22 February. Do write
immediately, I beg you, if this letter finds you still in London. If I
do not get any news from you while in Kiev, I shall take it that you
have left. In that case write to me immediately after your return
for if I get no news from your voyage I shall be 'like a cat on hot
bricks'. I shall get home from Kiev on the 1st March (old style). My
health is not too good. Old age makes itself felt more and more and
I have not much share of the joys of life. I am greatly worried about
you. May Providence keep you in her care.

I embrace and bless you from the depth of my unquiet heart.

Your uncle
T. BOBROWSKI.

As I shall wait for your letter I shall send your money order only about the 20th February (old style). Richard let me use his address for your allowance—he did not write about leaving M. So he is probably there?

12

18/30 May, 1880
Kazimierówka

My dearest boy!

You are worrying about me unnecessarily, for if I had given up the ghost you would be informed. Uncle Kazimierz, Mr. Tadeusz Zaleski, and Mr. Włodzimierz Czarnowski, whom I have charged with executing my will, would have informed you of whatever in it concerns you—you would say a little prayer and you would become a bit lonelier still in the world—which with you on it would carry on, less one heart and one head that loved you both (i.e. yourself and the world). That is the way with life. But as yet I do not plan to take refuge on God's acre—on the contrary I am quite well. And while suffering or even dying I would find consolation in doing so among my own people—which is something your profession denies you. So let your mind be at rest—I am quite well.

Why you do not get my letters I just do not understand as I always reply to yours. The last letter, dealing mainly with your naturalization, I wrote before our Easter holidays. Today I shall answer all your 4 letters, of 1, 6, 11, and 16 May—as I read them all at once on my return from Morozówka where I spent the Easter holidays and had to stay on because of Mrs. Lub.'s illness.

Your discomposure because of that madman Captain Munro[1] worries me not less than it does you, although I don't understand English logic, since if the Captain is a madman his certificate and commission should be withdrawn. Until he is judicially proclaimed mad his certificate must remain valid. Well, we won't change the English, so having to deal with them, we must adapt ourselves. I suppose that while I am writing, your *Europa* is in port and you have the testimonial from the present Captain, the previous second mate, and that you have either already passed your examination or are about to sit for it shortly. You can certainly believe that I wish you to pass this examination successfully and even with honours, so please accept my warmest wishes and blessings. Frania has promised

[1] The master of the steamship *Europa* in which Conrad served for seven weeks in December 1879 and January 1880.

62

to pray for you not only in the evenings but in the mornings and she keeps her promise.

What I had to say about naturalization I said in my last letter. It is impossible to be a 'Vogel frey' all your life. One has to acquire some civil status and sooner or later you will have to think about it and it is always better to arrange the matter calmly and not under the pressure of circumstances and necessity.

You would not be a Nałęcz, dear boy, if you were steady in your enterprises and if you didn't chase after ever new projects. This refers to what you wrote about Mr. Lascalle's proposal that you become his secretary and later make money on the railways! But I would not be myself and your uncle if I did not discourage you from changing professions and did not warn you that such changes make people become 'déclassé', who never having warmed a place for themselves nor having built anything for themselves (I don't even mention the good of society although it is only fair to think of it), bear a grudge against the whole world for not having succeeded. You must not, Panie Bracie, believe in either good or bad luck. Work and perseverance are the only values that never fail. In the life of every man a momentary success may occur, but a sensible and moderate man will not misuse it but use it, while a thoughtless and stupid man will either miss it or misuse it. But to expect that success should appear while one is on the threshold of life, and at any time it's needed, without any work or merit, is childish dreaming and a product of our epoch whose only slogan is 'enjoyment'. You must see it for yourself—does it agree with personal dignity and reason to tie oneself to the fate of another man—however great he might seem—and in this particular case to some American business-man or politician? It is much more dignified and sensible to devote your life and tie your future to a certain profession, putting into it your work and determination. You chose for yourself the profession of seaman,—you can expand on it further by trading—well and good —pursue this as far as you can and you will get somewhere. By changing from one career fortuitously to another you may encounter on your way nothing but deception and pain! Anyhow, that's what I think! You will do as you wish, for in all aspects connected with your career I leave you absolute freedom as I am a great believer in it on principle and I realize well that I cannot express my opinion, however firmly I hold it, without knowing the circumstances in which you are situated. As a man of a clearly defined position I feel sympathetic to people of the same kind. There is and never has been anything of an adventurer in me, so I sigh for a regular position for you as well. You know best what you want, what you are looking for,—and what can happen to you. 'You have made your bed and you must lie on it!' and whatever bed may be your lot, provided that you make it with dignity and diligence, you may be certain of my wholehearted blessing which I bestow upon you here and now.

Your uncle
T. BOBROWSKI.

13

5/17 June, 1880
Kazimierówka

My dear boy and Officer!

Two days ago I got the news (two letters together) about the fortunate outcome of your examination.[1] It has been a profound pleasure and my first reward to learn that you have received that piece of 'ass's hide' upon which so many terrible threats were written by the gentlemen of the Board Office in the event of your failing in the duties of your chosen profession, in the hierarchy of which you have now achieved the first step!! I fully share your satisfaction, which you can say arises from a twofold source. Firstly, Dear Sir, you have proved to our country and your own people that you have not eaten your bread in the world for four years in vain; secondly, that you have succeeded in overcoming the difficulties that arise from the language itself, and from your difficult position as a foreigner without any patronage to support you—and all this thanks to Capt. Wyndham, whom may God grant long life for putting the fear of God into you! And yet, that good old fellow of a captain let himself be disarmed, while that kind-hearted professor Newton who encouraged you while not mentioning Wyndham's prejudices, and those sailors who rejoiced at your success—they all seem very likeable to me at this moment,—for taking the stranger to their bosom. There are good people everywhere, one must only know how to find them and to attach them to oneself! You cannot complain of any lack of them on your path, from the beginning of your life among strangers—it is enough to recall the kind-hearted Solary and Richard and those good London fellows. This imposes upon you the duty not only of feeling gratitude to them, but of a general love of people and of helping others who need your help and whom you may encounter on your way through life. Let the

---

[1] For Second Mate. The examination is described in *A Personal Record*.

pessimists say what they will about the defects of the human race, but I will tell you from my own experience that there are more good than bad people;—it is only necessary to deal with them and approach them properly! Well now, my congratulations to you as Officer of the second degree in the British Merchant Marine. Peace to all men of good will whom you have met on your way!

Well, Officer! the first step is taken! Now we need work and endurance, endurance and work, to go further and to assure your livelihood, for you will soon be 24—in October 1881. You still have a year in which to find something which will assure you a living without your having to look to your Uncle. This Uncle will always carefully follow your progress—you can rest assured of that as long as you deserve his solicitude; only, while giving you a higher position in his heart he must lower your place in his pocket, for others are coming on who demand pocket-solicitude—your other Uncle's children.

Many thanks for keeping me au courant of your plans and hopes. I shall tell you now as I always do: do as you wish, for I am helpless in all that concerns your profession; you have therefore carte blanche to dispose of yourself as you see fit. I am not opposed to any of your projects—even if it is to become a Yankee. In my last letter I said what I think about that—namely that I would not be in favour of changing over from a maritime career to going into the service of an American politician, though even that would not scandalize me if you insist on acting contrary to my view; but always under two conditions: firstly, that you bear in mind our proverb: 'you have made your bed and must lie on it', and secondly, that you will never forget what is due to the dignity of the nation and families to which you belong—especially if you choose an American business life. So here are my conditions; I am not to be held responsible for your behaviour;—I am not to blush for your actions;—and as far as the rest is concerned—may God always help you!

I have not written to Richard for a long time,—not since sending him your allowance, and quite possibly I then complained of your silence—not having had a letter from you for some time. Now I have no complaints in that respect for I get them frequently and they are always welcome. Certainly I won't expect to get them so frequently when you are at sea, but I always like to get a sign of life from you once a month and details of your route so that I can follow it. However, I do not write to Richard frequently for I have nothing to say and I know that he has no time for odd letters.

Frania is triumphant at your becoming an Officer and attributes it to the skill with which she swaddled you, and to the efficacy of her prayers.

I bless your further successes.

I embrace you warmly my dear boy—write to me.

Your ever loving Uncle
T. B.

14

28 June (old style) 1880
Kazimierówka

My dear boy!

I have your letter of the 13th this month—it lay for some time on my table as I have been away for a fortnight. I see with pleasure that the Nałęcz in you has been modified under the influence of the Bobroszczaki, as your incomparable Mother used to call her own family after she flew away to the Nałęcz nest. This time I rejoice over the influence of my family, although I don't in the least deny that the Nałęczes have a spirit of initiative and enterprise greater than that which is in my blood. From the blending of these two excellent families in your worthy person there should spring a race which by its endurance and wise enterprise will astound the whole world! Pray God that may happen. Amen!

I am sincerely sorry, my dear boy, that you cannot find a suitable position straight away, but I do not doubt that it will come with time, work, and endurance. I am not distrustful by nature and I find it hateful to distrust people whom I love unless a person deceives me, in which case I withdraw both my trust and my heart. I have therefore not held the slightest suspicion that you have described the sad state of your finances in order to ask me for an advance. Even if your present financial situation, of which you yourself are the creator, were to move me, I could not do anything about it, as I don't manufacture money and my income comes in at certain times of the year and is spent according to a prearranged plan. Thus the money destined for your September allowance this year won't be in my possession till August. Should I therefore wish to show and prove my magnanimity towards you, I would have to explain to someone else, as you do to me, that I have no means of support till I get the money. So I cannot and shall not favour you particularly; you must wait, my dear boy, till October. Perhaps Richard could help you with one or two hundred francs? Then I would forward to him your allowance when it is due, for I undertook to keep up your allowance till you are 24 years old, that is till October 1881, and you can count on that. Then I shall expand for you, Sir, my heart, but squeeze my pocket, as I have told you before. And why? You know and understand well.

Therefore, my boy, manage your affairs as well as you can and acknowledge the fact—you, a Nałęcz—that economy and calculation are indispensable in every position, especially in yours! and even in mine!

Write to me what you have decided, and whether I am to send your September allowance to Richard or to some other person equally reliable and friendly towards you who at the same time I could trust like the worthy Richard. Write to me during your voyage at least once a month; but it will give me pleasure if you do it more frequently. I embrace you now, and bless you, my dear boy.

Your uncle,
T. BOBROWSKI.

Frania embraces and blesses you.

15

1/13 May, 1881
Kazimierówka

My dear boy!

I thank Heaven for bringing you safely back to the misty shores of hospitable Albion, for which country, by the way, in the depths of my heart, I do not feel a great sympathy. Thank you for letting me know immediately of your return, for since the 1st April I have counted the days and expected a letter with each post, even before our Easter holidays. I got it eventually on my return from Morozówka, five days ago. I am answering it without delay, in the hope that it may reach you in London before your next voyage.

Firstly, I was greatly pleased to be able to give you a surprise by announcing your half-allowance and not the quarterly allowance that you were expecting. Usually young people expect more than they should. This time, however, if I can believe in your assurance (and why should I doubt it?) you have shown a greater maturity for your age than could be expected. So all is well—we have both found pleasure in this surprise. The thoughts that led me to indulge in this munificence are the following:—I expect that during these three years you will sit for at least one examination if not two—and this allowance will enable you to stay several months in London for that purpose—a time when you would have no means of earning anything. Should that happen, your Uncle might possibly help you further. I am also pleased that you found the allowance on arrival, and that you therefore had no annoyance on that account. But my dear boy, don't count either on your good health or on an early departure; thus you should be careful with money so that errors you have made in the past do not recur, such for instance as made you lament last year when you fell ill and your purse was empty. Your own lack of caution brought suffering to you, as well as to me, for I had no means of helping, not from principle but chiefly because of my actual position then. You must believe me when I say that I do not accumulate capital, nor am I mean with it. But I have to calculate carefully, so that it suffices for myself and for others.

It pleases me greatly to see your 'professional fervour', which is proved by the efforts you are making to find a berth. May God help you to find one quickly, but although you say that it is all the same to you where you sail, I must avow that I would prefer you this time to sail somewhere nearer than Australia or Cape Horn. If you could for instance return to London by the end of September (new style) and spend a few weeks with me in Wiesbaden or nearby where I intend to undergo a grape cure—and I have chosen to take it there solely to make it nearer for you to drop in on me, should the opportunity arise. I plan to leave in the middle of July, via Lvov and Vienna to Ischl where I want to spend the 10th anniversary of the death of my Józieczka, the 26 July/7 August. Thereafter I would spend 4 weeks in Marienbad which would take me to the 10th September (new style), after which 4 weeks of eating grapes would bring me to the 1/13th October. Hence if you were free on the 1/13th I would willingly stay a few weeks longer in order to see you, for such an opportunity may not occur again. For someone who is already over 60 may expect anything! I shall therefore keep you au courant of my journey, and both from my journey and from where I shall undergo my treatment I shall write to you to the address 6 D.R.St.N.[1] so that you will know where I am and where we can meet if the gods are favourable.

I ask you, however, not to forgo for my benefit the opportunity of sailing somewhere more distant, for I know that staying on shore does not agree with you, and above all that it seems a waste of money to spend an unproductive 3 months on land while waiting for a fortnight's meeting, which although greatly desired by us both, has

---

[1] 6 Dynevor Road, Stoke Newington.

to be governed by a sensible assessment and judgement of the possibilities; such judgement in no way would diminish or weaken our
attachment; on the contrary, could render it stronger and more
agreeable; 'a word in the ear is enough for a sensible person'.

I don't know if this letter of mine will find you still in London or
how soon you intend to start on your next voyage. As I know, however, that it will be forwarded to you, I feel certain that it will
reach you sooner or later. I also hope that, however hurriedly, you
will write to me where you have gone. And you have not written
anything to me about how your health has withstood the voyage
and in what state you returned. I assume that your health is not bad,
but I always have a preference for certainty over conjecture, so
please write and bear that always in mind. And giving you an example to follow, I may tell you that my own health is not bad. I
don't experience any more the weakness I felt last year, but as I had
it mostly during the summer months it might return with the heat.
Well, I shall try to fight it with Marienbad and grapes—then we
shall see.

I embrace you and send you my blessing for your new voyage and
new work. With all my heart,

Your uncle
T. BOBROWSKI.

Send me your photograph. Frania embraces you.

16

18/30 May, 1881
Kazimierówka

My dear boy!

Thank you for your last letter, of the 8/20th inst., which, although it destroys any hope I had of seeing you this autumn, brings
me some pleasure at knowing you to be seriously engaged in your
profession and in winning for yourself a position which can only be
achieved by hard work—but one nevertheless which was your own
choice. I was very pleased that you look with adult determination
and common sense at all the difficulties which prevent our meeting,
instead of becoming submerged by grief and lamentation, which can
lead nowhere except to a loss of energy. We have explained matters
to each other, namely that you cannot wait three months for me
with folded arms, while for my part I can't wander about pur-
poselessly for three months, waiting for the grape season. We

must therefore submit to necessity;—which for sober minds is the ultima ratio.

Knowing your interest in my health, I may tell you that although there is no specific deterioration or damage in my organism, the marked loss of flesh, which was rather detectable, bouts of suffering from a haemorrhoidal condition, and particularly the lack of sleep are evidence that the machine is run down and needs repairing. I intend to take care of this, following without change the itinerary given to you in my last letter.

From the newspapers you probably have some idea, although undoubtedly an exaggerated one, of the happenings here, which were called by the Russian Press a 'Jewish pogrom' and by the German doctrinaire press a 'Judenhetze', but should really be called thieving. It all occurred mainly on the railway line between Kiev and Odessa, and in our part of the world, a further 8 or 9 miles away the villages are intact although fraught with anxiety, and it will probably stay that way. However, we all expect to be affected by a financial crisis resulting from the panic and stagnation of trade, mainly among Jews, who as you know hold 'nervus rerum' —money—tightly in their hands. I am mentioning this in order to reassure you that I am exposed to no particular danger apart from a general feeling of discomfort about what could befall all of us who live in this country.

There is nothing new to tell you. Mrs. Lubow., thank God, is a bit better, that is the progress of her illness has been arrested. The Zaleskis have returned from Warsaw to the country and the Montresors are in the country as well. For some months I have had no news from Uncle K. and I find this continued silence disquieting. Please do not neglect your catarrh and try to diminish its frequency with appropriate treatment. Write to me by the 1/13th July to Lipowiec as I shall remain there till the 10th/20th.

I embrace you and bless you.

Your Uncle,
T. BOBROWSKI.

Frania embraces you and sends her blessings.
Write and tell me where I should send your autumn allowance of 600 fr.—should it go as usual to Richard? You also have not acknowledged the receipt of the 1,200 fr. sent you in the spring.

17

16/28 June, 1881
Kazimierówka

My dear boy!

I was filled with melancholy and gloom at not having any news from you since the 10th of May, knowing you to be in London. However, the last mail (11th old style) brought me the welcome letter from you dated the 10th June; I found it all the more welcome and pleasing in that it was filled with the spirit of energy and enterprise—although our projects have failed to materialize. This disappointment perhaps affects me more than it does you—I don't say that by way of reproach. You can and you must believe more in the future, for you are young and you have not yet settled your accounts with fate while I have already done so. You believe that we shall meet sometime, possibly more than once, while I am in doubt; I expect and I wish it, but unfortunately I feel the whole uncertainty of my wishes. I must assure you, however, that this melancholy introduction is by no means caused by any deterioration in my health but only by a sober outlook on life.

Having thus given up this time the hope of seeing you, I have no reason to go from Marienbad to Wiesbaden, which—I don't know if rightly or wrongly—I considered to be the most suitable place for our meeting. I shall reach home on the 15/27th of July and on the 1st/13th of August I shall already be in Marienbad. I still don't know where I shall go for my grape cure, but shall write to you although I doubt if this news will find you in London. I cannot wish for it for that would mean upsetting your plans. For my part I would also prefer you to visit new lands and new seas, which I think would be useful for you, for I cannot help thinking how tedious it must be for you to visit the same parts of the world time and time again. As thank God you do not forget your Polish (may God bless you for it, as I bless you) and your writing is not bad, I repeat what I have already written and said before—you would do well to write contributions for the *Wędro-wiec*[1] in Warsaw. We have few travellers, and even fewer genuine correspondents: the words of an eyewitness would be of great interest and in time would bring you in money. It would be an exercise in your native tongue—that thread which binds you to your country and countrymen, and finally a tribute to the memory of your father who always wanted to and did serve his country by

[1] Well-known Warsaw weekly (*The Wanderer*), founded in 1863; published literary, geographical, and historical articles.

his pen. Think about this, young man, collect some reminiscences from the voyage to Australia and send them as a sample—the address of *Wędrowiec* is known in Warsaw. Six reports sent from different parts of the world during the year would not take much of your time: they would bring you some benefit and provide you with a pleasant recreation, while giving pleasure to others.

There is nothing new here; they have all calmed down, although neither Jehovah here nor Fo[1] in Australia has given any signs of his dissatisfaction at the worrying of his disciples.

Here, in the Ukraine, we cherish hopes of a very good harvest, but in Lithuania and in the depths of Russia, frost in May and even in June has spoiled any favourable expectations; even here the cold has affected the vegetables and possibly the corn that was in flower at the time.

Uncle Kazimierz is still on the railway, but at a different station, he has been moved from Mińkowice (on the Vistula line) to Leopoldôw. Dąbrosia is not here at the moment for she has gone to her brother in Zytomierz. I am leaving tomorrow for Kiev for my passport. If you send me a reply to this letter at once I may still get it by the 14th.

I embrace you and bless you.

Your Uncle,
T. BOBROWSKI.

Write to me Poste Restante Marienbad. I shall be there on the 1st/13th of August.

18

3rd/15th August, 1881
Marienbad

My dear boy!

Yesterday evening I received your desperate letter[2] to which I reply today with the remittance you want, in accordance with the proverb: 'bis dat qui cito dat', that is 'Twice gives he who quickly gives'. Your letter of the 10th reached me on the 14th, so I hope that mine will reach you on the 19th and that you won't die of hunger before then.

Thank God that you survived, that you are alive and only had

---

[1] Writing difficult to decipher. Fo is the Chinese name of Buddha, but it does not make the allusion any clearer.

[2] As Jocelyn Baines has proved (*Joseph Conrad*, p. 69), Conrad had invented the story about the 'wrecking' of the *Anna Frost*, on which he never served.

a few days in hospital, which this time has provided the necessary refuge, and that you had the uncommon luck to emerge safely from that ill-fated adventure! It is true that I should have preferred it if together with your bones you had saved your belongings, but what has happened has happened and we must both reconcile ourselves to that and patch up your present poverty as well as we can. Thus I send you herewith the 10 pounds you ask for and I shall not deduct it from your October allowance. You can have it as an extra—as a 'mariner in distress'. As, however, from October next you are to receive for three years only half your previous allowance, i.e. 1,200 fr. per annum, you can expect in October only 600 fr. and next April the same. You must manage on this, my dear boy, as best you can, for having decided to halve your allowance I have told Uncle Kazimierz that he will get more, so as to enable him to send his 4th child to school, which would have been done long ago but for the lack of means. What I was giving him hardly sufficed for bringing up three. As God is my witness, I have at my disposal no such capital as to be indéfiniment at the disposal of you all, to make good all your follies. By that I mean, with regard to Uncle K., the annual production of children without having the means to educate them or even feed them; and in respect of you, dear Sir: speculating on credit. I am by no means against speculation, providing it is done with one's own money which one has earned and saved, but I am when it is based on borrowed capital. 'Hope is the Mother of fools and calculation the Father of the sober-minded';—so goes the proverb. Since you are a Nałęcz, beware of risky speculations based only on hope; for your grandfather squandered all his property speculating, and your Uncle, speculating always with other people's money and on credit, got into debt,—caused many people disappointments, and died heavily in debt. Tandem speculate and trade, but firstly save the money you earn and speculate with your own capital and not somebody else's—otherwise you will always make nothing or, worse still, less than nothing, which is the situation you are in now. According to the present exchange 600 fr. makes 23 pounds, and if I understood you correctly Sutherland is ceding to you his profits from the transaction and will take only £21. 14s. instead of £30. So there you have all your October allowance gone in speculation and you will have to manage on account of the April one. That's what you have gained by speculation. In my opinion for the greater security of Sutherland your allowance should be sent to him. It makes no difference to me, so write and tell me what you wish to send him. I can give instructions for £25 to be sent to him every six months from Odessa. We shall thus save Richard trouble and give security to Sutherland. Write then what you wish. And write at least a few words on receipt of this letter to confirm the receipt of my remittance.

I have been here a week—I found Mr. Izydor Kopernicki[1] here who is in practice at the local waters. He assures me that my liver and spleen are in perfect order and that my sufferings are caused by haemorrhoids and nerves. To alleviate the first I drink the local waters; for the second as well as for the rheumatism in the right arm which I got on leaving home—I take cold rain-water baths and friction. Obviously your last calamity has upset me, for the worry gave me diarrhoea but this will settle down in a few days. So, as far as this matter is concerned, you may rest reassured and hopeful. Think about yourself; in the first place look for employment and write to me. I shall remain here till the 23 August/4 September, then I shall go to *Montreux-Vernet* (Suisse, Canton de Vaud) where I shall remain the following 4 weeks. On the 1st/13th October I hope to be back home. Please write to me both here and to Montreux according to the time of my stay given to you, and God grant that you inform me as soon as possible about your departure.

Mr. Kopernicki was most solicitous in inquiring about you. I read out your letters to him, having found one waiting for me. He is engaged on a great work which has already brought him European fame: 'Comparative studies of human races based on types of skulls.' This particular branch of science is called 'Craniology'. He earnestly requests you to collect during your voyages skulls of natives, writing on each one whose skull it is and the place of origin. When you have collected a dozen or so of such skulls write to me and I will obtain from him information as to the best way of dispatching them to Cracow where there is a special Museum devoted to Craniology. Please do not forget this, and do your best to fulfil the request of this scientist as by doing so you will bring real pleasure both to him and to myself, for he is not only a worthy, wise, and educated man but also most friendly and sympathetic to me personally. I go to him every evening for a chat as there is no other person I know here. Although there are many Poles here I don't feel inclined to seek their company as from conversations I have overheard I find them a rather empty-headed lot. The son of Izydor, who says that he recollects you well, takes me for walks and that somehow suffices—he is a very nice and hard-working boy. He for his part asks for Indian stamps. I should like to comply with both their requests, for I greatly respect the father and have grown to love the son. En revenant à nos moutons,—it seems to me

---

[1] Dr. Izydor Kopernicki (1825–91), well-known Polish anthropologist and physician.

that the owners of the *Anna Frost* in negotiating compensation for the ship should have included compensation for the things lost by her officers. That seems to me to be elementary! But perhaps it is not practised in a country where the rich manage well, while no one thinks of the poor???

Arrange your affairs with Mr. Sutherland as best you can, and rely on the half-yearly allowance which you can estimate to be £25 each half-year. I myself shall bear the difference, which will eventually be more than 600 fr. Otherwise manage for yourself, dear Panie Bracie, for I can't help you any more. If you previously expected to get some profit out of this speculation, it is fair that you should be the one who gets hit by the operation; and I have made clear the reason why my pocket is no more available for you: I can't create something out of nothing.

Write to me, my dear lad, at once and go on writing until you get back. Don't pay the postage; I shall willingly do it at this end and it will save you trouble. All I wish is to have news from you and may it, with God's help, become more propitious!

I embrace and bless you wholeheartedly.

Your Uncle,
T. BOBROWSKI.

19

22 August, 1881
Marienbad

My dear boy!

I received both your letters on the evening of the 19th and it surprised me greatly to realize that within 5 days both my letter to you and your reply had time to reach their destinations!!

I am also wholeheartedly pleased to have been able to come to your rescue so speedily and effectively so that you could show the people around you that you are not entirely devoid of support in life. Finally, it pleased me to hear from you that you had at last an opportunity to assure yourself of my real affection for you! None the less, I am pleased that you didn't waste your imagination or energy in searching for a new situation. May God help you to find one soon. Knowing to what extent my state of health disquiets you, I shall begin this letter by informing you that my treatment continues to take its course. I don't feel any improvement so far, but that will only show itself after a certain time. In 10 days I shall leave for Montreux Vernet (Suisse, Canton de Vaud—Poste Restante)—so write there, my dear boy, with all your news. First of all let me know definitely to which address I am to send your autumn allowance of £25—am I to send it to Mr. Sutherland, to Mr. Will. Ward whom you mentioned, or to Richard? Do these first two gentlemen understand French, or rather, does the one you ask me to send your allowance to know French, as that language is the only means of communication I can employ?

You let yourself be carried away quite unnecessarily by premature magnanimity declaring your wish to return to me during the next year the £10 which I have sent to you as to a 'mariner in distress'. I suggest another way of repaying me. Do you remember the large carpet which was Granny's and which belongs to you? It is now stored at Uncle Kazimierz's house. You don't need this carpet yourself and I had planned to get myself a new carpet for my study this winter. To tell you the truth, as I like your carpet very much I was going to suggest that you should let me have it. Therefore if I now offer you the £10 as a present and you offer me the carpet, we shall both be pleased, for each of us will have what he wants most at the moment and each of us will have the pleasure of offering what the other needs most. Please write and say if you are particularly attached to this carpet.—If you are I shall leave it at my brother's house where it has been since the death of my dear mother. It is the green and white one and is fairly large.

Mr. Kopernicki accepts as you give it your explanation about the skulls. Whether he can find any correspondents or not in the places you mentioned he will ascertain in Cracow from the list of correspondents of the Academy; and the instructions as to what he wants and how you have to set out collecting it and any letters that might be useful he will send through me in good time. In the meantime he sends you his regards. As a letter to London takes 3 days and so does the reply—with a bit of effort on your part you can still send me one more letter here but the next one should be sent to Montreux. It would please me to get news that you are sailing. The sooner the better!

What is the state of your health now that you have got over the effects of the disaster? It frequently happens that a shock of this kind is felt more severely after a certain time than immediately.

I embrace you and bless you with all my heart.

Your Uncle
T. BOBROWSKI.

76

20

30/viii/10/ix, 1881
Montreux–Vernet

The news you give me of yourself my dear boy is not particularly good! However, as you have still not lost your high spirits and hopes of a better future, it would be unbecoming on my part to dim this clear light of a youthful spirit with any words of doubt of mine;— which in any case wouldn't be founded on any professional know-ledge but would be the result of the pessimism of age,—which in the general order of things you yourself will experience in due course! and without the premature assistance of a loving Uncle. Thus, in spite of the oppressive thought that you chose for yourself so difficult and hard a profession, let us both pull ourselves together, my dear lad, for there is nothing else we can do! And although 'hope is the mother of fools', as the saying goes, for this once, we the 'sober-minded' will believe in hope, for there is nothing else left for us to do!

I left Marienbad on the 23rd August (4 Sept.) and on the 26th/7th, Wednesday morning, at 10 o'clock I arrived and went straight to the Hôtel Suisse, where I stayed 11 years ago with Józieczka. To an old acquaintance with such a good memory they offered the best they had: a room with a balcony, breakfast, luncheon, and dinner for 7 francs a day. It's very crowded here because of many people running prematurely away from cold and rainy places —but it's nice here. My hotel is full of French middle-class people. I know nobody personally and only answer their greetings when I pass them. There is only one friend of mine here: Mr. Konstanty Górski from Warsaw. He is a nice and sensible person and I take my after-lunch stroll in his company.

I shall begin my treatment in a few days, for it is only a week since I stopped taking the waters, and the grapes are not yet ripe. At 8 o'clock, fully dressed, I sit down to breakfast, till 11 o'clock I walk alone in the mountains, after which I take a cold shower. Luncheon is from 12 till 1 p.m., reading and correspondence take till 3 p.m., from 4 to 6 I take a walk with Mr. Górski (he stays in Montreux proper, I am in Vernet; the village is called Montreux Vernet), from 6 till 7.30 there is dinner, and then I take another hour's stroll along the streets. I read till 11 o'clock, then to sleep! As you see it is an existence which although not overburdened with work is quite respectable! And so it will be for another 4 weeks, for that is the prescribed length of the treatment and one more week will pass before I begin. As a result of the warm climate or possibly as a result of the quinine my neuralgia is much better so that for the time being I shall leave the electricity alone. If on the other hand the pain does not stop entirely within two weeks—at the moment I hardly feel it—I shall take a short course of electricity and thus have nothing to reproach myself with.

The reception given to me by that good Dr. Kopernicki was most cordial and his farewell was equally friendly. From him I heard about Pulman—apparently during his last examinations he tricked a number of people out of money, including Dr. K. out of 200 gulden. He turned a deaf ear to all calls for repayment, ignoring them as he did mine. Finally Dr. K. reached him at Czerniowce through his solicitor and after a court case recovered his money. According to what Leon Syr. says, Pulman apparently married a prosperous tradeswoman and lives at present in Sambor. I didn't expect him to behave like that and not even to answer my and Uncle Kazimierz's letters. One may be in a position where one is unable to pay back, but one should at least offer a justification. Write to him to Sambor; perhaps that will move him, for to your Uncle 600 roubles means a lot. Don't admonish him, just say that you have heard from me of his whereabouts and so you write.

I have not yet been informed of the date of Marylka's wedding. In any case I shall leave here on the 23 September/5 October and the length of my stay in Lvov and Volhynia will depend on the date of the wedding.

Mr. Buszczyński was in Toeplitz. He even sent me a pamphlet of his which, however, didn't seem to make much sense.[1] I gave him news about you and myself but I didn't refer to this pamphlet, which was extremely silly—this apparently offended him for he never answered. I have been told by everybody that he suffers from a literary monomania and a feeling of unrecognized genius.

Farewell, my dear Boy, may you soon have something pleasant to report—I am waiting—please write.

I embrace and bless you.

Your Uncle
T. B.

Mme Ofelia[2] was widowed and now, as they say, she is unhappily remarried! This has upset her Father very much.

---

1 Probably *Bestandtheiele der russischen Bevölkerung* ('The constituent parts of the population of Russia'), Dresden, 1875.
2 Stefan Buszczyński's daughter.

Dear boy!

Thank God that at last you have found a job and that you are on a ship! And thank you for telling me all about it and for not losing courage and confidence! . . . It seems to me that you are not very satisfied with your post: is it because being on a 'barque'[1] touches on your honour? Then, of course, £4 a month is disrespectful to your pocket, and, finally, the captain seems to you to be merely a 'creature', which gives me a sad picture of his intellect. However, perhaps the last point will enable you to distinguish yourself as a 'man conscious of his craft, and useful'. Anyway it's done— proceed in health and return safely. 'Deus te ducat, perducat, et reducat' as our ancestors used to say when setting out, sabre in hand, —and I say the same, bidding you farewell on your journey on an element unknown to them, embracing and blessing you with all my heart.

I shall send on your allowance to Mr. Ward as you request. If I at my age possessed the same rashness that is peculiar to those of another age—and to our whole race—I would have sent you from here the whole of your allowance. But I am afraid that what I have may not suffice for me and there is no one here I can borrow from. I expect the arrival of a neighbour of mine (Mr. Cieszkowski married to Ottolina Gruszczyńska). He will be my security and as soon as he arrives I shall try to dispatch your allowance plus possibly the £3 due to Mr. Ward.

What you write about our hopes for the future has really delighted me, for I see in it a sign of your interest in our national affairs and of your preoccupation with them in spite of your remoteness.[2] True, that is your duty and I counted on your remaining faithful to it, but many people although they live in their own country don't give it a thought. Thus you please me greatly, and for this reason I bestow a double blessing on you—may it bring you all happiness.

What you write of our hopes based on Panslavism is in theory both splendid and feasible, but it meets great difficulties in practice. You don't take into account the significance which actual numbers have in the affairs of this world. Each of the more influential nations

---

[1] *Palestine*, described as *Judea* in *Youth*.

[2] Undoubtedly Conrad and Bobrowski were exploiting the opportunity given by Bobrowski's journey abroad to discuss freely Polish national problems, avoiding the usual Russian censorship.

starts by relying apparently on the Panslavic ideal and by forgetting about its own interests—but secretly and almost unconsciously relies on some aspect of its existence which will ensure its leadership. You yourself have fallen into the same error, attributing to our country certain positive qualities, which are partly but not wholly true. And so Russia does not interpret Panslavism otherwise than as a means of russifying all other nations or even converting them to the Orthodox church, justifying themselves by the argument that they have a population of 80 millions (which is false).[1] And to our claim that we have a higher culture and a longer history they reply: this was only the life and culture of one class which claimed to be a nation (this contains a grain of truth) and that only she, Russia, will develop the real elements of the people. The Czechs are told: your nation is too small. Both they and we are accused of representing a bastard mixture of East and West while Russia's culture is real, being purely Eastern (which doesn't exist anyway). Other nations are told that they are small and all of Eastern origin as well and should therefore bow to a more numerous nation (Russian, of course!) in order not to perish entirely. They, however, maintain that as they are still in the cradle they are the true representatives of the pure Slavonic idea. And thus the argument goes on without end, with everyone believing himself to be in the right. I am certain that eventually out of this chaos some form of federation will emerge, but by that time I shall be long dead and possibly you too. In the meantime, since like pariahs we are deprived of our own political and national rights, we, more than the others, have to preserve our individuality and our own standpoint, till the time comes when Nemesis, as a result of our own efforts, spins out some situation which will give us the right to have a real national existence—and possibly something more.

However, one could write many volumes on this subject without solving the question, which will eventually be solved by time and events.

I embrace you a hundredfold and send you my blessing.

Write to me when leaving Newcastle.

Your uncle

T. BOBROWSKI.

PS. My arm still hurts—the pain, although light, sometimes affects the left arm and leg. Today I shall go to the Doctor to try out electric treatment. His mastics haven't helped at all so we shall try electricity.

[1] The statistics vary but probably there were by that time about 70 million Russians living in European Russia.

22

8/20 January, 1882
Kazimierówka

My dearest boy!

Your misfortunes of the past year fill me with despair! I purposely refer to the 'past year', for I hope and trust that this 'malchance' will leave you alone this year. Certainly your success depends to some extent on chance or luck, but your judgement plays an important part as well. This time at least, after the wreck, cool judgement seems to have deserted you when you accepted such a wretched ship as the *Palestine*. I quite understand, my dear boy, that you decided to do so in order to avoid being a burden to me by a long stay in London, and also by serving as a second officer to qualify for your examination for a first officer. But, my dear boy, you didn't take into account that if as a result of all the mishaps and accidents that are bound to happen in a situation such as yours you should become sick or injured, I would not abandon you! While if you get drowned it will be all the same to you whether you arrive in the 'Valley of Jehoshaphat'[1] with the rank of 2nd officer or that of candidate for 1st officer. I have never considered that I had the right to order you about, especially now that you are 24 years old, but all the same I sincerely advise you not to go to sea in such a lamentable ship as yours. Danger is certainly part of a sailor's life, but the profession itself should not prevent you from having a sensible attachment to life nor from taking sensible steps to preserve it. Both your Captain Beard and you appear to me like desperate men who look for knocks and wounds, while your ship-owner is a rascal who risks the lives of 10 good men for the sake of a blackguardly profit.

Consider well, dear boy, what you ought to do. I shall not hold it against you if you decide to return to London and I shall even try to help you, for as you can imagine, I do not want for the sake of saving 300–500 roubles to see you at the bottom of the sea, or ill or, worst of all, injured or crippled with rheumatism for the rest of your life!! Tandem weigh your good and bad chances of carrying through your project; curb your noble ambition and do what reason dictates, and this time you will not hear any complaints from me.

I am only writing to you today as your letter arrived while I was not at home as I returned only the day before yesterday, that is on the 6th. The pain in my arm still persists but it is not terribly bad

[1] The Valley in which the Last Judgement is to take place (Joel iii. 2).

and otherwise I am quite well. I had no news from your Uncle for a long time but I expect they are all well, and that they are getting along no worse than before.

I had qualms of conscience about distracting you in the autumn from looking for a job, not foreseeing the situation you have come up against. To this day I am under the impression that all 'engagements' are made only in the autumn. Is it so in fact? Do tell me. What had to happen has happened and now I shall think how to arrange for us to see each other next year. I take it for granted that whatever you decide to do, whether to return to London or to embark on a distant voyage, you will inform me. In the first case give me an address to which I shall send you a little money before I am able to send you your allowance from the fair. In any case, may your judgement guide your decision, and if my blessings may help I send them to you with all my heart, and I warmly embrace you.

Your uncle
T. Bobrowski.

23

12/24 April, 1882
Kazimierówka

My dear boy!

I am perfectly all right! I put this at the beginning of the letter so that you may be quite calm before I give you all the details of what I have done since your last letter. Firstly, I received no letter from you in Kiev. Your last letter, of the 12th April (new style) reached me on the 9th (our style) and this lette ris in reply to it. Your previous letter, of the 3rd of February (new style) had reached me before I left for Kiev. I did not answer it at the time as you wrote of your impending departure at the latest in 10 days, and by the time I received it 12 days had already elapsed. And in your last letter you said the same—and the same time had elapsed between your writing it and my receiving it. However, I have decided not to go by this any more, and seeing how you are repairing your old yawl for the third time, I write to the address you gave in case you are still there, and, receiving my letter, can depart with your mind at rest.

After returning from Morozówka, where I spent Christmas, I didn't leave home during the whole of January because of the bad roads (we had no snow at all) and also because of the trouble my arm was giving me, about which I wrote to you. On the 1st February, I left home via Morozówka for Kiev where I arrived on the 8th and stayed as usual in the Gr. Hotel till the 25th (new style). The worthy Dr. Krzyżanowski treated me for nerves during my stay and put me very thoroughly through a course of electricity. That helped me a lot for my nerves calmed down and the pain recurs only when I am subject to severe nervous excitement and to sleeplessness—which is not very often. As you see, I am much better!

On my way home I had to stay for some time in Morozówka to persuade my mother-in-law to take her medicine and to keep to her treatment, which she was trying to evade. I succeeded in influencing the patient, but my constant assistance was needed so that I could only get home on the 11th March. Hardly had I time to unpack when a messenger arrived on the 14th bringing the news that Mrs. Pruszyńska had died that day and that they all feared the effects which the news of this sad event (which occurred in Morozówka) might have upon the daughter.* They were waiting for me to inform her. Having then collected a few necessary things I set off on a whole night's journey, brought the news of the death and buried the deceased, &c. Afterwards, I remained there awaiting the arrival of one of the daughters: Mrs. Z. from Warsaw or Mrs. M.[1] from Nice. This all dragged on till after the Easter holidays, as the latter didn't arrive till the 6th inst. while the former was unable to come at all because of her health. Eventually I returned home on the 9th and on that day they brought me your letter from the Post Office.

This story will explain to you why in spite of my 'usual punctiliousness' (its recognition pleased me) I was unable to send at the usual time my dispatch to you through Mr. Ward; because in the haste of my departure for Morozówka I left behind my address book. From Morozówka I dispatched his allowance to Uncle Kazimierz; but was unable to send yours for lack of your address. Thus today I am sending instructions through Odessa to transfer £25 to Mr. Ward as you request in your letter of the 3rd February, and as in your last letter I found no mention of any change of address to which to send money.

To tell you the truth, it would suit my plans much better if we were to meet in the summer of 1883 (providing we are both still alive then) instead of in the autumn of 1882. I have a variety of reasons, the main one being that this year I have to hand over the estate to a new lessee, which procedure generally entails many formalities and even some expense; further, in 1883 my lease income will increase, which will better enable me to afford such a pleasure. True, that would postpone our meeting for six months, but bearing in mind that neither of us is a 'nervous little female' unable to survive without the other, nor who 'coûte que coûte'

---

[1] Zaleska and Montresor.

83

have to 'fulfil their hearts' desire', I hope that we shall somehow bear the burden of the postponement of this meeting which we both so much desire, and that we shall welcome it eventually with twice as much pleasure. Farewell for now, my dear boy. Write from your voyage, sending me your itinerary, and return safe and sound.

I embrace and bless you.

Your Uncle
T. BOBROWSKI

*These two ladies would not move of their own. One because of her age, the other one—because of ill health. The first one usually visited her daughter for a few hours in a wheeled chair.
Frania embraces and blesses you. She is well.
Nothing new at Uncle Kazim. and nothing worse than before.

24

14/26 May, 1882
Kazimierówka

My dear boy,

Your last letter, of the 11th May, gave me inexpressible pleasure, so full of energy, so full of exuberant ideas and the desire to work, and containing, as it did, the news of your excellent health. 'Mens sana in corpore sano.' If I contributed anything towards it with my speedy reply and my speedy dispatch of the 'filthy lucre' I can only congratulate myself on the result. I therefore repeat today the dose of the first medicine, and I am very sorry not to be able to offer you, my dear boy, a dose of the second one just as often. You have now lived for some years in England and have been taking part in the life there and you will have learned to respect money, and it therefore probably surprises you to hear me calling it 'filthy'. This expression is a survival from the 'romantic period' in which I was born and grew up, and to some extent it reflects our national character, a trait of which was supposed to be disinterestedness in money matters. I presume the latter to be an apparent rather than a real quality, for it arises rather from a carelessness than from a real contempt for money. This is because we did not work to get it but worked rather to squander it! Now our esteem for it has increased, mine possibly more than others, for we have come to realize that it is the 'nervus rerum' and the basis of both the external and inner independence of both an individual and a whole society.

You gave me great pleasure by writing again to your Uncle,

even if it was only to thank him for his speedy reply. I know your apparent indifference pained him greatly; he spoke about it to me with a sigh: 'Well, it is not surprising as he (that is you) does not know me.' He loved your parents very dearly and he loves you as well. Your Uncle's 'rôle d'équipage', as you call it, is as follows: (1) a son Stanisław (Kazio, the eldest, died) 17 years old, a good and hard-working boy but not gifted; the poor fellow is now only in the 4th form. (2) a daughter Zuzia, about 16 years old, hard-working, a gifted and good-looking girl; then (3) Marta—very attractive and (4) Maria. Then there is (5) a son, Tadzio; after him there was a girl who died, and (6) a son Michaś, born two years ago. He is very weak and apparently will not survive. It seems to be enough anyway and you will admit that your Uncle worked successfully in this field. I don't even know when he had time to achieve all that as at nights he always had to be on the look-out for trains. Probably between one train and another he devoted himself to 'social work' to keep himself from falling asleep! You said 'I don't know the "imieni"[1] of Uncle's children.' It is correct to say 'imion'. You ask why the older daughter Zunia, who is about to finish school, is not going to return home. It is because she has to prepare herself to become a teacher, find a job and earn her own living. This is always what happens when one marries without any basis of security, and brings children into the world without caring about the means of educating them or even feeding them. Uncle K. earns 600 roubles per annum, plus lodging, heating, and lighting. He does not even have enough to feed his brood. At first I would give him 1,000 then 1,200 and now 1,500 roubles, after cutting you down by 400. Your half-allowance is 500 roubles so that I should at this rate really give Uncle's children 3,000 roubles—going barefoot myself. As my brother and his wife would give way to temptation more than they should have done, they now have to suffer for it, denying themselves everything for the sake of their young. It is not my fault, and may God be my witness that at each fresh increase in their progeny I protested and cried aloud. The heavens heard it, but your good Uncle and Aunt remained deaf, they embraced thoughtlessly and now they 'sing Tadeusz' (this is a saying about someone who is in want)—but this time, however, they have no right to grumble about Tadeusz for without him things would be even worse. The fault is not yours either and yet you indirectly suffer for it as I would not have had to cut down your allowance if it were not for this large brood of your Uncle's. And so, all things in the world and in life are connected with each other. We are responsible for each other and the family

[1] Christian names.

spirit is based on that. One thing only in this whole problem is not quite clear: why should only I be responsible for all the 'family prolificity'? But, in time, the answer to that question may be found: perhaps these children will grow up to be good people!!?

Well my garrulity has filled so much space that I am on the point of putting my pen to the second sheet, with the object—even if it is only at the end of my letter—of reverting to its hero: Konrad.

You are obstinate, my dear lad, or is it the professional code of honour or the customs of the country you are living in that account for your sailing on such a miserable ship and risking your neck? Not being acquainted with either I shall refrain from comment, and I offer you nothing except a blessing and a wish for your safe arrival and return. I should be very pleased if you could return early enough next year for us to meet during the summer. I would very much like to get over to Cracow or Krynica for our meeting so that you could breathe a little of the air of your fatherland. If you get back early enough we could meet in Cracow and then go to Krynica for 4 weeks. If we meet as late as the autumn—then it would be in Lvov where we could also spend 4 weeks together. I shall arrange to leave at the first news of our meeting becoming possible; from the financial point of view it would also be easier to arrange it all next year. So consider our meeting next year as definite, providing of course that we are both alive at that time.

I shall send the usual £25 to Mr. Ward in the autumn for your allowance and the same in the spring. Therefore if, as you say, you are not a penny in debt, you will have £50 in reserve which will enable you to sit for your examination. You have still left un-answered my repeated question: did you get any compensation from the owner for the loss of your belongings in the *Anna Frost*? Answer, please. And if you didn't—give the reasons, for it is quite incomprehensible to me that the poor only should suffer because of an agreement reached by the rich. A second question—when on shore—do you now, apart from your salary, get your maintenance paid as if you were at sea? Please write before you depart, and write on your way as often as possible and especially when leaving Falmouth and Bangkok. May Sutherland rest in peace. He was a good fellow and was the first to offer you a helping hand in London. If he ever fleeced you—forgive him, I beg you.

Farewell dear boy, go, and come back.

I embrace you and bless you,

Uncle
T. BOBROWSKI

25

30 July/11 August, 1882
Kazimierówka

Dear boy!

As you wished I am writing now on the off-chance that my letter will reach you in time?! Firstly, I am sending you my blessing on your year-long voyage. Secondly, I am writing to inform you that I am in good health and am not feeling too bad. Go then, dear boy, in good spirits, and may you return safely, no matter when! And be sure that whether convenient or not I shall try to meet you, and I know I will, if I am alive. Anytime after the fair I shall be able to make this journey which we both so much look forward to. I shall save my pennies and look after my health so as to be able to meet you and spend a whole month together. Naturally, I should prefer this meeting to take place after your examination so that I could see your certificate with my own eyes and thus enjoy the high rank of my nephew! So it is fixed: after your return and your examination, we shall meet on our native soil! I shall send your autumn allowance to Mr. Ward and if you are still away by next April I shall do the same with the spring one, so that you will be able to take the examination.

The tergiversations of your Mr. Wilson are not to my liking either, but I can understand that after having wasted a whole year for the sake of getting your 2nd officer's certificate it would not be right to give up now in spite of the waste of time and the meagre pay. On the contrary, you are right to persevere to the end, and I admire your perseverance.

I have nothing new to report about myself, and the same goes for Uncle Kazimierz. His eldest daughter, the 15-year-old Zuzia, finished gymnasium[1] for girls with honours and is now preparing to become a teacher. The remaining youngsters are more or less successfully proceeding with their studies. In Morozówka things are as bad as ever, Mrs. Lubowidzka is worse, Mrs. Pruszyńska died in March. Marylka Tyszkiewicz gave birth to a daughter on the 16th/28th instant, the Zaleskis and Montresors are keeping well, the Karnickis are alive. Nothing is changed, only everything has grown older.[2]

I embrace you a hundred times and bless you.

Your Uncle,
T. BOBROWSKI.

Frania embraces and blesses you.

[1] The nearest English equivalent would be high-school.
[2] The last sentence is a quotation from a poem by Franciszek Karpiński (1741–1825), 'Powrót z Warszawy na wieś' ('A return from Warsaw to the country').

26

24 May/5 June, 1883
Kazimierówka

My dear boy!

Your two letters, of the 4th of April from Singapore and of the 13th of May from Port Said, reached me the day before yesterday and the news pleased me greatly. I am setting off now on a journey to Kiev where various business affairs require my presence. I shall take the opportunity of procuring myself a passport. Don't be disturbed by the news about the increase in the cost of passports here, for nothing shall stand in the way of our meeting—if anything can be certain in human affairs. It is a fact that the Minister of Finance came out with a project to raise the fee from 5 roubles to 162 roubles per passport, but the Council of State adjourned this wise project till their next sitting, thus burying it as gently as possible.

Presumably you got my last letter sent to you care of Mr. Krieger; —I hope you will have answered it before you get this one. On my return from Kiev about the 5th/17th June I should get your reply, and depending on the news in it I shall make the final decision about our meeting. It will probably take place in Cracow but not sooner than on the 5th/17th July or possibly a day or two later, as I have a lot to do at home and I only hope I shall finish it all by the 1st/13th July. If I leave on the 1st/13th I can get to Lvov on the 3rd/15th, where I have to spend at least 24 hours, so I can't get to Cracow any earlier than the 5th/17th. I dislike being pressed for time and would therefore prefer to have 5 days 'de marge', and thus fix your arrival for the 8th/20th July.

I shall repeat again what I already said in my previous letter: namely, that as you will be staying in London for your examination it would seem most suitable that you should apply then for naturalization and be at last finished with it. I am allowing you up to £25 for it. If you can, pay the cost out of your own pocket and I shall refund you the money when we meet. If you haven't enough money write to me and I will send it immediately; but that would postpone our meeting for a few weeks because from the day of receiving your letter at least that amount of time is necessary to send my draft to Odessa and thence to London. I must admit that I should prefer to see your face a little later, and as that of a free citizen of a free country, rather than earlier and still as that of citizen of the world! However, you must decide all this for yourself, for it is really a matter of your looking after your own best interests. So now I await news

from you, and if in the letter that I expect from you I find a mention
of money, i.e. of sending you some, you may be certain that I shall
not wait for a second appeal but shall at once dispatch it, about the
8/20 June (on the 5th, 6th, and 7th we have Whitsun here and the
post office is closed).

Well, my dear boy, you now have everything that concerns our
meeting. Don't worry any more, concentrate on your examination,
and get yourself naturalized—and in all probability we shall see
each other soon. I am feeling reasonably well. I mentioned to you
that Mrs. Lubow. had died. This must have had some effect on my
humour and my disposition. But this, as well as the other numerous
sufferings of my life, has to be borne. In a few days' time the Zaleskis
will leave for Marienbad, and it is quite likely that on their way back
they will find us in Cracow. The Montresors are in Ems and they also
will be returning home at the begining of July, but probably through
Warsaw. You inquire after your Uncle's daughter, who was forced
by illness to return home. It is his third child, called Maria, who
greatly resembles my late Mother. She, poor thing, is not the only
victim of scrofula, for the second one, Marta, is scrofulous as well
and is losing her hearing, but most of all the youngest son Michaś;
the older children are affected by this illness as well. Being unable
to send the whole bunch to Ciechocinek[1] I sent your Uncle some
help to assist in the journey of the mother and these three children
who suffer most, and to render their 6 weeks' treatment possible. It
is a nice prospect to be penniless all one's life and ill as well. And
these are results of heedless marriages, where hunger and desire
combine to produce misery and illness. C'est le cas de Votre cher
Oncle. 'Marthe hath chosen the better part'—that is production of
children, while I have to feed and nurse them.

Trêve des bouderies. I embrace you a hundredfold.

Your Uncle,
T. Bobrowski.

[1] A popular Polish health resort.

12th/24th June, 1883
Kazimierówka

My dearest boy!

Your two letters of the 5th and 13th June were brought to me simultaneously from the post office on the 10th/22nd, which means that the first took 17 days and the second 9 days to reach me. The only possible explanation is that the first letter lay a whole week in the post office in Lipowiec and was late in being delivered here, as half an hour's really fierce rain is enough to convert all the side roads into lakes, thus holding up for days on end all correspondence in this part of the country. We can't do anything about it, but may this be a reminder to you how little we can rely on the regularity of our post and how necessary it is for us *to decide in advance* on the place and time of our meeting.

Since my last letter to you, the functioning of my gastric organs has shown certain catarrhal symptoms, and the pains which have bothered me for two years have begun to move from my arms to my legs. Before this slight complaint could develop into an illness I consulted Dr. Krzyżanowski and decided to go to Marienbad. I shall take the waters there for my stomach trouble and mud-baths for my rheumatism. It follows from this that we shall have to meet *in Marienbad instead of Cracow*, and this month spent together will be a rest for you, a cure for me, and a long-awaited pleasure for us both.

There is just no possibility of my leaving home before the 1st/13th July, or of my getting to Marienbad before the 10th/22nd. Taking into consideration all you have told me in your two letters, *I now send you my final decisions:*

(1) We shall meet *in Marienbad*, where I am sure to arrive not later than the 10th/22nd *July.* You should arrive on the 12th/24th of the *same month*, so that I shall have had time to settle in and get our lodgings ready. You can find my whereabouts from *Dr. Kopernicki*, who two years ago and even last year used to live near the *Kursaal, villa Zeidler.* If he has changed his address you can find it in any house at Marienbad, where on each gate a list of the doctors practising there is fixed.

(2) *Your journey.* I think the shortest way would be through Brussels, Frankfurt, and Egger, from where a train will get you to Marienbad in 40 minutes. Anyhow, I leave it all to your judgement. You are quite right in saying that if you travelled by a slow train your night's lodging would cost you more than the supplement you would pay for a fast train.

(3) It is extremely convenient for me that you are able *to pay for your own journey.* It would otherwise mean the trouble and waste of time dispatching the money to Odessa first, and then on to London. *The cost of your voyage will be refunded to you immediately on your arrival.*

(4) If you have to deposit anything towards *the cost of your naturalization* and are unable to do it out of your own money— borrow £10 from Krieger or some other friend, on the understanding that the day after your arrival at Marienbad you will send it back to him. As you will be there about the 25th then your creditor may be certain to get his money back by the 31st July or 1st August. Sending money abroad from our village here is a long and complicated business, but in Marienbad the whole transaction can be completed in a few minutes and the money will be delivered within 5 days. It is understood of course that *I shall cover the cost of your naturalization.* It is up to you to decide the right time for it, for as we are to meet abroad it is all the same to me whether it takes place earlier or later as long as I know that it will eventually happen, and I prefer to have less expense than more.

Here you have *my final decisions* regarding our meeting. I don't expect there will be any changes, but in case of something unforeseen happening I shall notify you by telegram as I can do it now from *Lipowiec.* If for your part you are delayed, write to me to *Marienbad —poste restante.* If there is nothing awaiting me on my arrival there I shall expect you on the 12th/24th July. You will find the Zaleskis in Marienbad—they have been there since the 1/13th June—and possibly Staś[1] as well who is now taking the cure in Kissingen. Probably I shall not be writing to you any more, unless when getting into the train I send you a line to say that I am starting the journey.

Farewell my dear Boy and 1st Officer. Please bring your Certificate with you as I should like to see it. I embrace and bless you, Your Uncle

T. BOBROWSKI.

28

27 June/9 July, 1883
Kazimierówka

My dear boy!

Two weeks ago I sent you a registered letter containing my final decisions as to the time and place of our meeting. I suppose it

---

[1] Stanisław Zaleski.

has already reached you? Then I received your last letter bringing the news that for the time being, because of the work connected with your examination, you have given up the idea of naturalization and that you will sit for your examination on the 4th July. More than once did I think of you on that day, and always with confidence and hope that you would pass successfully.

However, as you know I am a very careful man! Perhaps my letter went astray and you have been tormenting yourself over my silence? I shall therefore repeat briefly what I have already said: (1) We shall meet in *Marienbad* where I have to take the waters and the baths; *I shall arrive* there on the 10th/22nd July at the latest and you should arrive by the 12th/24th July. You can find my address (which is also yours) from Dr. Kopernicki. His address, together with those of other consulting doctors, can be found in a list on any house inhabited by foreigners. (2) Go by fast trains—it will be cheaper than going by slow ones and stopping for the night. I shall repay you all the expenses of your journey. As you have written that you prefer to pay them out of your own pocket (knowing that I shall refund them) in order to spare me the trouble of transferring the money for the journey, for which I thank you, I have not sent you any money. If, however, you should find yourself unable to cover all the expenses out of your own pocket, borrow some money, which we shall send back to your creditor the day after your arrival. Now, in any case, it is too late to consider sending you money, for I am leaving in three days. I don't expect anything will detain me or prevent me from arriving at Marienbad on the 10th/22nd July.

I shall end my epistle with an 'au revoir', which should ring pleasantly in your ears, and it gives me pleasure as well to say this to a first Officer of H.M. the Queen of Great Britain which you no doubt are by now.

I embrace and bless you my boy.

Your Uncle
T. BOBROWSKI.

The Zaleskis are staying at the *Goldene Kroone on the Church Square* in Marienbad. I wrote asking them to take rooms there for me. On your arrival, therefore, ask to be driven to the *G. Kroone* and if you should find me not yet there and the Zaleskis already gone—make inquiries from Dr. Kopernicki.

29

Friday 19/31 August, 1883
Toeplitz[1]–Schönau

My dear boy!

Your letter from Dresden gave me real heartfelt pleasure. Everything you said I am keeping 'sealed up in my heart' as Bohdan Zaleski[2] says referring to feelings that do not seek the light; and again—'constantly pursue with the senses' the image of my nephew, who has left me! You were right in supposing that on returning to Toeplitz I was sad and melancholy, sitting down alone to my evening cup of tea, opposite the empty chair of my Admiral!!!!

However, apart from the pleasure which you gave me with the words of your letter, you have caused me an even greater pleasure by an act seemingly of no importance! You are mistaken if you think that I found no other pleasure but that derived from just reading a letter written in your usual style. You are mistaken once again if you think that your deed would pass me unnoticed! On the contrary, I noticed immediately that you had gone out of your way to give me pleasure, and this small fact gave me a far deeper joy than the most eloquent words, for it is in itself much more eloquent. I therefore thank you for it, and you may be certain that each similar act will never be unnoticed by me but will be remembered in my heart and mind.

My pains still persist. The doctor seems to be quite satisfied with this, and predicts that the pain will go on up to 6 weeks after finishing the treatment. It has been decided that I am to stay here the full 4 weeks, that is till the 28th August/9th September; and as after every 4 baths I have a day's rest, that means that in all I shall take 24 baths. I am rather feeble and can walk less and less: I perspire profusely, which also pleases the doctor who maintains that the sweating prevents the formation of uric acids and salts which are what cause the swelling of the joints and the arthritic pains I suffer from. On the 28th August/9th September, after my last bath, I shall leave for Prague. As you know my plans, I shall not repeat my itinerary. About the 15th/27th September I hope to be back home. That is enough about my feelings and health, so now to your business!

(1) As for going to sea again the sooner you do so the better, and the shortest sail possible before your examination would also be to

---

[1] Cieplice in Polish, Teplice in Czech.
[2] Polish poet, 1802–86. The quotations are from his poem 'Duch od stepu' ('The Spirit from the Steppes'), 1836.

your advantage; but you must make certain, my dear lad, that the B. of Trade will be satisfied with 6 weeks, so that you do not have any more trouble. Anyhow you are now a sufficiently experienced 'sea dog' to decide this for yourself.

(2) As to your naturalization, I should wish you to obtain it at the very earliest moment and that the 'brass' which has been put aside for it should not be used for any other purpose. If you are contemplating postponing these formalities till your return, it is up to you to do what is most convenient for you. My only advice is that in addition to the £10 deposited by you with Mr. Naunton, you should deposit another £10 with Krieger for that purpose. You would then be able to feel satisfied that the financial side of the business is taken care of.

(3) As to your going into partnership with Messrs. Krieger and Mering,[1] I am very pleased that they are prepared to accept you. I shall willingly increase your share from £300 to £350, but no more. Please let me know before the 18th/30th January, 1884. Should it have to be postponed my promise will stay valid for January 1885. If I am notified in January I shall send the money to Mr. Krieger before the 18th/30th March. During the year I shall accept any date, provided that you warn me 3 months in advance. I shall feel bound by all these conditions in peace-time only, but I must be free in the case of war between Russia and any other country, for then the value of our money will drop terribly and the price of a pound may reach 15 roubles or more. Even today our position is not particularly strong, for as you saw we paid 10 roubles 31. As you can see, we treat the issue en grand, linking it with the question of peace in Europe. As you requested, I am enclosing a letter in French, setting out my position. My conditions in respect of yourself are much as you mentioned. I make but one observation: you did not say for how many years your association is to last. Secondly, as to the division of profits I should consider it more advisable to decide at first on some percentage on the capital, supposons 4%: and then share the profits in the proportion of 4/5ths and 1/5th, which here is the usual basis of companies. Thirdly, are your investments to be equal, or different in size? That you didn't say. Please let me have all this information, and when writing address your letter to Kazimierówka. (Perhaps one more letter *would* reach me here. Your letter I received on Thursday after lunch.) I shall certainly get it there, but if sent here, it may get lost for I am definitely leaving on Sunday, the 28th.

[1] Spelling incorrect; the name of the firm was actually Barr, Moering & Co., and Adolf Krieger, a friend of Conrad's, was associated with it.

Well, my dear boy, keep well and manage as best you can. I embrace and bless you.

Your Uncle,
T. BOBROWSKI.

I shall not write again from here, but only from home.

From Kazimierz Bobrowski[1]

8.XII. 1884
Leopoldów

My dearest Konrad,

It was a real surprise to get your letter yesterday. Though all news about you was already known to me from a letter of the 5th instant to my brother Tadeusz, I am nevertheless sincerely grateful to you for remembering us. We are truly pleased with your success and congratulate you on your newly acquired rank[2]—and above all on your winning the case against your ex-captain![3] A failure in the former matter could have been amended but not so in the latter, which moreover would have unfavourably affected your whole career! Thank God you came safely out of this affair.

Tadeusz's health is far from perfect; it can't be helped—he has been knocking about the world for 56 years and approaching old age does not improve his health; I am 8 years younger than he is and yet with every day I feel the burden of years more acutely. However, as far as I can judge from his letters and from what one of our friends who visited us has told me, there is nothing dangerous about Tadeusz's health: according to the last opinion of the doctors his bad digestion was responsible for his heart palpitation, otherwise the condition of his heart and the whole organism is quite good. I expect that by the time you get my letter you will have already had Tadeusz's reply to your letter and he is sure to inform you about his health.

Our news is not too good: my wife is still ill and the state of her lungs deteriorates steadily. There is no hope for improvement, chiefly because the land around Leopoldów is marshy and the air

---

[1] Tadeusz Bobrowski's letters to Conrad written between August 1883 and July 1885 have been lost. To compensate partly for this gap I include here one of the three existing letters to Conrad from Kazimierz Bobrowski. The others are dated 13/25 December 1869 and 18/30 April 1882; the earliest one is now in Yale University Library, both later letters are in the National Library in Warsaw, sign. 2889.

[2] On 3 December Conrad passed his First Mate examination.

[3] This refers probably to some court action following Conrad's quarrel with Captain L. B. McDonald, the commander of a sailing ship *Riversdale* on which Conrad served between 10 September 1883 and 17 April 1884. On Conrad's Certificate of Discharge (now in Yale University Library) Captain McDonald refused to answer in the space provided for comments on 'Character and conduct'.

unhealthy. I am ageing rapidly, the arthritis in my leg troubles me more and more, frequently disabling me entirely. My eldest daughter Zuzanna is staying with us this year—she is very much like your late Mother! My little darling—amongst my daily troubles she is the only consolation! My younger daughters Marta and Maria are still at school in Lublin. My elder boys Stanisław and Tadeusz are in a Gymnasium in Radom in 6th and 1st forms respectively. They learn well, especially the younger one. The youngest, 4-year-old Michał, is of course at home. He is rather sickly. I am expecting my whole brood for the holidays on Christmas Eve. On those occasions, my dear Konrad, you are, although not in person, *always* present among us for we place on the table for the Christmas Eve supper all the photographs of our dear ones who are either far away or have gone from this world: my always mourned Mother, your Parents, all my three brothers, Józieczka, Tadeusz, my Kazio and yourself! And thus in our hearts and thoughts we break the wafer[1] with you, but our wishes for you cannot increase in number for they are always there.

You mention in your letter our rare correspondence. You are right. The reasons for it are the uncertainty of your whereabouts and our lack of an address at the proper time. If you let us know each time you are back in London and send us your address you will give us great pleasure and we shall write to you by return post. Both my wife and I send you our warmest love; keep us in your heart.

Your loving
K. BOBROWSKI

Taking advantage of my stay at home I am adding a few words to my dear Father's letter in order to send my best Christmas wishes to my cousin the Sailor and to remind you of myself your affectionate sister,

Zuzanna Bobrowska.

30

1st/13th June, 1885
Kazimierówka

My dear boy!

I am taking a chance in sending this letter, as a reply to yours of the 14th May and in the hope that it may still find you in England,

---

[1] It is a Polish custom to break a wafer with everybody present at the Christmas Eve supper.

which is possible as your loading and unloading usually take longer than originally planned. As I was away from home from the 16th to the 29th May, your letter lay on my writing desk for a whole week, which explains why I didn't answer it immediately it arrived.

Let's begin with the 'Barataria'[1] and your explanation of the metaphor, which you did in such perfect Polish that reading this part of your letter gave me real pleasure. But I must correct your unjustified assumption: the work of the famous Cervantes is well known to me; in fact, last year in Cieplice I read it again. Many of our younger generation could say the same, but neither to me nor to these younger and more 'enlightened' fellows (and this statement should not surprise you, for it is only natural that youngsters know more than their elders—thanks to the work of the previous generation) whom I asked did it occur that you were playing with metaphors! 'Sans crier gâre.' This is the origin of the whole misunderstanding, and if my memory serves me correctly, the 'New Robinson'[2] does mention Barataria, which would justify my supposition that some island or some small country in Africa had the honour of being called by that name!

Your whole explanation of the safety of your intended voyage to India, and of your abstinence from wine and rum, which are well known to me and have been well tested, appease me only to the extent to which any irrevocable or already accomplished fact can do. As usual under such circumstances I am left with hope which, according to the proverb, is the mother of those who are not specially wise! Sooner or later however it befalls us all to join them!

Having returned home the day before yesterday I had a day's rest and have now started taking the Marienbad water—a cure which lasts 21 days, as ere in Marienbad. I expect good results from it. But something that gives me no pleasure at all is the recurrence of arthritic pains both in the right side of the jaw and in the right arm, the latter being responsible for my illegible writing. What is old age for? Does it need any explanation? It is only a week ago that these attacks started. In any case, I shall not go to Teplitz: the baths there aggravate my haemorrhoids to such an extent that so far I have been unable to soothe them.

The harvest is good beyond our best expectations, but this good result wrinkles our brows, for last year in spite of a poorer crop our wheat and sugar fetched no price at all. They fell to 60 copecks and 3.80 per pood respectively, whilst before we used to get 1.20 and 6

---

[1] In *Don Quixote* the island-city over which Sancho Panza is appointed 'governor' (vol. ii, ch. 45).
[2] *Swiss Family Robinson*, by J. R. Wyss (1813).

roubles per pood. We shall walk barefoot among the haystacks and shall cover our roads with sugar! So life will be bitter in spite of all this sugar! If you can, dump into the sea the load of wheat you will be bringing over from America! Perhaps the prices will then go up? And help yourself to twice your usual amount of sugar. It will be a service to us!

Staś Zaleski who is here just now sends you friendly regards. He is going to marry Miss Zaleska, his cousin.

I embrace you a hundredfold and bless you.

Write and give me your 'itinéraire'.

Your Uncle,
T. BOBROWSKI.

31

2nd/14th August, 1885
Kazimierówka

My dear boy!

In the last letter I got from you, dated the 3rd June, you asked me to write to you towards the end of August to Singapore, so that my epistle could find you there. I am choosing a middle way, via London, as my letters sent you last year via Odessa and Brindisi never reached you. I suspect the Italians to be just as disorderly as the Russians in matters of mail and as we have no business ties with India it is quite probable that my letter was the only one of its kind in the post office at Odessa addressed to India. It may still be lying there and waiting for some fellow-letters. So I am writing via London.

First of all, in accordance with your wishes, I report that from the 1st till the 21st June (our style) I have been drinking Marienbad water at home, observing the same conduct as in the watering-place itself. Up till now I see no very obvious effects of the treatment. My stools during the time I was drinking the water were very gentle. Possibly, the whole thing was not necessary? Since the cure, the attacks are rarer, but have not been eliminated entirely. The arthritic pains have gone but neuralgia in the jaw and teeth bother me from time to time. On the whole I don't regret not having gone this summer to a spa. I couldn't have drunk the Cieplice waters, for they aggravate my haemorrhoids, and the Marienbad water I drank at home with the same result as if I had drunk it there and I avoided the boredom and expense of the journey. In general, my

98

2/14 August 1885

condition is not worse, possibly it is even better. I shall expect that this detailed report of my health will be repaid by your writing to me about yourself, about your health, and your precious little liver in particular. In spite of your assurance that from September till December the climate in India is good, I am not convinced and I would have preferred you to aim in a different direction; for if your first Indian voyage has already affected your liver, the second one could cause serious harm. This possibility is not an enviable one, even if for the price of it you were to become an admiral! Well, it's done! I pray to God for your safe return without your having done yourself much harm, and I vow to God on your behalf that you will give up further experiments. Panie Bracie! Don't make a liar out of me!

What local news shall I give you? Our good companion from Marienbad, Karol Zagórski, has gone abroad again for a cure, according to his father. His brother Tadeusz, about whom I wrote to you last year, telling you that he was at Cieplice after a severe attack of venereal disease, has gone there de noviter. The two poor old Zagórskis, weary with life and its troubles, are lonely in their old age and Zagórski himself is threatened with serious lung trouble. Karol and his wife, who moved to Warsaw a year ago, now have a second daughter.

The wedding of Staś Zaleski, who as I informed you got engaged to his cousin, will take place only towards the end of February next year. The Zaleskis always ask very kindly after you, and I gave them your regards. The Montresors are at present in the country. They returned recently from a spa and in the winter they will drag themselves somewhere else.

Frania is not too well. She can hardly move about now, but always thinks of you fondly and is touched by your remembering her. Uncle Kazimierz is living in Leopoldów (on the Vistula Railway), as poor as ever. Zunia has gone somewhere in Lithuania as a governess, and Marta, the second daughter, returned home from school to look after her sick mother and the house. Well, that is all for now, my dear boy. Write to me.

I embrace you a hundredfold and bless you.

Your Uncle,
T. BOBROWSKI.

In October as usual I shall send your £30 allowance to London to your partners.

Mr. Conrad N. Korzeniowski.
Singapore p/Londres

32

24 March/5th April, 1886
Kazimierówka

Dear boy!

On your return to London I would like you to find this letter to greet you, and for that reason I am not asking for it to be forwarded on to you. The last letter I had from you was dated the 8th January, and it reached me at the end of the month. Previously I received letters of the 28th November, 14th October, and 3rd June, the last informing me of your departure for India. I only wrote to you the two letters which you received in Singapore, as this was the only definite address you gave me. As you know, I don't like to write letters that there is not a good chance of your receiving. Had you given me a detailed itinerary I could have written to you oftener, to the places you might have mentioned in it, but as I didn't know where you were calling for certain, I preferred not to write. What is done is done, and there is no use talking about it now. Meanwhile, as you are about to return, I hope safe and sound, you must consider seriously, Panie Bracie, your examination for a captaincy, and also your naturalization;—the final steps in your career, which I still insist on; first get your captain's licence and your naturalization, then you can do, Sir, as you please. Your old Uncle will have no choice but to rejoice in your projects and happiness, providing God grants that the former bring about the latter. In November I sent £30 for you to Mr. Krieger, which you will find at your disposal. As to our meeting this year, which you planned and I in a way looked forward to as well, it seems to be rather doubtful as you will realize from the following.

In mid-December my brother and your uncle, Kazimierz, fell gravely ill with pneumonia. It almost sent him to his grave and left him an invalid for the rest of his life. Desperate telegrams from his wife brought me to his bedside, where I remained for several days. Being obliged to return home on account of the Kiev fair, I left with but a very faint glimmer of hope. However, God has mercy on his servants, and eventually kept him alive. He even got out of bed, although he lost his left lung, and the condition of his already weak heart deteriorated, while his right lung which was already not good is damaged further. As you can see, his situation is not an enviable one; it is just a slow, prolonged death. In the conditions in which Kazimierz exists there can be no question of his living very long. At the same time there are his sick wife and 6 children, of whom only one daughter can earn her keep. I cannot tell you what

I went through last December and January. Anxiety, sleeplessness, and nerves have affected my own strength. I can't say my health has suffered, for I am quite well, but my strength has visibly deteriorated. Of course, my brother's illness also affected my pocket, in addition to the usual help I give his children; and now there is the prospect of further medical treatment, possibly abroad. In the meantime my income has fallen! The good days of Aranjuez,[1] or in plain speech, the big dividends from the sugar shares, are finished, and instead of getting from that source the usual 1,500–2,000 roubles annually, I got for the past year a meagre 400 roubles. Thus I am obliged to tighten 'les cordons de ma bourse', especially where expenses are concerned that are not absolutely necessary, so as to be able to meet those that cannot be avoided. Among these I include saving my brother's health and educating his children; so I cannot regard meeting you as absolutely necessary and dare not dream of your coming over to see me, while on the other hand I cannot even think myself of going abroad. Am I not right, Panie Bracie, under the circumstances to reach the above conclusion? Apart from that, if, as I deduce from your and Krieger's letters, you intend to devote yourself to trade and stay in London, I would think it only right for you to stay put till you have got quite familiar with the routine of your new occupation and that you should not tear yourself away from it till you have mastered all its difficulties. In view of these and possibly other reasons which may appear on the political horizon, I believe that the only sensible thing we can both do is to give up any hope of meeting each other this year, either here or abroad, as both duty and necessity require it!! Whatever you may decide as regards your future, I emphatically beg you not to postpone either your examination or your naturalization. I shall cease to make a nuisance of myself once you have settled these two affairs; these are now the only things I insist on your doing.

For your information and that of your partners, in case you decide to embark on business, I would strongly recommend a thorough investigation in London of two possibilities: *trading in wheat-flour*, for here milling has become very popular and eventually wheat will be exported in the form of flour; and *trading in granulated sugar*. In both these articles you could with my introduction do big business, providing you were quick and thorough. It would be essential at first to get well acquainted with the market conditions and with the qualities and imperfections of the goods as well; also with the conditions and shortcomings of our market. Observing the difficulties

---

[1] A town on the Tagus, at times the seat of the Spanish royal court. 'The sweet days of Aranjuez are over' are the opening words of Schiller's *Don Carlos*.

that are caused here by the problem of sugar and wheat, and seeing that these products are dealt in mainly in London, I felt that it would not be amiss if at least some of the profit reached you and your partners instead of flowing into the great London houses through our banks as the sole intermediaries. This is why you should act more speedily, cheaply, and profitably than these big dealers, and this is also why you should investigate the position in London, Odessa, Libau, and Królewiec and should be prepared to content yourselves with a smaller profit in order to secure more orders. I shall not expatiate upon this any further, for as you know I am not an expert on commercial affairs. Here, however, is my idea and it is for all of you to consider how to realize it to your advantage. Maybe you and one of your partners could come here to get acquainted with the local conditions and clients. But first find out all you can yourselves. The main thing is from the very beginning to avoid making mistakes, and to meet the competition of the big firms. There is still time until the next harvest and the new sugar campaign.

Write to me on your return and after getting this letter, and now farewell to you. I embrace you heartily.

Your uncle,
T. BOBROWSKI.

33

12/24 April, 1886
Kazimierówka

My dear boy!

I would like you to find some fresh news on your return to London and therefore although you should find waiting for you at Mr. Krieger's the previous letter I wrote, here you have a second and more recent one, by which I welcome you back and embrace you. Send me as speedily as possible all your news, for I miss it badly, as the last I heard from you was from the River Hooghly, dated the 8th January. I will begin with news about Uncle Kazimierz which after reading my previous letter you will certainly be most anxious to get. Well, he is alive, minus his left lung and still very feeble. He doesn't leave his room. He intends to come and stay with me for a few weeks, but so far he is not strong enough to make the 30-hour journey by rail followed by eight to ten hours by coach. One needs some strength for that. He is rescued, but how long can he live? When I tell you that apart from losing one lung the other one is affected, and in addition his liver and heart have been in a bad state for years—there is no sense in deluding oneself. You will also understand my calling his condition a 'slow death'. True, that is better than death itself, especially for his wife and children, for death is irrevocable; true also that some people go on living with similar complaints, but not in conditions as bad as his! Would to God I may be mistaken, but my impression is that he will not live for long. All the same, one should and one does do everything to sustain his flickering life. So, if he is strong enough, he will come to me for the summer.

Obviously, I won't spare any material and moral efforts over this! As he is coming to me—but it is uncertain when—I shall have to remain at home to await his arrival, and then keep him company and look after him. So in addition to the usual expense connected with his health and with the maintenance of his family, and of their education, his medical treatment has already cost me an extra 800 roubles. In this state of affairs I cannot think of myself. Luckily, my own health is quite good and I neither contemplate nor need a cure. Other pleasures, such as meeting my nephew, have to be postponed till a more favourable moment, for I cannot leave the country nor even find the money for doing so! I must stay at home and sustain myself with letters instead of personal contact, my dear Panie Bracie! 'Tenez le pour dit' at least for this year of 1886 which, according to a prophecy of some medieval monk, is supposed to be a terrible one for the human race. Perhaps all the Germans with their progeny will go to the devil, or perhaps only Bismarck with his master—that would be at least something!

Please write to me: (1) How is your health? (2) When is your examination for a master's certificate (for I am not going to give way over this!)? (3) What are you going to do next?—this you may decide as you please. (4) What about your partnership—will you find it advantageous if you leave the Mercantile Marine? (5) Finally —when will you get your naturalization? And don't forget to draw the attention of your partners to the possibility of trading with Russia in sugar and flour. These branches of trade hold great possibilities for the future as they have not yet been methodically exploited. There is a good profit in it for a middleman who is prepared to go in for it after a thorough investigation and with reliable management. We suffer here from an over-production of these articles which are essential for you. Well, that is enough for now: I embrace you a hundredfold.

Your Uncle,
T. BOBROWSKI.

34

24 June/6 July, 1886
Lipowiec

Well, you are back at last my dear boy, and I was already getting very anxious about you as you could see from my letter addressed to Barr, Moering & Co. Four days ago, together with your letter, I got the reply from these gentlemen; please thank them for it on my behalf.

Under the influence of the recent loss of my brother I was obsessed by gloomy thoughts about you which now, thank God, I can put out of my head. Really, quite apart from that, I had many worries and expenses this year. The family by now have probably settled in Radom as by the 1st July they were due to move. They are certain to have done so, as in any case since the 20th April, the date of your Uncle's death, for a period of a full two months they were allowed on compassionate grounds the free use of their flat together with heating. Now they have taken a four-roomed flat which for a family of 6 is barely large enough. The annual rent is 300 roubles. I have fixed for them 1,500 roubles, hoping that they will get 300 roubles by way of pension and about 200 roubles interest from the small capital left by the children's grandmother—Mrs. Marciszewska. However, apparently they may not get the widow's pension after all as according to the regulations they are short by just under one year. This question is not settled as yet, but if our hopes fail I shall have to provide this sum myself, for 1,500 roubles is far from enough for such a large family. It's a pretty kettle of fish to find oneself in in one's old age, and I must confess that I consider it a 'cas pendable' for which I blame my late brother himself. But may he rest in peace, for he was a good and honest man although he lived all his life on the principle that 'somehow it will work out', and was strangely thoughtless in the matter of producing offspring. And, indeed, it always does work out somehow and always will, but at the expense of the person least responsible for it all; of the person who had no say in the matter and no pleasure out of producing this progeny. I don't remember if I told you that apart from the family who need supporting he also left me debts amounting to 1,000 roubles which I had to pay. Well, what's done can't be undone Mościa Panno![1] Let's hope it will all work out for the best! Zunia, the eldest daughter, became engaged during her father's lifetime and is now to marry a 'chemin de fer'-man, Mr. Meresch. The

[1] 'Mościa Panno', literally 'Gracious Miss', was the old Polish form of addressing unmarried girls of gentle birth. The whole sentence is a popular expression.

wedding is to take place in November, which means another unforeseen expenditure to be taken into account in this year's budget.
However, this also must be borne, and to cover its cost and the repayment of debts I have had to break into my capital to the extent of
1,500 roubles.

My health is good, but even had it been otherwise I could not
have considered this year taking any cure or making any excursion
abroad—it is hard to make ends meet as it is. Anyway 'Boh
kryw',[1] as our peasants say, and at least in that respect I am not
troubled. What about your health, my dear boy? For you said
something, you hinted something about some 'dyspepsia' and about
being 'a weakling', as if you had some incurable disease! Please make
yourself more lucid on the subject. Anyway, at your age you are too
young to get some chronic complaint and it would really be too
much for one to bear, to be both poor and ill! Write to me as well
about your further projects—when you've passed the examination
and have got your master's certificate. Do you intend to go on
sailing? Or will you stay in London in business? These are just my
questions and you will settle them for yourself as you wish and in
the light of such experience as you have—without taking me into
account. It's all the same to me what you eventually do as long as
you do it and find it satisfying. Everyone approaching the age of
thirty knows or should know what he wants and what he is aiming
at—provided that he is self-supporting. According to my point of
view, no one, not even the most loving Uncle, has any right to
interfere with that. To close our accounts for the past I permit
myself to demand from you only two things—a master's certificate
and your naturalization; and I ask this in the hope that you will
shortly be informing me that both matters have been successfully
settled. Furthermore, and only if asked explicitly, I shall permit
myself to give you my opinion about your career, rejoicing in its
success or, God forbid, being grieved by its failure. We shall surely
come back to this subject in the future, and not only once. For the
time being, keep well, settle your old affairs before starting new ones,
and write to me. Accept my warmhearted embraces and blessings.

Your Uncle,
T. BOBROWSKI.

[1] 'God is cross', or 'angry' (Ukrainian).

35

8/20 July, 1886
Kazimierówka

My dear boy!

Our letters must have crossed as I answered your first one straight away; and I am answering the second one now.

From the phrase in your last letter, 'I decided to try my luck, providing my health is good', I deduce that you are not absolutely well. Why don't you write explicitly what is the matter? I don't imagine that this phrase relates to your preparations for your examination. I most emphatically request you to write to me clearly about the state of your health. And as the examination will be over by the time you answer this letter, let me know how it went. Finally —has your naturalization gone through—and if not, why not, and when will it be finally settled? Please answer each of these questions categorically. And just one thing more; did you get the £30 sent to you in the autumn, and did you get the agreed interest on your investment? Finally, on what sort of terms would you be working in the Agency? I am quite ignorant about this. I am not surprised in the least at your intention to make another voyage, even if only one, in the rôle of a captain. Anyone who has devoted 14 years of his life and work to attain a certain position should cherish it and desire, if only once, to utilize it. Good luck to any enterprise of yours in whatever direction!

As to the problem with which we are preoccupied, i.e. flour and sugar, after having introduced you to the idea, I feel it my duty now to suggest a mode of action and to acquaint you with people with whom you might have to do business.

As to the method, I suggest that first of all one should investigate the trade in flour and sugar not in its accidental but typical symptoms. Granulated sugar, for instance—what type is in demand? What is the average price?—I mean en gros, for we cannot do business en détail. As to the flour—what kinds are looked for by the bakers? This latter question, in fact, is the obstacle which has hitherto upset all endeavours. Having examined both questions, two separate reports should be prepared, one about sugar, the other about flour. The producers are only interested in their own branch of trade and would not read a memorandum devoted to both. The reports, in both Polish and French (here English is likely to be known only to a few women), could be sent out and if the idea meets with approval could be published later in Russian. The French part of the prospectus could be written by you, while the Polish text you could send to me for correction to ensure that the Polish is good. One could try to get a translation of such a prospectus published in the Kiev newspaper *Zorza* and in the paper of the Association of Agriculturists in Kiev. For the sake of creating a good impression it is essential that this memorandum be signed with your name. This will ensure that 'on viendra aux renseignements' to me. Explain this to your colleagues (Barr, Moering & Korzeniowski). Here, the period of greatest business activity in sugar and grain is September and the following months, for then begins the production of the first and the threshing of the second.

Now, something about the people you will be dealing with. The producers of sugar, and of flour as well, have no idea of trade and especially of foreign trade. You cannot therefore expect them to act in the way real business men do and to which you have got accustomed. Our producers like to have a free hand and don't care a bit about having promised to send goods for sale on commission. As soon as a producer is offered a good price on the spot—he sells, not bothering about his commission agent. This is a difficulty where trading with us is concerned and that is why the commission has to be higher, usually 1% to 2%.

Therefore it is not possible to rely on promises, but only on goods which have been delivered, and therefore a journey to Kiev might not bring any result even in spite of many promises. The working-up of a clientele here is a slow process and in addition depends on prices being low (the sugar-beet harvest is likely to be bountiful); if the first deals prove successful, then it would be time to think of coming here and settling in Odessa, or better still in Kiev which is the centre of the sugar and flour trade.

In the meantime carry on your investigations and write your memorandum. My letters will keep you informed how things are here.

I embrace you a hundredfold.

Yours,
T. B.

36

12/24 August, 1886
Kazimierówka

My dear boy!

You worry about me quite unnecessarily and your impatience, my dear boy, serves no purpose. I shall not answer the questions you put to me before it is possible for me to do so thoroughly, so far as I am able to, in order to give you all a fairly accurate picture of the local situation and of the people. In spite of my best intention to satisfy you with an exhaustive survey, or even because of it, I am unable to give it to you as soon as I should have liked. I have been busy working on it for the past few days, but in spite of my zeal I cannot expect to have it finished either today or soon enough to satisfy your impatience. The reasons are as follows: To begin with I was absent from home till the end of July, our style (from the 10th to the 28th), when I found your two letters and settled down at once to work, not only to reply to the questions you asked but to deal with all that I considered essential. However, here a country squire, unlike in the rest of Europe, is not master of his own time. It is not customary here to invite people specially; neighbours and friends call when they wish, they are boring or entertaining as they wish, and they depart when they wish. Thus a squire becomes a slave to his visitors, while someone wishing or needing to work is a prey to idlers. The summer encourages such visits and I myself have to make and receive a certain number of them. In fact after having been away for a couple of weeks, my door is now never closed, what with one arriving and another departing, each visit taking up time and rendering one unable to think or write. I have already written part of my memorandum and I had hoped to complete it and send it off this week, but an unexpected accident calls me away from home. Spasowicz,[1] who was due to come here, had an accident; he was very badly bruised and telegraphed for me to come to him. Kalixt Bądarzewski is seriously ill and also called me to his bedside. In view of this, I have to interrupt work and go to them. Luckily they both live in the same district and on my way to Spasowicz I practically pass the estate of Bądarzewski. This will delay for a couple of weeks my letter to you, or rather to you and your colleagues, for it will be in the language of the Gauls. My excursion will take about a week and let us hope the reply will eventually be dispatched during the week after next, especially as about this time my monthly Court session is due and also the visit of Mrs. Leonowa Syroczyńska who stays with her husband's brother and who on her last visit to me inquired after you in the most friendly terms. As you can see, my dear lad, although I do not work in any profession and can permit myself to take things easy—as a well-bred country squire and proprietor of an estate is not born to overwork himself—I have a lot to do and am

---

[1] Włodzimierz Spasowicz (1829–1906), well-known conservative publicist and literary critic, one of the main exponents of the loyalist pro-Russian line among Polish intellectuals; a friend of Bobrowski; later wrote an introduction to his *Memoirs*.

sometimes short of time in which to accomplish it quickly. Thus please accept my excuse for delaying my answer, but believe that the matter is close to my heart and you will get a reply as soon as possible and as thorough and detailed as is possible for me. In case of your absence please authorize your partners to accept the letter, on which I shall, in any case, put their address. In September I shall send you £30 for the current year. I am not sure how much longer I shall be able to assist you, for it will depend on how much supporting Uncle K.'s family costs me.

Finally, let me put on record that since your return to London I have had four letters from you and this one is my third to you. I am quite well. I embrace and bless you with my whole heart.

Your Uncle,
T. BOBROWSKI.

37

28 August/9 September, 1886
Lipowiec

My dear boy!

I am engaged in sitting here in the Court, and this of course has delayed for a few days the completion of my report which however I now enclose. To the best of my abilities I have put into it all my thoughts and observations on this subject of trade which is alien to me.

Your fifth letter, of the 13/25th August, reached me when I was just about to finish my report. I presume that you received my third letter written two weeks ago and that you are now at peace. How could such an idea as writing to Dr. Kopernicki enter your head? Why, I am quite well, as I wrote to you; I don't think of going abroad —I just can't afford it, Panie Bracie.

I presume therefore that nothing but impatience could give you such thoughts. You know me well enough to know that I keep all my promises, particularly those made to you, and if I am not speedy in carrying them out there must be a good reason. And so it was on this occasion. After reading my lucubration you will appreciate that some time was necessary for drafting it and then copying it; and I am not always the master of my time. Thus, you yourself and your friends should regard me as excused, for, as our late Uncle Adolf[1] used to say: 'he is a rascal who does more than he can'. Draw up

---

[1] Adolf Pilchowski.

such agreement as you and your partners may fancy, but don't drag me into it. For whatever I do or may be able to do I am doing only for you and not for what I can get out of it. Think then of yourself, dear Panie Bracie, and only of yourself. I wish you every success! As to myself, I want to remain apart and disinterested, so please make this clear to these gentlemen so that they should not regard me as their agent. Remember, Panie Bracie, that you vouch for their character, both to me and to anybody else who, the Lord grants, will contact you.

The address of your Uncle's wife is:

Royaume de Pologne à Radom,
Ul. Dmitrowska 132, d. Ziętkowskiego.

I am extremely glad that you have completed your naturalization and I embrace my Britisher and nephew wholeheartedly.

Your Uncle,
Tadeusz B.

PS. Write to me, my dear lad, as often as possible.

Vos lettres sont toujours les bien venues.

38

18/30 September, 1886
Kazimierówka

My dear Panie Bracie,

Simultaneously with this letter I am sending money to Mr. Heisman in Odessa to buy £30 and dispatch it instantly to you care of 'Barr, Moering et Cie'—as you have not given me any other address and you told me some time ago that your friend Krieger was very ill. I could, therefore, see no other solution but to burden these gentlemen with my dispatch, for which I apologized politely in my letter to them. The rest is now up to you. The money will probably arrive about a week late for it will take at least that time for it to reach Odessa and then be posted on to London. I am now just telling you that it will arrive, proving my constant solicitude for you. I do not know how much longer I shall be able to manifest my remembrance in such a tangible form. For if Hamlet said 'Something is rotten in the State of Denmark', so it has been the case for some time in our agricultural affairs. The fall in the prices of grain (in spite of the bad harvest this year our local needs can always be met) and sugar affects the rent one can get for one's land. The leaseholders are losing badly and I have my land leased for only two years more at 10 roubles per dziesięcina (about 2 morgs, a morg is somewhat more than a hectare). What will eventually happen I do not know, but one thing I do know is that whatever the price of land may be I am not going to farm it myself, so I shall let it for what it will fetch. My income from this source is certain to decline; it only remains to be seen by how much. It might go down to 3 roubles per dziesięcina, although now they still give 8. The capital invested in the sugar refineries' shares brings me as little as 5 % as compared with 30 and 35 % in the past. A loss of capital may even follow. My source of income is thus threatened, and the remaining capital invested privately at 8 %, however carefully invested, may be endangered as well as a result of the general poverty. As you see, the position is not to be envied and I can say with Hamlet 'something is rotten' while not, however, taking the matter as tragically as he did. Let us, Panie Bracie, wait and see what happens. In the meantime you can be certain that I both like and desire to think of you and to give you visible signs of the sincere uncle-like interest that I cherish for you, and if they should come to an end, it would not mean that my feelings had come to an end too, but that the bottom of my pocket had been reached. Meanwhile let us praise God that this is not yet the case.

My trade report can surely not have made particularly enjoyable reading. Possibly I painted it in too dark colours, but it is always more pleasant to be surprised by things turning out better than by their being worse than expected. I expect to get news from you soon as to what you have decided on for the present, as well as for the future. I also expect to find in that letter some information about your master's examination; I hope it went off successfully. This, together with the completion of your naturalization, would mean the fulfilment of all my desires for you, leaving everything else to you!

I am going to pay farewell visits to Śnieżna and Nŏwofastów before they depart for the winter to Warsaw and abroad. Thereafter I shall retire for the winter, which, judging by the early frost (on the 7/19 inst. we had 3° of frost), will be long and hard. I shall thus stay at home writing my memoirs. My health is good, and I am used to being alone.

Write to me, Panie Bracie, what your plans are for the future. Meanwhile I embrace and bless you,

Your Uncle,
T. Bobrowski.

Dąbrula, although with one foot in the grave, still carries on. She sends you her embraces.

39

28 October/9 November, 1886
Kazimierówka

My dear boy!

Your two letters of the 21st September and 29th October reached me simultaneously and I shall answer them, but in the reverse order, replying first to the proposition you made in your last letter. Apparently, my dear fellow, amidst all your business activities in London, you have confused people and facts. I have always told you what I said at the beginning of my memorandum, and I will now repeat it again: I was never either a speculator or a trades-man, for I do not feel that I have the right flair. Having thus for 57 years preserved the innocence of my soul, I have no intention now of selling myself to Mercury or possibly even to the devil himself with the object of exploiting other people's poverty, need, or stupidity! So much for the principle. From the practical point of view I must tell you that at present we pay 10 roubles 45 kopecks for £1 sterling, and that our sugar shares, although they may not have fallen below par, find no buyers, and finally, that I get here 8 %, and that in advance. If I pressed hard I could get as much as 9 or 10 %—without moving my capital out of the country. This year I could not even do so if I wished, because of the bad harvest and general depression, especially as all my debtors are friends. I feel sure, my dear Panie Bracie and nephew, that you would say about me 'dementus est', if in spite of the above situation I transferred my funds to England and put them into the hands of a stranger who would pay me a smaller rate of interest,—and above all earn the name of usurer; 'Noli me tentare'. I would like you to realize that it was not in order to speculate that I parted with some of my 'precious metal' and sent it to London—not for speculation but to help my nephew who chose to live there. The Scriptures say: 'Where my treasure is, there also is my heart'; and shall I dare to improve on it thus: 'Where my nephew is, there is my gold!'

So much for the business you propose, and now I ask you to let me know clearly and definitely what is in fact being done with the £350 capital which I put up and sent you to London. Does it re-main entirely in the hands of Krieger? Or is it in the business of Barr Moring & Co.? For if, as you say, Krieger is ill and might 'kick the bucket', who will be responsible for the capital involved and who will look after carrying out the Agreement? For as you will remember I signed an Agreement with Mr. Krieger, putting in a clause about the 'réversibilité' of this sum on specific conditions, in the case of your death. Be kind enough to write to me clearly and definitely how this matter stands. Secure this money in the event of Krieger's death and meanwhile remember that in the event of your losing it you will not get a penny from me till my death. Take care of it, for it is all you have for the time being and I am not in a hurry to go ad Patres. Before you depart let me know how matters stand and how you have secured your affairs. Write this to me in French so that I can have a document comprehensible to both parties. Also, before leaving, take the necessary steps at the Russian Embassy, particularly as you are leaving for several months. By the time you return the permission will be granted, and the sooner you get it, the quicker will be the moment of our meeting in our country. Don't put it off, dear lad, and make it a rule not to put off till tomorrow what you can do today. The same applies to the examination for your Master's Certificate. Get done with it once and for all, my dear boy, and may God help you to do so successfully. Write to me about it soon and about all the matters I have mentioned above. Your philosophical acceptance of the news about sugar has pleased me greatly:—'C'est le sentiment d'un vrai fils du pays, mon cher', in what you said about it, and that has much gratified me. I enclose herewith the latest French report about the situation. Write to me as well about the state of your health.

The wedding of your cousin Zunia with Mr. Meresch of the Vienna Railway will take place on the 8th/20th. Their engagement took place while Uncle K. was still alive. 'Je n'y suis pour rien, hors d'avoir fourni le trousseau comme toujours.'

That is my lot! I embrace you, my dear lad.

Your devoted Uncle,
T. BOBR.

40

14/26 November, 1886
Kazimierówka

Dear boy!

Long live the 'Ordin. Master in the British Merchant Service'!!¹ May he live long! May he be healthy and may every success attend him in every enterprise both on sea and on land! You have really delighted me with the news of the 'Red Seal' on your certificate. Not being an Admiral I have no right to give orders to a newly created Master and I leave to his own discretion the solution to the question—whether he is to change his O.M. into E.M.??²—which

¹ English in the original.   ² Probably 'Emeritus Master'.

depends on your prospects and plans for your future career. As the humble provider of the means for this enterprise I can only rejoice that my groats have not been wasted but have led you to the peak of your chosen profession, in which Mr. Syroczyński,[1] the heir to the virtues of the Romans and Greeks, drew twelve years ago such an unfavourable horoscope for the young aspirant to Neptune's service. You are, my dear Sir, now 29 years old and have mastered a profession; it is for you to know and understand what you must do further.

My last letter, with a reply to your proposed transport speculation, has by now doubtless reached you. The reply was what you expected. It seems to me, however, that the right conclusion occurred to you only after some thought and after you had written to me. I am not going to read you a lecture and there is no reason for you to feel 'trepidation'. I am neither cross nor surprised. I simply refuse for the reasons I have already explained. I am left intact with my groats while you acquitted yourself of a friendly commission, 'e sempre bene'. Far more important to me is the news of your own money deposited jointly with that of Krieger. My concern for the health of this worthy man is certainly to some extent due to his being your partner. Thus be kind enough to appease my anxiety over this and before leaving, satisfy my curiosity. Secure the only capital that you possess, in the event of Krieger's death. From what you tell me, I see you are a protector of widows and invest their capital well. This is very noble, but for God's sake think of yours also.

Once again I shall repeat my remark, or even my demand, that you must before departing take the necessary steps at the Russian Embassy to obtain release from their citizenship. The correspondence could be completed during your voyage and on your return you could find the matter settled, I hope favourably. Then you could come and visit me, which we both desire. The sooner that happens the better I shall be pleased, for in the 57th year of one's life, pleasant events should not be postponed for long. I feel better, the dizziness caused by digestive disorders has subsided; I have not had it for at least a month. About a week ago, that is on the 8th/20th, Zuzanna, Uncle Kazimierz's eldest daughter, entered into wedlock with Mr. Meresch, a railway official, to whom she was promised by her father when he was alive. I was not present at the wedding, but sent a telegram. We shall see what will come of it—most probably another 'bare-foot' generation. On this note at present, I shall end my speculation as to the future of this couple.

---

[1] Antoni Syroczyński (cf. Introduction).

As yet, nothing definite is known about the sugar question. We have definite news, however, that regulations have again been accepted in principle, but the other terms are unknown. I shall inform you when the regulations are officially published.

Set off, Panie Bracie, once more on your journey over the seas, as apparently there is nothing for you to do now on land. Let me know when, where, which way, and for how long? Write to me during the voyage. Now I embrace and bless you.

Your uncle,
T. BOBROWSKI.

41

5/17 April, 1887
Kazimierówka

Dear boy,

You asked me to write to you in April. I am responding to your request so as to spare you any worry and anxiety you might feel about me. I hope that, in return, you will take the first opportunity of letting me have some news of yourself.

Your last letter reached me at a very distressing time for me, namely, on the death of our good Dąbrosia. Although it had long been expected and in the natural course of events it had to happen, nevertheless I felt it, and still feel it, very deeply. As you know, two years ago she was stricken with paralysis, but got over it. Last year she had another stroke which was, however, so mild that no one, not even she herself, realized when it happened. It left her, though, with a difficulty in speaking and swallowing. On the evening of the 3/15 February without any warning there came a third attack which knocked her unconscious and took her away after 60 hours!

My last link with the past has been broken. An ever-growing emptiness surrounds a man, till at last he falls himself.

Immediately after the funeral, I had to hasten to Kiev for various reasons. I consulted doctors there: Krzyżanowski, Bądarzewski, and Orlikowski. After a most careful examination, inspired by feelings of friendship, each of them pronounced my organism to be in good working order and blamed my way of life for my occasional indispositions. Unanimously they ordered me to eat less, to forgo my afternoon nap, to take more exercise, and, in springtime—to drink buttermilk. I am fulfilling the first three orders, leaving the last one till the spring. I have not suffered from dizziness since the end of January, thanks to the diet and exercise I had prescribed myself, while as to my appetite I must confess it has diminished of its own accord and is not as great as it used to be.

I was in Kiev till the 24th February (old style). There was a good deal of work but the justice was not affected by your uncle's health! Experience has shown that I don't get ill when having less food, less sleep, and much exercise—which, due to my engagements in Kiev, is exactly what happened. As you see, I am ailing from 'rozkisz',[1] as our rustics say.

I stayed in Lipowiec from the 24th till the 28th of February for the Congress of Magistrates and I didn't get home till the 1st March. I have not stirred out since then and have hardly seen anyone because of the terrible state of our roads. Today is the first day of our Easter. Snow fell in the night and the temperature is −2° C. The snowfall is as deep as it should have been at Christmas, when in fact there was none. That is why we have this cold spell now.

I have no local news to give you. Uncle Kazim's family, all complete, live in Radom. The eldest one, Stanisław, will leave them after the holidays to go to the University, probably to Warsaw. At present, he is finishing school.

Both the Karnickis are alive but have aged a lot; they were no longer young when you knew them as a child and you are now in your thirtieth year. The Zaleski parents are in Warsaw for the winter, while the young ones are in Śnieżna, and are already enjoying having an heir.

The Montresors, on the contrary, are glad not to have one. They flit around the world searching for something they have not lost. At present they are near Vienna, in Kaltenleitgeben, taking a hydropathic cure. They went there after the fair. You will have a full picture of our financial situation when I add a word about our pauperism; our rouble is now worth only 179 marks and £1 is worth 11 roubles 46 kopecks. If, in addition to this, you recall the tender and increasing attention bestowed on us by Bismarck and Katkov,[2] you will have a foretaste of our moral and social situation. He is blessed who can settle down in Patagonia and enjoy the fruits of freedom and civilization—to say nothing of Java or Samoa.

This is all I have found to say and now it is for you to write and tell me how you are and how you prosper.

I embrace you a hundredfold and bless you.

Your uncle,
T. BOBROWSKI.

---

[1] Pleasure, delight (Ukrainian).
[2] Mikhail Katkov (1820–87), the editor of *Moskovskiya Vedomosti*, reactionary and violently anti-Polish journalist; exerted strong influence on the Tsar Alexander III.

42

8/20 August, 1887
Kazimierzówka

My dear boy!

I received your letter of 2/14 July yesterday—on the day of the solar eclipse, which was very appropriate because your letter completely eclipsed the good and tranquil thoughts I had had about you. I had expected you by now to stand on your own feet; that I had guided you to the right destination; and after 14 years of work and endeavour you were on the right road. And now 'pas de chance', as you say![1] And indeed it looks like that if our mariner, who risks death, is later to be faced with the prospect of rheumatism! This is too early for you, and once you have had trouble in your leg I very much doubt if you will ever quite get rid of it. You did not write to me exactly what the trouble is; is it ordinary rheumatism? or sciatica?—or perhaps paralysis? It could be any of these. I am racking my brains to think what it can be!? I would like to think that it is something slight, but the sad experience I have gone through with persons dear to me continually eggs me on to think the worst. With old age comes doubt! . . .

In the postscript you write that before your letter reaches me you will probably have been able to leave Singapore; but all the same you want my reply. I give it to you, but what else can I say but words of sympathy, for I live in the depths of the country and in addition it is one that has no direct contacts with India. The only thing I can say is that without any delay I shall send £30 to Krieger. Then, if you already need or at any time in the future will need some money, you may apply (if you have not done so already) to Krieger, asking him to help you from London by means which you may know (but which are unknown to me). This assistance could even be taken out of the small capital which is deposited with him, if you do not find it possible to return to London as a mariner. No other solution can I see—which is a direct outcome of the difference in our professions; I tied down to one place, while you roam the seas. But since for years we have been aware of this state of affairs, we have no right to grumble about the consequences, but must accept them as the logical outcome of our deliberate plans. At times we may feel them painfully, but there is nothing to be done

---

[1] For reasons of health (possibly after an accident on board) Conrad had to leave the *Highland Forest*, in which he had sailed from Amsterdam in February, in Singapore on 1 July 1887.

about it. The only hope is, as with many other setbacks, that this one will also pass! I suppose that on your return you can apply again to the same ship-owners—for it was illness that interrupted your service, which, as you state yourself, was quite creditable to you in other respects. But this is a matter for the future. My thoughts today are chiefly directed towards the recovery of your health and to your return to London, and I close this subject, so unhappy for both of us, with an ardent wish that it may be as soon as possible.

You will be very sorry to learn that Tadeusz Zaleski, who was so greatly liked by you, died suddenly in Warsaw in May. The whole tragedy happened in a few minutes. After an ordinary evening spent at home he woke up during the night complaining of an acute stomach pain. He got up, walked across the room, and fell— dead. What happened in fact is not known as his wife would not allow a post-mortem. This fatality caused me great grief and a lot of trouble, for it is impossible to bear with indifference the loss of a friend of almost 40 years, and it was equally impossible not to attend to the affairs of Cecylia Z. She has borne the blow with courage, or rather with an energy and submission that no one suspected her of. In London you will find a 'lettre de faire part'—Mrs. Z. herself remembered to send it to you.

During the summer I also visited your late Uncle Kaz.'s family in Radom. They are not doing too badly. Your Uncle's wife, although ailing, is still alive and, thank God, is keeping up. Stanisław, the eldest son, has finished gymnasium and is going to the University. Tadeusz, the younger son, passed into the 4th class and learns well. Zunia is married but apparently not very successfully; he is some kind of a milksop and his mother and sister bully her. Certainly Mme Kazimierzowa herself has never had such security as now, but this costs me 1,800 r. a year and it will probably eventually be more, as I shall have to add something extra for Stanisław at the University.

I am fairly well. During May I took a whey cure, but had to interrupt it when T. Z. died. In July I drank Marienbad water till the 31st and I found it rather beneficial.

Farewell, my dear boy, return in good health and write as often as you can. I embrace and bless you.

Your Uncle,
T. Bobrowski.

43

6/18 December, 1887
Kazimierówka

Dear boy!

The day before yesterday I got your letter of the 3rd November so that it took a full 6 weeks to reach me. It is therefore quite probable that before you get my reply the year 1888 will be over the horizon everywhere—even here! This fact, and even more your recent 30th birthday, account for my sending you my best wishes, embraces, and blessings. May God give you the best of everything, the best of health and prosperity! . . .

You have relieved my anxiety by your assurance that you are well as far as your leg and liver are concerned, and still more that you are assured of means of returning to Europe at any time you notice that a longer stay in India is likely to affect your health. I ask you earnestly to be careful for at your age and in your condition, as indeed at every age and in every condition, nothing is more precious than health! I suppose, however, that your 'objectif' is to await a suitable occasion to return to Europe as an officer, 'sans bourse délier', and in the meantime to accumulate a certain sum in dollars or guineas? and to save what has already been accumulated. Is that so?

Krieger wrote to me some time ago, and you now repeat it, that 'business in London is doing well'. That is all right as far as it goes, but I am not aware to what extent you participate in this? You wrote to me, at the time of joining the partnership, that while not working in it yourself, you may get 6% on your investment, and your share of the profit only when engaged personally in the business. Has there been a change in the agreement? Or was the original agreement binding only for a certain time? I would like to know. As you can appreciate, I cannot derive full enjoyment or even pleasure without knowing to what extent this satisfactory business affects you personally. Such knowledge would mean more than the Platonic pleasure caused by your friend's success, to whom of course I wish all the best while thinking nevertheless mainly of you. Write to me therefore, dear young man, how things really stand, so that I may know within what limits I may give rein to my joy!

I had anticipated that you would not be indifferent to the premature death (for he was scarcely 60 years old) of that good and worthy Tadeusz Zaleski, whom you grew to love so well in Marienbad, and who is sincerely mourned by all who knew him. His wife, although inconsolable, does not lament but bears her misfortune with the fortitude which is habitual in the Lubowidzki family. She has gone all on her own to Warsaw for the winter and there she leads a lonely existence. Her children visit her in turn, staying a few weeks; and it is surprising how she, who never attended to any business affairs and took no interest even in household matters, now wants to know about everything and to decide everything herself—causing weariness in her family, who in the end have to give way. Her affairs, in spite of there being considerable property, have turned out to be rather complicated. We are engaged in trying to sort them out and she seems ready to follow my advice, which she sought herself. Time and work alone will bring her peace and tranquillity.

I am quite well, considerably better than last year, and I attribute this to the Marienbad water, which I shall be taking again in the spring. It is impossible to think of going to Marienbad itself—there is a smell of war in the political air, and there is great poverty at home, for in spite of a good harvest the grain and sugar business is entirely at a standstill. A pood of wheat stands at about 70 kop., sugar—4 r. 30 k., while for £1 we pay 11 r. 40 k. and for 100 roubles we get 176 marks. The tax on land has gone up by 30%, and that is without counting the surtax paid by us Poles just because we are Polish, and which amounts to 100% of the basic taxes. Purchase taxes keep going up as well, and we shall soon have to pay excise tax on paraffin, on stearin candles, and on matches. How can one think of a cure abroad? Thank God one can afford to buy medicine at home, and drink.

Enough of this jeremiad which commenced so well in respect of my person but ends so sadly in respect of my purse. Write to me, Panie Bracie. I embrace and bless you.

Your Uncle,
T. BOBROWSKI.

44

1/13 January, 1888
Kazimierówka

Dear boy!

I got your last letter, of 1 December, yesterday evening as a New Year's gift and I cannot make better use of this day, which I usually greet and pass in solitude, than to transfer myself to the realm of recollection and talk to those who link me to those irretrievable memories! Thus I am writing to my brother's wife, and to my friend for 50 years—Sobotkiewicz, whom you must surely recollect from Granny's at Cracow. I am writing to you, sending my New

Year's and whole year's wishes and blessings! You really did give me bon-bons for a New Year's present (although it is a French custom, and not ours, to offer bon-bons), telling me about your present state of health as pronounced by the physician who treated you; although as you rather slightingly point out this pronouncement cost you 6 dollars, which struck you as too expensive, I permit myself to be of an entirely different opinion and would willingly offer the doctor a second 6 dollars out of my own pocket for relieving my anxiety. Therefore, Panie Bracie, organize your life and your return to Europe according to your own judgement, but never cease bearing your health in mind and at the first sign of a liver attack don't hesitate to return at once—or sooner—for there is nothing like health![1]

I do not demand now, and never did, that you should return from India, and this was not my intention when sending you the money through Mr. Krieger. The money this year was always meant for you, only it was intended to be sent a bit later. The news of your illness has only hastened its dispatch. As I did not warn you in advance of the cessation of your allowance, I would regard it (in spite of your sagacity) as a 'felonie' [*sic*], as the English call it, to withdraw my assistance now 'sans crier gare' when you are God knows where and above all ill. This is why I felt it my duty to give you a year's warning, so that you would be able to make your plans accordingly. Not for a minute did I think that the information about your illness, which I ought to be informed of in any case, could be interpreted as an indirect appeal for cash. Being myself straightforward I value straightforwardness in general and I have the right to expect it from all my relatives to whom I have given and still give proofs of my solicitude. I therefore assume that if it ever happens that you do not see any other way out, either now or at some time in the future, you will admit it openly, just as I would indicate to you in full honesty what I both can and intend to do in any specific case. Although in principle you must be self-sufficient, once again I ask you for absolute frankness. Bear in mind that you have an Uncle who is not indifferent to your fate and who is always ready to come to your rescue in any rational and genuine need—except that of marriage, for in regard to this extravagant need everyone has to look after himself. 'Nous n'en sommes pas là, Dieu merci, je pense!' but 'j'aime les avertissements', as you can see by my anticipating events which may never even have entered your mind.

I do not ask you to sacrifice your intentions as to staying or

---

[1] The last words are a quotation from a short verse, 'To Health', by Jan Kochanowski (1530–84).

returning, but none the less I do ask you for one sacrifice—a small but a valuable one to me, namely: buy yourself, Panie Bracie, some decent writing paper and good ink, and use them when writing to me. Your paper smudges and the ink runs so that I have to strain my eyes to decipher your letters; and as I usually re-read them several times— my eyes suffer even if my heart is gratified. You can cause them both to rejoice by doing what I have suggested and using it for my benefit. Do you agree?

In Radom all are well. Stanisław is at the University in Warsaw. His private tutorship brings him in 40 r. a month, and I give him 200 r.

Here, prices for leaseholds have fallen. I am not being offered more than 8 roubles for a dziesięcina (1¾ of a morg of land), while for the past 6 years I was getting 10 r. I have decided to accept this price although it means an annual loss of income of 1,000 r. and it seems that I shall be able to complete the arrangement here before going to Kiev. For the past two years my sugar shares have brought me no dividends, while at one time they used to bring me on average 1,200 r. or even 2,000 r. At present there is a slight improvement in the sugar business. We are getting 4 r. 50 kop. on the spot but I suspect that price to be artificial and that the crisis is not yet on the way out and has only subsided for the moment. We can never expect the price to go over 5 r. as the Minister of Finance is entitled to let in foreign sugar as soon as the price on the Kiev and Petersburg markets reaches 5½ r. and 6½ r. per pood respectively. What it all amounts to, both in respect of the leases and the sugar, is that the value of my estate has depreciated in the relation of 10 to 8 and my income still more. I am 2,000 r. per annum worse off although my expenditure is roughly the same as it used to be, for whatever I deduct from your allowance I add (and even more) to my brother's family, consisting as it does of 7 persons. This is the reason why I am so apprehensive about my relations getting married, as it always affects me in the end.

I embrace you a hundredfold. Write to me.

Your Uncle,

T. BOBROWSKI.

I am going to Kiev fair on the 3/15 February. I shall stay there till the 24th at the *Grand Hotel*.

45

19th March, 1888
Kazimierówka

In Kazimierówka there are the following things belonging to you:

1. A canteen of silver for 12 people marked with the 'Jastrzembiec' coat of arms—the property of your late mother.
2. Two Fraget[1] silver-plated trays—the property also of your mother.
3. An antique 16th-century clock—from your late father, left to him by the Driakiewicz family, that is from your grandmother's Korzeniowska side.
4. A Voltaire arm-chair which stands at present at my desk. It was given by your grandfather Korzeniowski to your mother when she was expectant.
5. A small table standing in the hall used formerly as a dressing-table by your grandmother Korzeniowska, a very worthy woman.
6. Some table linen and various knick-knacks, neither beautiful nor valuable, deposited in a separate chest.

All this was sent to me from Żytomierz to Nowofastów whence it was transferred to Kazimierówka temporarily at the time your parents left for Warsaw in 1860. Here it has remained for the last 28 years.

T. Bobrowski.

To: Mr. Konrad Korzeniowski.

46

10/22 May, 1888
Kazimierówka

Dear boy!

I have written to you twice c/o poste restante, Sydney, since February, that is since learning of your departure for Australia, and not a line from you has reached me here. Possibly you never got my letters, for although our post is quite efficient in regard to European mail, when its destination happens to be Africa, India, or the like—small country officials are frequently bewildered as to the choice of route. Yours however, had you written any, should reach me! Tandem you wrote none!!—you were not able to write—and this is

---

[1] A well-known plate factory in Warsaw, established 1824.

what disturbs me as I don't suppose that you would willingly have exposed my solicitude to such a long suspense. Nevertheless I am determined to seek you with my present letter, this time addressed to London and not to some outlandish region,—which you were due to leave anyway about now. I may or may not succeed in finding you thus, but my conscience will be clear and at least one of us will cease to fret—i.e. your mind will be at rest about my well-being. This in turn vous engagera d'honneur to reciprocate by sending news of the person of the esteemed Commander! . . .? Hence, here am I, awaiting the Captain's compassion, which I pray he may exercise speedily, and in favourable conditions.

As to me, I have been ailing constantly since the fair. In December my former nausea and dizziness reappeared and since my return from Kiev they have troubled me more and more frequently—one week I had about four of them! By careful dieting and attention, and with the help of medicaments, I have remedied and restored my health temporarily and I have managed to see the month of May in with its relatively warm weather. On the 5/17 May I began drinking Marienbad water as advised by 6 doctors: my family doctor and five physicians who are friends of mine in Kiev, who recommended it after examining me. I have always found the effects of Marienbad water very beneficial and I hope it may do my heart good as well. In the autumn I plan a visit to Odessa for a hydropathic cure and massage, which have also been recommended. A cure during the autumn is supposed to be more effective and as life in the country is then devoid of attractions, I would like to leave in the latter part of our October and devote myself to the double pleasure of this cure till the end of November. I cannot afford to contemplate a cure abroad—unless it should become an absolute and proved necessity—in view of the bad rate of exchange of our rouble coupled with the fall in the income from leases and from the sugar business. Anyhow, as you know, I do not care for roaming about foreign countries if I can help it, and it is cheaper at home too. That is all about me!

I doubt very much if on your return to London you will find an answer from Petersburg—for the reason that the question of naturalization is at present à l'étude and it is customary here to postpone the settlement of such issues till legislation is actually in force. Anyhow, Panie Bracie, don't let the grass grow under your feet, and when in London knock at the door of the Russian Embassy or Consulate and renew your application if need be. Don't forget to inform me how the matter stands, for our hope of seeing each other depends on that and I greatly desire to embrace you, my dear lad, at least once more. There is nothing new here. The fear of war has quietened down a bit, but the economic situation has not improved, since preparedness for the first eventuality hampers the second. This apparently is the case everywhere, but that's small consolation! We hope to have a reasonably good harvest, and the American famine brings no tears to our eyes! However, in spite of that, the prices of grain and sugar have not risen at all so far. I hope that by 1890 we shall have a railway station 8 versts from where I live, which I would like to live to see as it would facilitate the honourable Captain's journey to me.

I embrace you a hundred times, my dear boy, and I await with impatience a letter from you.

Your Uncle,
T. Bobrowski.

47

12/24 September, 1888
Kazimierówka

Dear boy!

Your laconic letter of the 6th August contained nothing but your address. It reached me a few days ago and now to clear my conscience and to mend the errors resulting from my misunderstanding of the address you sent me, without delay I take pen in hand to give you a sign of life.

In your letter just received you say you had given me your address in the two preceding ones, when in fact I have received from you only two letters since your return to your Head Office: one, of the 5th May, written on your arrival at the port of Sydney, the second, of the 29th June, written from Melbourne on your return to your shipping company. The latter one did in fact contain your address. However unpleasant it may be to admit it, your uncle was so impetuous that he failed to understand that 'Mauritius' meant 'St. Maurice', and took it to be the name of some firm or company; and addressed his last letter 'Sydney—Mauritius'; this will surely result in a mess which will prevent the letter ever reaching you. Or perhaps it may arrive after all? This double address might be regarded as an extra prudence on the part of your uncle and it might be eventually posted to 'Mauritius'. This is but a guess. To correct my error I shall now repeat what I wrote before.

My health is neither good nor bad, swaying from indisposition to robustness—as is usual in an old man of 60. Always the same

125

digestive and nervous afflictions; nausea and dizziness occurring more or less as frequently as before. I live a life of moderation, denying myself the joys of taste and appetite—the only remaining pleasures at my age—because overloading the stomach is just as harmful as some dishes. And so self-restraint has to be observed daily.

At the same time I am grieved by the death of my friend of 40 years' standing known to you, Mr. Włodzimierz Czarnowski, who died as suddenly and unexpectedly as Zaleski last year. He became ill at 9 p.m. on the 1st/13th August and at 1 p.m. the next day he was already gone. He died from a burst intestine. It was a most painful loss to me . . . and on top of all the previous ones!

You didn't tell me in your letters how long you think you will stay in Australian waters, but this nevertheless is of great interest to me. I do not wish to influence you either to prolong or to shorten your stay, if you are satisfied with it, but for an old man who has not long to live, time is a matter of some interest as it is also to know that he may possibly see again those who are dear to him—in this particular case: you! Could you not ask Mr. Krieger to make inquiries for you at the Russian Embassy in London whether they have news concerning your application for your discharge from subjection? I have read in the Polish newspapers that 27 people have this year been relieved of Russian subjection although no names were given; possibly you are amongst these 27 persons. The settlement of this problem is most important for both of us for we could then begin to plan a meeting in our country.

Here, with us, everything is much as it was—the harvest has been quite good and there is a steady demand for our grain products as our crops are the only ones that have been good. Sugar is improving as well, and the value of money has risen by over 30 marks since January. During the fair it fell to 172 marks and now it is 204 marks. I can boast to you about a railway station which is in process of construction 8 versts from where I live. It will be ready by 1890. It remains to be seen how long one may be able to use it. . . . However, I don't lose hope that one day you will arrive by it to see me. Meanwhile I embrace you and bless you.

Your Uncle,
T. BOBROWSKI.

48

22 December, 1888/3 January, 1889
Lipowiec

Dear boy!

Your letter of the 18th November, written on your departure from St. Maurice, reached me yesterday while I was engaged here in the Magistrates' Court. As you complain about lack of news from me, I answer it 'stante pede' today, hoping sincerely that you will get it on your arrival at the port of Adelaide.

As far as I am concerned there is nothing new. Since September I have been following a cure prescribed by our worthy Dr. Krzyżanowski and by Professor Fritschel, who were strongly opposed to the hydropathic cure in Odessa (they were against fresh water as applied 'ad hoc' in the cure baths—but had nothing against the salt water in the sea!), arguing that as I had a fatty heart anything that might cause congestion of the brain should be avoided. Both Doctors Bądarzewski and Orlikowski agreed with this opinion, which they themselves had advanced prior to the two celebrities. Only two voices were in favour of the hydropathic cure (Dr. Janiszewski and Dr. Dynowski, the latter not the one from Czernihów but from somewhere else)—so, following the voice of the majority I have not gone to Odessa and since mid-September I have been taking a cure which is designed to last six months, and is supposed to dissolve the fatty tissues. I am experiencing a certain relief, and the dizziness that troubled me for over a year is much less frequent and acute although it returns from time to time (about once a month). Dr. Krzyżanowski maintains, however, that one must not expect these symptoms to disappear completely in less than six months. Therefore I am patiently waiting; meanwhile I eat as little as a young maiden looking for a husband, and I run around my house and yard like a pointer, indifferent to the cold and frost. None the less my sixty-year-old mechanism is constantly falling down on me: either it is my teeth or my eyes, which have served me faithfully up till now—altogether I have reached the conclusion that there is nothing as silly as the sixty years themselves! And my advice to you is to put off reaching this age as long as possible. Drag it out as long as you can, Panie Bracie—that is my advice! Anyhow, I hope to God that whether healthy or sick I shall see my beloved Captain at least once more—at home or abroad as the case may be. You have done well to write to Krieger and instruct him to make inquiries at the Embassy. For my part I am studying our official Gazette (called *Pravitelstvenni Vestnik*) where such news as naturalizations and discharges from subjection are published. However, during the whole of 1888 your name has not appeared, which is not in the least surprising for they have to find out all about your doings from Berdyczów where you were born, Czernihów whence you left with your father, &c.

I have asked you once before: firstly, what remuneration do you get as a ship's captain? Secondly, how long do you intend to remain with Messrs. Simpson & Sons? As you haven't answered my questions I repeat them again.

Wishing to spare you trouble in the future, I have arranged my affairs as far as you are concerned by depositing 15,000 roubles with Mrs. Cecylia Zaleska, and in the event of her death with her son Stanisław. After my death this money is to go to you—directly into your name and without your having to pay any death duty on it. You should get it one year after my death. Both executors of my will have been informed about it: *Mr. Stanisław Syroczyński* (Province of Kiev, post office Glińce-Jurkowce) and *Mr. Tadeusz Horkowski* (Province of Kiev, post office Lipowiec, village Skała) and in my will you are not mentioned. The document is deposited with *Stanisław Zaleski*. Do not think that I am straight away setting off ad patres—I am writing all this for the sake of order. Keep this letter as it contains the addresses. Now I embrace you a hundredfold.

Your Uncle,
T. BOBROWSKI.

49

12/24 June, 1890
Kazimierówka

My Dear Boy![1]

I do not know if and when you will receive this letter, but nevertheless I am writing to you as my heart will feel easier after a little chat with you instead of having my thoughts chasing after you in space and asking myself for ever how you are. I feel confident that sooner or later I shall hear from you, provided that you have not been already cooked on a spit and eaten as a roast (or in a stew as the case may be). . . .

Up till now the last letter I received from you was dated from Teneriffe. According to my estimate you are by now already in Leopoldville.[2] You are probably looking around at people and things

[1] In English in the original.
[2] Conrad reached Leopoldville only on 2 August.

as well as at the 'civilizing' (confound it) affair in the machinery of which you are a cog—before you feel able to acquire and express your own opinion. Don't wait however until it all crystallizes into clear sentences, but tell me something of your health and your first impressions. I await patiently a letter from you together with your address—meanwhile I am writing via London with news of myself.

My health is reasonably good. Since my return from Kiev on the 12th May I have for four weeks been drinking whey scrupulously and in spite of the cold rain, as I have been recommended to. Three days ago I finished this treatment and I began another one: morning and evening I am eating wild strawberries and cherries. Jakub, when serving me with this fruit, or rather berries, says frequently: 'It's a pity the Captain is not here'—and I think to myself: the Captain would like them, as they even bear Anglo-Saxon names like 'Victoria', 'Albert', 'Jenny Lind', 'Peabody', and they really do honour to the race they represent.

We did not have a single warm day during April and May and I had to go back to my woollen quilt. The crops seem to be promising, providing the excess of humidity in the form of the so-called 'rust', that is fungus, does not hinder the formation of the grain. This would be disastrous coming on top of last year which was a very bad one. We shall not be able to say anything till the end of the month. As a rule, July is decisive, but this year everything is one month ahead—we already had asparagus in the first part of April instead of in May as is usual; the wild strawberries were ripe at the end of May instead of between 10–12/24 June—everything is one month early! The beets are not particularly good, they are uneven in size, but they will improve after all the rain that we have been getting almost daily. The price of corn which was low has fallen further; sugar somehow maintains its price. I shall inform you of any further developments. 100 roubles is equal now to 233 marks.

Our local news: the day before yesterday, the 10/22nd, the marriage took place of Maria Mniszek and your favourite Marchocki. On the 3/15 July the wedding of your cousin Maria will take place. Mrs. Bobrowska, who used to be extremely 'engoué' with Mr. Dąbrowski, at present 'a prise en grippe' Marta to the extent of complaining loudly about her, even in front of me. I think she exaggerates: it is simply a case of a woman nagging at her daughter because she loves her husband more than her mother. That good fellow Stanisław repeats everything after Mamma, in which he reminds me of your good father who, although he always contradicted his wife in conversation, nevertheless eventually looked at everything through her eyes. I shall see in August 'ce qu'il en est'.

Tadzio passed his examinations successfully and moved up to a higher form. Finally, poor Gaba[1] still conceals the death of her brother from people upon whom it would in any case not inflict mortal pain. Mrs. Koprowska[2] still deplores the fate of her daughters and grandchildren—'Ainsi va le monde'—my dear lad, and I embrace you, bless you, and await your letter.

Your Uncle,
T. Bobrowski.

[PS. inside the letter.] The Jakubs have got a daughter at last. They regretted that the Captain was not here or they would have asked him to be a godfather—evidently they take me for a 'heretic' as they did not ask me.

50

Kazimierówka
10/22 July, 1890

My dear boy!

Your letter, written from Libreville on the 28th May (new style), reached me a few days ago, so it took about seven weeks to get here. You wrote it while you were still on the border-line between civilization and the wilderness, but what can one expect once you had set out for the depths of the African continent, whence the mail goes to Europe once a month? Firstly, we must fortify ourselves with patience, secondly with a certain amount of optimism;—which will come more easily to me sitting here in Kazimierówka than they will to you. I cannot even rely too much on your 'youth', when everything seems rosy, for at Christ's age no room is left for illusions. The only consolation you can find in perfecting your perseverance and your optimism amidst your present struggles with life is in the exclamation of Molière with which you are familiar: 'tu l'as voulu, tu l'as voulu, Georges Dandin'. One thing that is certain is that I shall count with an impatience no less than yours the days and weeks of these three years that will keep us apart —and always with the doubt whether my 'carcasse' will hold out that long, although at present it is quite sound. However, let us live in

---

[1] Gaba (Gabriela) Zagórska was a sister of Aleksander Poradowski (who died in Brussels on 7 February 1890; cf. Conrad's letters to him) and the wife of Jan Zagórski. They were the parents of Karol and Aniela (born Unrug) Zagórski, with whom Conrad was in correspondence.

[2] Konstancja Koprowska, born Pilchowska, Bobrowski's aunt.

130

hope in spite of our proverb that 'hope is the mother of fools'—for without it even the wisest of men couldn't survive! Let us then be fools, but let us live and hope! . . .

Since the 10th May this is the third letter which I have sent via London, always awaiting your address.

I have stopped wondering if they will ever reach you, and I write for the sheer pleasure it gives me and because you have asked me to.

I have just returned from an excursion to Śnieżna and Nowofastów where they inquired after you in the most friendly terms. Mrs. Zaleska, trying to please me, offered me some copies of the 'Mouvement Géographique'—which the good Mme Marguerite had already done;—my reply to both ladies was: the Congo interests me only in so far as you are there. I made an arrangement with Mrs. Z. that on returning to Warsaw she will send me a good map of Africa together with just those copies of the 'Mouv. Géographique' where you are mentioned,—authorizing me not to read the rest. We spoke a lot about you and Mrs. Z. concluded, 'providing Konrad is wise enough not to get married, he may have a very pleasant and happy existence'. As you see—she does not believe in marriage, and she said it in front of her son and daughter-in-law! We all laughed at this aphorism. The Châtelaine and her husband have also inquired most warmly after you. She is not well—extremely enervated and, oddly enough, she avoids people and locks herself in her room. She told me these are attacks of melancholy— I am afraid this might indeed be the case and I was always afraid of this for her. She is well aware of her own state—and this frightens me. The little boy is well and I have just become godfather to the other little boy, Staś's son.

Maria Tyszkiewiczowa is also subject to such anti-social fits, and old Herbert Mikołaj, in order to disperse the gloomy mood of his favourite neighbours, has announced a 'Grand Bal' for the middle of August. Miss Maria has married Count Serbor—she sent to London for you a lettre de faire part. Cecylia on the other hand is seriously contemplating going into a convent, which she wanted to enter immediately, but we stopped this religious impetus by exercising our power of 'veto' as her guardians till she reaches the age of twenty-four. . . .

As to our neighbours: Granny Karnicka has not yet gone to Warsaw but she will go any day now. The Misses Nikorowicz have gone to Odessa with their married sister to take the baths; meanwhile their parents may 'console' themselves by producing another daughter. . . . Cziszkans, poor fellow, a few days ago buried his last brother and his niece's husband—he is deeply grieved; and

Florek has gone to Zoppot (between Połąga and Heligoland) for the sea-bathing.

The harvest which seemed promising at first has not turned out so good, as the so-called 'Hessian Fly' destroyed some of the wheat, —the beet is only medium while the spring corn is beautiful (that is the oats, barley, &c.) but these fetch no money. Things are therefore not so good, either for the nobility or for the plebs.

I am only planning to go to Radom on the 8/20th August, when both Tadzio and Stanisław will be there. Miss Maria got married on the 3/15th July; afterwards her mother planned to take a month's rest in the country with the youngest 'Mizynek'. The excursion to Radom together with the visits on the way will take about three weeks and I shall be back about the 1/13th September. By then I hope to receive a letter from you from your last stopping-place.

I embrace and bless you.

Your Uncle,
T. BOBROWSKI.

51

28 October/9 November, 1890
Kazimierówka

My dear boy!

I can't think of a better way of starting and celebrating this day, which as you will realize is my name-day, than by joining you in my thoughts by recalling the pleasure of your stay with me at the beginning of the year; and I embrace you a hundredfold as if I were receiving from you the greetings appropriate to this day. Therefore, my dear lad, I embrace you twice as strongly as usual. My health is reasonably good on the whole. If I get occasional fits of dizziness —which are fairly rare—or arthritic pains in the left leg or arm, or if I suffer from sleeplessness, I still consider that to be all in the natural course of events for a man over sixty years old who should be thanking Providence for not inflicting on him an incurable disease—as was the case with the dear and good Zagórskis! Just imagine: Jenny[1] has been paralysed for two years, as you saw for yourself; poor Jan, who is quite a monomaniac, obsessed with the idea that Ołdakowski took some of his money, nags his wife and makes terrible scenes daily,—which I witnessed myself with great grief last August in Lublin. Since I left, poor Gaba has become paralysed on the left side of the body, and is quite unable to move,

---

[1] Johanna Poradowska, Mrs. Gabriela Zagórska's sister.

which for her, with her passion for movement and visiting (which was always both her entertainment and her consolation) is a real torture! Thus three people under one roof are incapacitated, and both the moral and the financial burden falls upon poor Karol whom I sincerely pity. The worthy Marguerita, whom they are all very fond of, is still there, and according to the letter I received from her intends to remain there till Christmas. In the light of such a misery as this which has befallen my favourite relations who were always the closest to me, how can I possibly complain about some occasional pain!? . . . This reference to the plight of the Zagórmans,[1] whom you as well liked best of all of the family, has caused me to diverge from the subject I usually begin with, so I now go back to it. Three days ago I received a letter from you forwarded by good old Krieger. It was dated the 3rd August from 'Stanley-Pool'. Prior to this I had letters from you from 'Manyanga', from 'Matadi', from 'Banana', from 'Libreville', and from 'Teneriffe', and on receipt of each I always sent a reply via London. I have thus written five letters, the present one being the sixth, but up till now in none of yours did I find a hint confirming the receipt of mine. I don't suppose that you suspect me of negligence in correspondence but all the same I would not like you to worry about my silence. . . . Let me know if any of my letters reached you and if so,—how many?

I see from your last letter that you feel a deep resentment towards the Belgians for exploiting you so mercilessly. In general there is no love in your heart for the Latin races, but this time, you must admit, nothing forced you to put yourself into Belgian hands. You can say to yourself: 'Tu l'as voulu, Georges Dandin'; and if you had paid any attention to my opinion on the subject when discussing it with me, you would have certainly detected a lack of enthusiasm in me for this project.

As a traditional Polish nobleman I value more the certain and less glamorous than a more glamorous uncertainty! . . . In the first place, whatever happened, I ask you most sincerely to calm down and not to get worked up lest it should affect your liver, 'Ne vs gâter pas le sang et le foie.' Secondly, let me observe that by breaking your agreement you would expose yourself to considerable financial loss, and you certainly lay yourself open to an accusation of irresponsibility which may be harmful to your further career. Unless your health becomes affected you should stick it out; at least that is my opinion. And let us both (for I also share in your disappointment!) find consolation in the thought that after your period of captivity—not Babylonian this time but Belgian—we shall

[1] i.e. Zagórskis.

be reunited for several months, resting our bodies and souls—God granting that I shall live till then! . . .

I always remember you to your friends—many never fail to ask after you themselves, especially the Zagórskis, Mrs. Koprowska, and Tadzio—the mariner;[1] whenever they write to me they always inquire most kindly after you.

And now, my dear boy, keep well, hope for the best, and stay calm; God granting we shall still see each other!

I embrace and bless you.

Your Uncle,
T. BOBROWSKI.

52

15/27 December, 1890
Kazimierówka

My dear boy!

Three days ago, that is on the 12th/24th inst., I received your letter of the 19th October from Kinchassa, informing me of the unfortunate outcome of your expedition to the Congo, and also of your return to Europe. At the same time I received the same news from good Mme Marguerita from Lublin (which she has left by now) who was informed about your return by the Company's Manager, whom she asked after you.

In spite of your assurance that the first sea breeze will restore you to health, I found your handwriting so greatly changed—which I ascribe to the weakening and exhausting effect of fever and dysentery—that I have since then given myself over to far from happy thoughts! I made no secret from you that I was absolutely against your African plans and more than once expressed myself in this spirit during your stay with me, but faithful to the principle 'laisser chacun être heureux ou content à sa manière' I did not oppose your decisions, particularly as I felt sure that you would have yielded out of deference to me while I of course could not be expected to have a thorough knowledge of things and situations beyond my experience—while you might have had it. Thus your intentions were realized—to your confusion, for neither the people nor the circumstances responded to your expectations. This in my view would be only half the evil—although a year lost at whatever time of life is not a good thing—but what worries me most is your health and what will happen to it in the future. I am very much

---

[1] Tadeusz, Kazimierz Bobrowski's son. 'Mariner' was for some reason his family nickname.

worried lest it was permanently damaged or at least affected for a long time? This is the question which torments me and takes away my sleep—for you and for me it is of prime importance—I ask you to answer as speedily and as thoroughly as possible immediately on your arrival in London. Please begin by calling the best specialist for dealing with people who return from the tropics, the Indies, &c., and get his opinion. Our physicians 'n'y entendent goutte' and therefore there is no point in inviting you for a rest to Kazimierówka: on the contrary, I believe you should let yourself be treated by people who are particularly well acquainted with these specific ailments. This I most seriously request you to do. Secondly, I beg you to inform me without delay what the specialists suggest and how long they estimate for a sufficiently thorough treatment—for you to be restored to your normal health? My third and final request is for you to tell me openly what is the position of your capital funds, so that I can think as far as I can of sending you such help as may be essential. If your health is not as badly affected as I fear, and if you quickly regain your normal state of well-being—you can decide on your own future. My sole concern is that my beloved nephew should get well as quickly as possible, and when that is achieved he himself will think of further work! I shall wait with the utmost impatience for news of your return and for the opinion of the doctors.

Mme Marguerita said in her letter that she was returning to Brussels before the New Year and that she hoped to see you au débarqué. We shall see what she has to say about you after seeing you. I keep thinking that you have grown grey hair?

I was recently in Warsaw, where I was forced to go for a few days. Mrs. Zaleska showed me the 'Mouvement Géographique' where your departure for Stanley Falls was mentioned.[1] She will certainly be sorry that you have had to return, but it is one thing to read in a comfortable arm-chair and another to produce and carry events on one's own shoulders.

I shall be in Kiev between the 10th and 20th February, 1891 (our style). Our railway has not been opened officially yet, and one is allowed to travel only 'as a special favour'—and most uncomfortably. However, we expect it to function regularly by the New Year. I am quite well. I embrace you and bless you while waiting impatiently for news of your return and of your state of health.

Your Uncle,
T. Bobrowski.

[1] Issue of 21 September 1890.

I get ordinary letters now at the *Oratów* railway station; registered letters always at *Lipowiec.* My address for ordinary letters is:

Mr. Thadée Bobrowski,
Russie Méridionale
Ligne Koziatyn-Odessa
Station 'Oratów'
à Kazimierówka.

53

26 February/10 March, 1891
Kazimierówka

Dear beloved boy!

I received your last letter, of the 4/16th February, on my return from Kiev, and I share with you the regret you feel at the deformity of your legs (one of which is still swollen while the other is its normal size) and I also deplore the thinness of your hair, presaging as it does future baldness. But, in the store of my life's experience, I find no remedy for this; and we must therefore pass from this touchy matter to the next item on the agenda, and patiently await whatever the gods of hair-growth decide!

I went to Kiev rather early, on the 8/20th February, on Tadeusz Syroczyński's business, which was an idea of mine, in which however I was not successful. Unaccustomed as I am to the bustle of business and to the multitude of people, I soon became weary—and, feeling fatigued, I gathered my belongings together and left for home on the 18th (our style). On my return I found your letter, which does not, however, constitute a reply to my long letter of the 6/18th February in which I invited you to Kazimierówka for your convalescence—not for a cure, and announced the dispatch of some of our precious metal with the object of saving your health. As I had advised you, immediately after having secured some funds on my arrival in Kiev, I sent them via Odessa through Mr. Heisman, my usual contact. I have had a note from him, dated the 16/28th February, confirming the purchase of £35. 10s. for the 300 roubles I sent him, and informing me that the money had been dispatched. I hope that by now, as I write this letter, you are in possession of it. Possibly the messenger who takes this letter to the post office will bring me an exhaustive reply to my last letter, written before leaving for Kiev. Whatever you may decide to do about my invitation for the period of your convalescence—whether you refuse or accept my proposal—I request you solemnly to bear in mind every possible consideration of your own well-being before making up your mind and not to make a premature move till you receive my further letter. The snow has now begun to thaw, the dampness to rise from the earth, and there are other signs of spring—which occasionally hinder the proper functioning of the railway—all of which are to be avoided as not being good for a convalescent. Apart from this the trains still run irregularly—once a day each way—I would have to describe all this to you in detail and suggest the right route should you decide to come.

Now, my dear boy, with hope and desire to see you—or not: ignorant as to how things will work out in spite of our best sense and judgement—and not inspired by the kind of sentiment that women are governed by, I embrace you a hundredfold, prepared for anything that circumstances may bring.

Your Uncle,
T. BOBROWSKI.

54

12/24 March, 1891
Kazimierówka

My dear boy!

What can I say to your last letter of the 21st February/5 March, written from hospital? What else can I say but this: it grieved me deeply and gave me the impression that you are dispirited and weak, in spite of kind Krieger's vain attempts to erase such impressions from my mind by including a little note giving Dr. Ludwig's[1] opinion. But an old man is always more inclined to see human affairs in darker hues than perhaps they really are—I pray to God this is the case as far as you are concerned, and that your speedy return to health may prove my fears to be unfounded and Dr. Ludwig thereby be raised in my esteem to the rank of the best specialist in either hemisphere! His patient, however, must co-operate by not yielding to lassitude or depression—for as you say: 'le moral réagit sur la phisique' [sic]. And so my dear lad, let us be of good heart and keep our spirits up, each one for his own part; this certainly will do no harm even if it does not help!

While waiting patiently for your recovery, let us in the meantime

---

[1] Dr. Rudolf Ludwig worked in the German Hospital in London, where Conrad was a patient. The hospital was primarily intended to serve German nationals and Conrad was admitted there probably through Adolf Krieger.

talk of your convalescence. I am still awaiting a reply to the proposal I made last February, to which I have found no reaction in your last letter and to which I am still looking forward eagerly—not because of my having in view the pleasure which we should both derive from the meeting, but solely from the point of view of what is rational and advantageous for your health and further plans. In my letter to Krieger, in which I thanked him for writing, I hinted something of my proposal—under the impression that as he is a friend of yours you will ask his advice.

Here, within a few days (between the 5th and the 10th of March) the snow disappeared, having left no damaged dikes or mills behind. In contrast with most of Europe the corn here is also unharmed. There is hope that in a few weeks' time the roads will dry up, the spring sowing can commence and the winter corn will become green —provided of course that the March winds, which are dry as a rule, do not upset the 'farmers' hope'. . . .

I have no special family news to pass on to you—except possibly this: Mrs. Koprowska, Maria, and Tadzio inquired warmly after you and the last two demand replies to their letters. I have told them all that you returned ill and do not yet feel like correspondence, and I questioned whether you received the letters they wrote to you. Poor Mrs. Kopr. complains about the deterioration of the Prophet Samuel's[1] business, which places them under the threat of expulsion from the estate, which is mortgaged to the Agricultural Bank. Sooner or later this is bound to happen—as is always the case with those who think only of their comfort and of gratifying their whims. Nevertheless I feel sorry for Mrs. K. who indeed is unhappy in her family life and who has got so used to grumbling that it is difficult to distinguish in her letters of grief between the truth and idle fancy. Thus, she constantly has occasion to importune me with requests— which it is difficult to leave always unanswered, all the more so as I am often assumed to be more wealthy than is really the case.

About your cousins: first, Zunia has given birth; second, Marta is about to give birth; third, Maria will give birth, for she writes that she is pregnant.

Since the New Year I have had no letter from Staś, who is, how-ever, not given to writing without a purpose. Tadzio is the only one who writes regularly every few weeks. He is doing well at his studies and we are getting on splendidly together. Staś and Tadzio are to visit me during their holidays, but I do not yet know when. Uncle Kazimierz's wife seems to be sulking for I have only had one letter from her since my last visit to Radom in August. I suspect

---

[1] Samuel Koprowski, Mrs. Koprowski's son.

that she is displeased by the fact that some time ago I put 2,000 r. at her disposal and now I am deciding myself how much I assign to whom, leaving for her and Michaś 1,200 r. It seems to me that being the donor entitles me to say how much I give whom? However, it is always a problem with females, who have a logic of their own and forget easily what they owe to anybody if it happens to conflict with their own views.

Keep well, my dear boy, and hope for the best. I embrace and bless you a thousand times.

Your Uncle,
T. BOBROWSKI.

55

30 March/12 April, 1891
Kazimierówka

My dear boy!

Yesterday I received your last letter, written on the 30 March (your style). Thank the Lord that you have left your bed, but from your description, which you try to make comic, I see that you are still very enfeebled and very exhausted—and the slightest thing may lay you prostrate again. For God's sake, take care of yourself, for I have reason to suppose (you hinted this indirectly) that you have overtaxed your strength during your stay in Africa, and Mme Marguerita said the same in her letter, and that instead of taking a rest either in Brussels or in London you dashed off to Scotland.[1] Thus I have bad reports about my dear and honoured Sir, in respect of his senseless behaviour towards himself. I appeal for and demand more sense and the utmost prudence in the treatment of my beloved young Master, and I await the fulfilment of my wish!

You have just informed me of the recommendation made by Dr. Ludwig: that you should go to Switzerland. The fact that previously he had in mind the seaside, makes me think that you are very exhausted and he hopes that the bracing air of the Swiss mountains will help you to recover your strength and put on some flesh. Some place like Interlaken or Righi-Culm. If that is the case then we must give up the thought of Kazimierówka. While we are allowed to suppose our climate in the spring to be refreshing and beneficial, when conditions of life are comfortable,—the same can by no means be said of our climate in the summer. On the contrary, our June and occasionally even May are so stiflingly hot that

[1] Conrad went to Glasgow at the beginning of February, looking for a command.

breathing is practically impossible, let alone July with its usually hot and dry winds;—it all makes our summer rather oppressive. From what you say, I deduce that you could not come to us sooner than May, which means losing all the smell of spring. I may add however that up till the present it is very cold, never more than $+3°$ C. and we have not thought yet of the spring sowing. Do you remember what it was last year: never less than $+12$ to $+16°$ C. from the middle of March?! This year is different: and the later spring comes, the more torrid it is—it's almost always the case.

Discuss it all, my dear boy, with the doctor. But do not insinuate anything yourself and do not give any erroneous information about the peculiarities of our climate. Weigh together all the considerations from the point of view of your own advantage and welfare— even if it means something less pleasurable—and decide what you are to do. Switzerland is not very expensive. Interlaken is regarded as the most expensive, but even there—and in the neighbouring Unterseen—one can get a very decent 'Pension' for 6 fr. per day. In Unterseen it is even less: 4 fr. per day. The saying goes 'A word is enough to the wise'; so why should I try to teach you what to do? Now your health is our greatest concern and for its sake we have to renounce all personal pleasure and concentrate all our thoughts on this one object.

Write to me, my dear lad, how you stand financially at present; have you still got anything in your pocket? What do they charge for a month's stay in a Maison de Santé? Panie Bracie, let your answer be as sincere as my question is. You know me not to be over-generous, but if there is need for it I shall draw what's necessary to save your health. Parsimony must give way!

Keep well, my dear lad, and send me as often as possible news of yourself. You have no reason to doubt the promptitude with which I shall reply.

I embrace you a hundredfold and bless you.

Your Uncle,
T. BOBROWSKI.

56

25 May/6 June, 1891
Kazimierówka

My dear boy!

After having waited a week for news of you—I received at last two letters simultaneously (of the 20th and 28th May from London and Champel-les-Bains)! I tormented myself a great deal after receiving your last letter but one on the 2nd May, full of sadness and despondency (I think on the 3/15th inst.)—but I shall refrain from describing all I went through as it would serve no purpose— unless it were to prove to you how dear you are to me. But you knew this quite well before this date—just as well as I know it— and as it is a subject that may only interest us both, I shall not dwell upon it at greater length. . . . Thank the Lord you are better and that the cure at Champel is beneficial to you! . . . Let me, however, comment: when beginning a cure a patient is not supposed to determine in advance the length of his stay: four weeks! He might have to stay six or eight weeks. You will lose all the benefit of the cure by not doing it thoroughly and by travelling quickly immediately after, or—worse still—not completing it at all. This way you can even do damage to yourself. . . . So my request and advice is: stay there till you have completely recovered your health. Foreseeing this eventuality I am sending you 200 r. via Odessa– Heisman–Krieger. This, according to the present rate of exchange, is approximately £23, the equivalent of 660 francs. You might think that I could have sent it directly from Lipowiec in our money. However, I wanted to settle the matter as quickly as possible and this made me do it via Odessa and London. Otherwise I would have to make a special journey to Lipowiec (30 versts each way is too much for my old bones) to write postal declarations in Russian and in French, while by means of Mr. Heisman and Krieger I have settled the matter from my desk at home. The money sent today will be dispatched to London in three days' time, that is on the 28th inst. It is sure to be there on the 3/15th inst. and knowing this you may return to Krieger the money he lent you, and if necessary, request what is left. I can see from the way you arranged the cure that you are not well acquainted with Switzerland. You are reckoning too much for the doctor's visits. The 'sommités' are satisfied with 20 f. for a consultation and 10 f. for a normal visit. Physicians practising at watering-places and spas are pleased to get 5 f. per visit—I paid that myself during my stay in Interlaken and Montreux.

You speak so enigmatically about your plans for the future that I can understand nothing: were you referring to your professional plans or to the possibility of visiting me towards the end of your convalescence? State your thoughts, Panie Bracie, with more clarity and lucidity, as I have never been any good at solving 'rebuses'— as I love God, I have never cultivated this pastime. I was correct in my judgement of the peculiarities of our climate in summer.

I have recently seen Dr. Orlikowski, whom you know, and Dr. Raczyński with whom you are not yet acquainted—and they both praised me for having discouraged you from coming here in the summer to convalesce. They confirmed my view about the depressing effects of our climate in summer. However, truth compels me to confess that up till now we have had dry and cold winds, together with scorching sun above. In general, the weather at present is abominable—the crops are threatened, but it is impossible to foresee what June and July will be like—the heat and sultriness might be even greater than usual.

Did you receive a letter from Samuel who some time ago asked for your African address and has now requested your present one? Obviously, the prophet has some important business for you, probably connected with postage stamps? . . . I shall send him your address.

Mrs. Zaleska and the rest of us are deeply grieved by Mrs. Tyszkiewiczowa's illness—as a result of childbirth she is threatened with tuberculosis. Now she has been taken to Warsaw. There they will decide if in fact it is malaria or tuberculosis and further treatment will be advised. I do not know if the Montresors are back from abroad. In the middle of June Tadeusz Syroczyński[1] is leaving for Reichenhall; he promised to visit you in Champel—providing you are still there—to renew your acquaintance, and to see you in order to appease my anxiety. I am well, and as you are now getting better I expect to get a letter from you every week—I shall send my replies punctiliously. Write to me, my dear lad; I embrace and bless you heartily.

Your Uncle,
T. BOBROWSKI.

57

15/27 June, 1891
Kazimierówka

My Dear Boy![2]

I once knew a man of the gentry who 'per fas et nefas' acquired a beautiful farm. On one occasion when he was winning a game of billiards at his neighbour's house one of the onlookers remarked:

---

[1] Tadeusz Syroczyński, one of four brothers (the others were Leon, Agaton, and Stanisław) of whom Bobrowski was the guardian, was the son of Antoni Syroczyński and brother of Tekla Syroczyńska (cf. Introduction).

[2] English in the original.

142

it's a joy to see a gentleman play so well. On hearing this he turned round and answered sneeringly: it's a fine gentleman for you who resides in Zbarażówka!—resenting not having been called 'Sir'. And so you may tell me: it's a fine 'boy' indeed who is already 34 years old! However, I shall apparently call you this till my dying day for I have grown to like this expression and to me you will always be a 'dear boy'! . . .

Thanks be to the Lord and glory be to Messrs. Ludwig and Platz for having raised 'my boy' from his sick-bed and restored his health, to the joy of both of us! Yesterday I received your letter of the 2/14th June, written when departing from Champel;—today in thought and with words I hasten to London in pursuit of my dear boy. I hope that Dr. Platz did not let you go off too soon or that you didn't run away too soon from him. This is the important question, for indeed I fear a relapse. For the Lord's sake, take care of yourself, Panie Bracie, for a worsening of your condition would be tragic for both of us:—for your health and for my peace of mind. I did go through a lot as well, during your stay in Champel— especially the time between your first letter of the 8/20th May and your second one of the 2/14 inst. which arrived only yesterday;— and you did announce in the first one that you would write in a week's time. Well, I forget it all now after having read the news that you are well and have departed. . . .

Now we must be careful not to allow your health to deteriorate and to find an acceptable position for you. If, as you say, you have had enough of Africa—although I suppose the Niger is not the same as the Congo—then you are right to have refused. I perceive that you are inclined to settle in London for good, and I see that in this matter you rely on Mr. Hope's[1] help: his friendliness and eloquence are to persuade Capt. Noble to resign in favour of Capt. Nałęcz. However, I doubt if things will work out this way, for as far as I know the English character, reasons based on 'sentiment and eloquence' don't appeal to them as much as well-understood and personal interest, which in this particular case doesn't seem to point to resigning the job for 'the most honourable Nałęcz'. We shall see! . . . I only keep asking myself the question: why, having decided to remain in London, you don't take a job with Barr, Möring & Cie? This is how I explain it: you have no capital and not wishing to become a subordinate where you might have been a partner, you have decided to look straight away for other employ- ment. Anyhow, this is the impression I got from a paragraph of

---

[1] G. F. W. Hope, director of the South Mercantile Company in London, Conrad's closest friend at that time.

a letter you wrote before departing for the Congo. You then informed me of your wish to leave to Mr. Krieger whatever sum is left on your account. As it is a weakness shown by all the dreamers known to me to leave a legacy behind them (remember what I told you about the projected last wills of the late Adolf Pilchowski and of your Uncle Hilary?) so I deduce that you are, firstly, penniless, and, secondly, a dreamer. Is that so, Panie Bracie?—no offence meant. If my experience has misled me I shall withdraw this remark with pleasure.

Things are not good with us. A bad harvest and even hunger threatened us in the spring, and then rain! During the second half of May the situation improved, but even so we cannot expect anything better than results below the average. As this has been the case for the third year in succession it makes things hard, very hard. As far as I am concerned I feel certain that my lessees will not be able to stand it, and will eventually leave me. I already have this possibility in mind, and thinking about it I tighten my purse, which is now considerably slimmer. This is the reason why I had to give up the hope of meeting you, my dear Sir, this year in Kazim. However, it should not interfere with our future as we planned it at the time of our farewell last year, for our next meeting is to be in three years from then. This plan will be fulfilled, providing the Lord gives us life. I am reasonably well, apart from the rheumatism which troubles me frequently in the left hand and forearm. Next year I might have to go to Toeplitz. I am unable to give you such good news as you expected of Mrs. Tyszkiewiczowa. At present she is staying at Nałęczów, drinking koumiss. For the winter she is to go south, but it has not yet been decided where. The Montresors are still abroad. My two nephews are to come to me for a few weeks during August—the good Tadeusz has been lamenting for a long time that he will not recognize you—but this is how it is and nothing can be done about it for the time being. Write, my dear boy, I embrace and bless you.

Your Uncle,
T. BOBROWSKI.

PS. [At the top of the page.]
Please thank Mr. Krieger for his letter and give him my best regards.

58

20 June/1 July, 1891
Kazimierówka

My dearest boy!

My heart is overjoyed at reading your last letters from which I can see that you have recovered your old health and humour, which go in harness with you—as indeed with anybody—but particularly in the case of highly strung people, and when I tell you that I am capable of reading between the lines, you will easily understand how perturbed your previous letters made me—not by what was stated in them in black and white, but by what was between the lines. Thank God—from the minute you put your foot down on Swiss soil—your letters have changed 'du tout au tout' and somehow peace descended upon my soul. Your last two letters telling me how you had now got back to a normal condition, allowed me also to think of you in normal terms. All this you have in reply to your last letter of the 12/24th inst., which arrived yesterday. To this I add my request: do be careful to avoid a relapse; for you must admit yourself that I cannot rely too much on your inborn sense of caution,—as Tante Margot may confirm. Now I may add, in order to complete this report, that I enjoy good health apart from the rheumatic pains I have mentioned, that trouble me slightly. But those will have to wait till next year as I would have some considerable trouble in getting a passport, for as a Justice of the Peace I would have to apply for it to the Minister of Justice. I shall apply for it next year in the early spring. Tante Margot has not yet written since your return via Paris—but no doubt she will do so soon. If you talked about Lublin, you must have gone through in your mind a whole gallery of 'snobs'—both alive and dead—and I shall tell you of a different group of such 'snobs' whom I have in Radom, represented by Kazimierz's widow and Mr. Dąbrowski, her once beloved and now hated son-in-law. The latter got the idea—I do not know where from—that the late Kazimierz died of grief as his wife had left him alone and ill at home and had gone to Warsaw and apparently spent all the money allegedly given by me. Actually, just before the late Kazim's death, his wife went to Warsaw to fetch some things, which he, in the capriciousness of his mood, desired to have in readiness for the journey to me, where he was to have spent his convalescence. Poor Kaz. died the day after her return. Anyhow, she has always been better than her husband at arithmetic and has never deserved any criticism as a wife (except possibly for bearing fruit more often than necessary). This gossip, which originated from the ill will of her son-in-law, eventually reached the ears of Mrs. Bobrowska who swore a life-long hostility towards him. He for his part is a petit bourgeois right through—and full of spite;—so they entertain Radom with their accusations. Poor Stanisław is summoned alternately by his mother and his sister (the latter, a rather narrow-minded female, as you have seen for yourself, feels entirely out of her depth in this situation): and he racks his brains as to how to soothe his mother, who on the subject of her son-in-law is practically suffering from monomania and is quite unable to talk of anything else but him. We shall see how long this state of war will last, which means constant suffering for Staś and Zunia who love their mother very much—and are, as is only natural, deeply afflicted by their brother-in-law and pity their sister. Amidst all the altercations in the Radom family I adopt a defensive position: I wrote both to Kazimierz's widow and to Maria that I can't come to Radom to face such quarrels. It might, or might not, result in moderating the grief of the former and spurring on the latter's efforts to bring her husband round to a reconciliation even if it is only for the sake of appearances. I am not in the least concerned that they should in fact love each other, and Mrs. B. probably feels about it in the same way, for she knows full well that she will never have to depend on her son-in-law and as long as I live she will have all she needs from me—and after I am gone, her children will support her. Mr. D., on the other hand, who does not know me at all, might fear that my quarrel with his wife's family could eventually in the case of her death deprive him of any benefits from an 'Uncle's munificence'. I suppose that this practical consideration is more likely than anything else to lead him to moderate his actions and to control his speech. There is the épopée of the Radom 'snobs' 'pour vous désopiler la rate dans vos moments perdus'.

As, thank God, you are now quite well, I remind you that you are indebted to the good Karol (as you are fond of him—you may have thought of it yourself), to the kind Tadzio, who loves you in spite of not having ever seen you, and to Maria and apparently to Zunia, as it seems they all wrote to you either when you were in Africa or since your return:—so if up till now you have not answered one or other of them, do so now, so as not to be accused of indifference. Samuel, the prophet, also pestered me for your address. I do not know if he has already written to you, but I did send him your London address. Business with him does not seem to be good, and Mrs. Koprowska still pours out to me her lamentations and complaints.

Write to me, Panie Bracie, about your hopes and projects as

they occur and you can always count fully on my sympathy. Now, I embrace you a hundredfold and bless you.

Your Uncle,
T. BOBROWSKI.

59

18th/30th July, 1891
Kazimierówka

My Dear Boy,[1]

We are writing to each other nearly every week now—I had your last letter but one, of the 7th, and yesterday I received the one dated the 18th. I have sent my answers to you last week and today.

In my previous letter, unasked and unquestioned by my dear Sir, I touched slightly on certain defects in my Dear Boy,[2] defects with which, for that matter, it is possible to live and be loved. Today, you yourself ask me to indicate those shortcomings of your character that I have observed during the thirty-four years of your life, with the help of my 'cold reason'; shortcomings that make your life difficult, as you yourself admit. You state in advance that you cannot perceive them yourself, and you therefore request me to conduct this operation upon your person. If this is an oblique way of evoking my assurances, and even of my swearing that I have not perceived even the slightest shortcoming in you and that I consider you perfection without flaw, then forgive me, Panie Bracie, but I shall not say that, because I regard you as an ordinary mortal with ordinary shortcomings, since who is free from them? . . . Well then, I consider that you have always lacked endurance and perseverance in decisions, which is the result of your instability in your aims and desires. You lack endurance, Panie Bracie, in the face of facts—and, I suppose, in the face of people too? This is a trait of character inherited from your Grandfather—your paternal Uncle—and even your Father:—in short the Nałęczs. The former two were always involved in various projects, most diverse in nature, mostly of a practical type—they hatched them in their imagination and were even offended when anyone criticized them—considering their opponents to be 'idiots', but the facts most often gave the lie to their dreams, hence bitterness towards those who saw more clearly. Your Father was an idealistic dreamer; he certainly loved people and he certainly wished happiness for them—although he usually

[1] English in the original—as in all future letters.
[2] 'Dear Boy' in the original.

147

applied two measures to them:—he was a lenient judge of the poor and the weak of this world—and he was very sharp and pitiless towards the rich and powerful;—hence we have a cleavage. They all had a high opinion of themselves and suffered much after their failures—suffered more intensely than appeared or could be expected. Thus, Panie Bracie, you also are subject to these inherited short-comings and you too bear their punishment. In your projects you let your imagination run away with you—you become an optimist; but when you encounter disappointments you fall easily into pessimism—and as you have a lot of pride, you suffer more as the result of disappointments than somebody would who had a more moderate imagination but was endowed with greater endurance in activity and relationships. This is what I think in this matter, and let me repeat again what I said in my last letter: these are short-comings, but even with them one can be loved, while life itself will in time teach you a better perspective when judging people and facts.

Why do you say that you are one-eyed: do you suffer with your eye—or is it only a metaphor inspired by your being Tante Margot's 'support'? Well, it seems to me that you both fail to see that you are only flirting with each other since the death of poor Oleś—as an old sparrow friendly to you both I advise you to give up this game, which will end in nothing sensible. A worn-out female, and if she is to join up with somebody, it will be with Buls[1] who would give her a position and love—of which he has given proof. It would be a stone round your neck for you—and for her as well. If you are wise you will leave this amusement alone and part simply as friends: if not, however, you have been warned!—and you will not be able to say later on that you were not warned! I suppose that the locomotive which you say in your letter found itself in Aunt's life and 'a écrasé son cousin' is in fact the very nonsense which has arisen in the minds of one or both of you. A word is enough to the wise—you know this proverb of old.

Keep well my dear lad—please write, we can differ in our views while loving each other with all our hearts.

I embrace you a hundredfold.

Your Uncle,
T. Bobrowski.

PS. [At the top of the letter.]
Please explain what I am supposed to understand by the passage in your letter: 'I am feeling quite well, although mentally only so so, but this will improve.'???

[1] M. Charles Buls, the burgomaster of Brussels and an old suitor of Mme Poradowska.

60

My Dear Boy,

If the Prince of Benevento[1] of 'accursed memory' was right when he said that: 'Speech (in this case the written word) was given to us to conceal our thoughts', then, Panie Bracie, you have coped most efficiently with the task, telling me on five whole pages about all the young and old, ugly or beautiful, English women you know, who importune you to flirt with them successfully or unsuccessfully, —God only knows which!—and all this to omit The Only One whom I suspect of such practices with you:—and she not a flat-footed English woman but a certain Margaret well known to me!!

There is no need for you to carry into effect the aphorism of that lame Prince and to lie both to me and to yourself, for I am an old bird and I have got eyes to see with (this time for reading with), and ears for hearing with, and I know what I have read and it is there to stay—'pas de mal en tout cela': this is but human. 'L'avertissement est donné' and I wash my hands of the affair. 'Salvavi animam meam'—as foolish Pilate thought, and I now repeat it after him, so regard yourself as warned. . . .

Your cousins and my nephews depart today after having been on a visit to me. Stanisław arrived two weeks ago and Tadeusz stayed here only one week as his whole holiday is only 2 weeks of which he devoted one week to me and the other to his mother. He passed his examination successfully and has moved up to a higher class—he has still two years of school ahead of him and intends thereafter to spend another two years in the Academy—which he will have to repay by 9 years' service. He is a nice boy and quite good-looking. It seems to me that he will be like my Father—quite a 'bel homme'. In the meantime, he is a 'bon enfant' of good disposition and good health, well built and of a lively temperament. Stanisław has a worthy character and is already a man, but less pleasant—very presumptuous and rather a doctrinaire. Possibly he has, in fact, ultra-democratic notions which, however, he keeps to himself either out of consideration for his paternal Uncle or else not wishing to 'cast pearls before swine'. He is rather reserved and rather cold. He reminds me very much of his own father in respect of qualities, shortcomings, and general appearance—which when added up is not a cheerful forecast of his future—especially since, although a serious judge of people and things, he is a harsh judge as well, and this influences his

[1] Talleyrand, created Prince of Benevento by Napoleon in 1806.

actions—I very much doubt qu'il vincisse jamais? Tadeusz on the contrary I expect to be a success in his life. In any case they have both made a favourable impression on me—in fact I invited them here to get to know them better. My observation of them served only to confirm my previous impressions of them. Tadzio is going to his mother's, and Stanisław to Warsaw. Mrs. K.B. is still at war with her son-in-law and the others have no great love for her either. Stanisław and I are trying to persuade her to move away from Radom but she is a determined and obstinate female and stays put. 'J'ai lâché mes grands chevaux'—I have written to Radom and said that I shall not be coming this autumn—we shall see if that has any effect.

About myself there is nothing more to say apart from this: that I am well and will leave in a few days' time for Śnieżna and Nowofastów for my annual visits. Poor Mrs. Zaleska is in Nałęczów with her sick daughter, whose health is deteriorating and nobody knows if she will be strong enough to travel abroad this winter? I await news from you as to what you will decide for yourself—will you stay on shore or will you go to sea? No matter: here or there—as always I embrace you with my whole heart and bless you.

Your Uncle,
T. B.

61

26 September/8 October, 1891
Kazimierówka

My Dear Boy!

Your letter of the 14/26th instant reached me yesterday in Lipowiec during the session of Justices of the Peace. Unfortunately the tone of your letter—it is not difficult to read between the lines—shows that neither your state of health nor your state of mind is satisfactory. Having expressed your sympathy for poor Mrs. Zaleska at the death of her daughter you follow it with a most melancholy paragraph which—for me—constitutes a sufficient indication of your frame of mind. To philosophize about death in such a way as to maintain that 'en fin de compte' 'it is better to die young as in any case one is bound to die sometime', one must feel 'profondement découragé' or ill—or both? At your age, 'soit dit' at the age of thirty-four—such a philosophy does not even enter the head of anybody young and healthy, and this worries me greatly, my dear lad;

or maybe it is just a case of autumnal 'spleen'? May the Lord grant that in your next letter, after your return from Mr. Hope,[1] you will sing a more cheerful tune! But please, do not pretend to be gay if you do not feel it in your soul—I have a good enough knowledge of people—and of yourself—to be able to recognize an artificially produced gaiety, which will neither gladden my heart nor reassure me. Let us leave things to take their natural course, but should this emissary of heaven and the natural companion of youth really visit you, please let me know—it will make me happy.

One beautiful night—after I had returned home from the funeral of Mrs. Tyszkiewiczowa—something began to shift at the back of my head as if the Devil was stirring it up with a spoon. I felt certain that it was either the beginning of an inflammation of the brain or a tumour. The only fact that I found reassuring during that night was that I did not feel the slightest temperature. In the morning I sent for the doctor who reassured me straight away, not only theoretically but practically, by his statement that the pain in the head was rheumatic. Within 48 hours the suffering subsided to such an extent that on the third day I was able to travel to Lipowiec for the Court Sessions—which shows you my present state of health.

We are having a beautiful autumn here, but . . . when can there be no but?—the lack of the rain which is usual at this time of the year makes one anxious about the success of next year's harvest, the failure of which after the three bad years we have had would be quite disastrous. Now, some family news: poor Mrs. Koprowska was so miserable with the Prophet and he was so unhappy with her that they decided to part—but how was it to be done? He can't pay or rather does not think of paying back what he owes her. She wails and laments to me, imploring me to intercede; I refuse, knowing that even if I rebuke and quarrel with the Prophet, no money will come out of it. I had already once gone through a similar case with Uncle Adolf, and it ended in exactly that way, but in that case I had a good reason to speak, for he was pestering me for a loan. The Prophet is clever enough to keep silent and not to ask for money, so what right have I to kick him even though I know he deserves it? Mrs. Bobrowska is again at loggerheads with her son-in-law, the Right Hon. Mr. Dąbrowski. Poor Stanisław finds it all utterly loathsome, and together we try to persuade his mother to move out of Radom—which she will most likely do in the spring. She will probably settle down in Łowicz—2 hours' distance by railway from Warsaw on the line to Częstochowa and Cracow. Meanwhile, I

---

[1] With whom Conrad was yachting on the lower Thames.

took advantage of these disputes not to go to Radom at all this year, giving them as an excuse for staying away.

Keep well, my dear boy—be more full of hope than you have been up till now and write, Panie Bracie, bearing in mind that I care for everything that has to do with you.

I embrace you a hundredfold and bless you,

Your Uncle,
T. Bobr.

62

28 October/9 November, 1891
Kazimierówka

My Dear Boy!

I begin as usual,—though I should perhaps begin with 'My Dear Pessimist'[1] because that at least suggests the aroma which your letters have for some time been bringing me and that and no other is the proper way to address you. I can't say that I am pleased with your state of mind, and having now recognized it for what it is, it is difficult for me to contemplate your future with equanimity; however, I thank you for your openness, and I ask you not to hide from me your real state of mind while this mood persists;—that would be dangerous. In general I know people too well—and I love you in particular too much—not to be able to read between the lines of your letters. By being open with me—a quality which is highly desirable between people who are close to each other—you will lose nothing, my dear boy; on the contrary, my words may bring some consolation and some appeasement to your troubled mind? . . .

It is certain that in the depth of the soul of every reasoning human being, even of one who is not properly brought up and educated, there is a certain amount of pessimism—as well as a certain amount of optimism—perhaps not evenly balanced—which, depending on favourable circumstances, act in various directions: personal, domestic, or social. Either one or the other must prevail and will determine the individual character and all the activities of a man—most often adversely. Pessimism ruins the individual and his life and stultifies his actions; on the other hand excessive optimism may, in its worst form, render a man stupidly self-satisfied and absurd. . . . Between these two extremes there is the 'golden mean' which contains, I suppose, the basic truth of life—for those who do

---

[1] English in the original.

not work on the basis of a philosophical system but who in their existence abide by simple rules and who apply them in judging both themselves and their fellow men. Pessimism develops either during the early youth of one who is still ignorant of all the obstacles and failures that life brings, one who is still childishly over-sensitive— as the result usually of feelings not yet equipped with the resilient strength which can only be acquired by life itself. Or else pessimism may come at an advanced old age when one is battered by a life during which the resilient strength earlier acquired has become lost —an old age which can give nothing except memories and which has taken away hope—the chief motive force! . . . There is still a third, transient, ground for pessimism, which I call 'diseased'—when as a result of bodily sickness the resilient strength—both physical and moral—has become exhausted, or else when, as a result of a diseased imagination, of exaggerated demands and of wishes either for one-self or for others—in the positive or negative sense—one's whole power of resistance has become consumed in dreaming and there is none left for the sober judgement of facts and of the various problems of life, and there is none left for action or counteraction. . . .

After deliberating on the possible causes of your pessimism, I find I can't call it either symptomatic of 'youth' or of 'old age' for the thirty-four years of your life with all its vicissitudes doubly bear witness against that interpretation; I am therefore obliged to call it 'a sickness', and I feel justified in doing so because of your recent experiences in Africa and your ensuing illness during which you had plenty of time for sombre meditations, and because of—as it seems to me—my observation of the structure of your character and mentality. Both in you as an individual and in what you have inherited from your parents I detect the dreamer—in spite of your very practical profession—or perhaps because of it? Perhaps my supposition is wrong, but I think that you had the same pessimistic disposition in Marseilles years ago—only that was against the back-ground of your youth—and this reinforces my point of view that being endowed with a melancholy disposition, you should avoid pondering on anything likely to bring you to pessimistic conclusions —you should lead a more active life and possibly seek to lead a rather jollier one. Modern physicists suppose that on the earth there recur alternate periods of dryness and humidity every thirty-six years. Why, then, should we not suppose that in the world of humans there are organisms subject to periodic rises and falls of spiritual aridity—by aridity I mean pessimism. . . .

My dear lad, whatever you were to say about a good or bad balance of the forces of nature, about good or bad social relationships, about right or wrong social systems, about the boundless stupidity of crowds fighting for a crust of bread—and ending up in nothingness—none of this will be new!! You will never control the forces of nature, for whether blind or governed by Providence, in each case they have their own pre-ordained paths; and you will also never change the roads along which humanity goes, for there exists in social development an historical evolutionary compulsion which is slow but sure, and which is governed by the laws of cause and effect derived from the past and affecting the future. If, on this road, the will and work of man mean anything—if in this field all the endeavours of men and their chosen individuals—the geniuses—are effective—everyone may and even ought to contribute to it his hand or head, according to his strength and talents—but not himself dreaming of being the chosen Apostle of the people—for that way he may only meet with bitter disappointment—but rather thinking of himself as a modest tiny ant which by its insignificant toil in fulfilling its modest duty secures the life and existence of the whole nest! Certainly humanity has a lesser need of producing geniuses than of the already-existing modest and conscientious workers who fulfil their duties; nobody has the right to call himself the former until he has proved it by deeds, just as nobody has the right to withdraw from the work of the latter because of his conviction that he is not part of the team. This unfortunately happens frequently—with us here more than anywhere else! Our nation unfortunately, as Słowacki so truly remarked—although he himself was not immune from the accusation—is a 'peacock among nations',[1] which in simple prose means that we are a collection of proclaimed and generally unrecognized celebrities—whom no one knows, no one acknowledges, and no one ever will! So that if both Individuals and Nations were to make 'duty' their aim, instead of the ideal of greatness, the world would certainly be a better place than it is! And those crowds 'aiming instinctively at securing only bread', so detestable to all visionaries, have their raison d'être: to fulfil the material needs of life; and they no longer seem detestable when, as often happens, a more thorough evaluation reveals that they embellish their existence, their work, and often even their shortcomings, by some higher moral idea of a duty accomplished, of a love for their family or country to whom they leave the fruit of their endeavours and labours in the form of sacrifices or bequests.

Thus my assertion is: that although this world is not the best that

---

[1] Famous expression of Juliusz Słowacki in his poem *Podróż do Ziemi Świętej z Neapolu* (*Voyage to the Holy Land from Naples*), part viii, 'Grób Agamemnona' ('Agamemnon's Grave'), 1839.

one could imagine, it is nevertheless the only one we know and it is
tolerable to the extent that we neither know any other nor are we
able to create one; that society is not quite as bad as some seem to
think and that it can't be different from the people who constitute
it; and that it is open to improvement provided that individuals try
to improve themselves,—which in turn is bound to take place
provided that with the idea of duty (already recognized as the guiding star in human ethics) they will combine, not the idea of compulsion and necessity, as it has been hitherto—and that is especially
so in the 'quasi' intelligentsia the members of which are mainly
concerned with enjoying life and not with its duties—but the
thought and conviction of the satisfaction arising from fulfilling
altruistic duties—the origins of which, as well as of the pessimism or
the optimism, are contained in the soul of a newly-born man
though their development and application are the flower of a
Civilization which has been well absorbed and well directed;—this,
in my opinion, will be a matter for the future. One must be able to
look closely in order to see the good or at least the tolerable side of
life and of people, in the light of the worldly order, the fate of which
is not entirely in our hands—but one thing is certain and that is that
if one must judge with one's intellect one must appraise with one's
heart, obeying the order of nature in so far as it is necessary, with an
understanding of the shortcomings of the order of society in so far
as they can be and should be rectified; with sympathetic understanding for the clumsy creatures which men are, provided that they act
in good faith (although frequently inspired by blind prejudices). On
this soil pessimism, which is the aridity of soul and action, will not
grow; for the steppes of life are filled with the warm glow of the
love of one's fellow men as well as of personal satisfaction and
appeasement.

Perhaps you will tell me that what I have said is but the words of
a man who has always been comfortable in the world, 'qui a eu
toujours chaud'; but this is not so—you know this well. I have gone
through a lot, I have suffered over my own fate and the fate of my
family and my Nation, and perhaps just because of these sufferings
and disappointments I have developed in myself this calm outlook
on the problem of life, whose motto, I venture to say, was, is, and
will be 'usque ad finem'. The devotion to duty interpreted more
widely or narrowly, according to circumstances and time—this
constitutes my practical creed which—supported as it is by the
experience of my sixty years—may be of some use to you?—I shall
probably learn the results from your next letters! Faithful to the
principle 'mens sana in corpore sano' I wholeheartedly pray for

your health—for it is obviously the main cause of your low spirits; and I am glad of what you write in your last letter—may it continue to be so—and the pessimism will then be conquered, I hope! In return, I regret that I am not able to pass on to you any good news about myself, for on the 27th instant, while at Lipowiec, I had a severe fit of dizziness (I have not had one for a year) which forced me to return home immediately. Now I am quite well again, and I am writing this letter on my name-day, which I can't spend more pleasantly than by communing with you!

I embrace you a hundredfold and I send you my blessing on your road to optimism.

Wholeheartedly,
Your Uncle,
T. BOBROWSKI.

63

20 November/2 December, 1891
Kazimierówka

My Dear Boy!

Yesterday I received your letter of the 8/20th November—informing me of your immediate departure on the ship *Torrens*—from the brevity of which and from the reference to the previous one—'immediately the contract was concluded'—I am bound to assume that one of your letters missed me, which does not surprise me in the least in view of the present disorder in the distribution of the mail since the opening of the Railway line. My ordinary letters are transferred from Lipowiec to the railway station 'Oratów' where there is no proper Telegraphic or Postal Service, whereas in Lipowiec I collect the registered letters and 'chargées'. This duality is responsible for a frequent loss of newspapers and ordinary letters. In order to learn in detail something about your future plans I shall specially send faithful Jakub to Lipowiec and to the station to search for your last letter—even if it means moving heaven and earth and . . . the disorder at both stations which are paid 1 rouble a month by me, supposedly to look after my correspondence which they do so carelessly. . . .

I am not waiting till your mislaid letter turns up although I am fully aware that this letter will not reach you for 3 months—nevertheless I am writing it today, for the illusion of conversing with you makes my heart lighter. This does not prevent me from writing some more, so that on your arrival at Adelaide you will find a complete set of my letters which will constitute a reflection of my feelings and thoughts during this period;—I shall write every month.

The best news I had in your last letter is that you are 'quite well' and although it was short and to the point—as was necessary in the hurry of an immediate departure—it had about it an air of satisfaction and energy—which had been lacking in your letters since your return from the Congo and which had not pleased me and had given me some anxiety. An active life, even the most commonplace one, is the best remedy for pessimism. In fact, in my last letter, which you couldn't have received yet, and which was in reply to your ultra-pessimistic one of the 11/23rd September,—when considering your temporary disposition, I advised you, my dear lad, that a return to active professional service was the most effective remedy. I assume that my letter will be forwarded to you to Adelaide and that you will read it together with the present one. If I am not mistaken I imagine that you didn't want to take a position below that of a captain and as none came your way you waited in London becoming more and more embittered, helping your friends who deep inside might have been surprised—or else might have shared your opinion? until at last, bored and tired, you finally decided to accept a less brilliant position, but one which would prevent you from sinking deeper into pessimism. Or perhaps your financial position made you do it?—and 'le fond de votre bourse' was more eloquent than any arguments of your own and your Uncle's logic! In any case, you couldn't have acted more wisely—that is under the circumstances—for I would also have preferred to know that you had gone as a captain with a £1,000 salary instead of what you have got! One has to submit to necessity, and the moral advantage derived from the present decision will compensate you for the lost chances. Who knows—it may be that in Australia you will find what you were waiting for in vain in London? . . . indeed, should it in fact happen, I ask you most emphatically: forget all about our idea of meeting and take whatever is worth while that comes your way in the other hemisphere, if this one has proved unfavourable to your plans and 'crescence' (as our ancestors used to call it). . . . I have no intention of dying so soon—during your absence and without at least once again seeing and embracing you. If my likeness to my paternal Uncle is to be complete—then I should add that he lived till the age of seventy-five and I am now only 62—tandem 'vous avez—nous avons de la chance encore . . .' all the more so that —reciprocating your last letter—I am still feeling quite well! Although lately the rank and file of my contemporaries have thinned out considerably, I myself am not suffering any organic damage, and I hope that if I am unable to do as much as your Uncle did—as far as age is concerned—I shall at least do half as well as he did, which gives us another six years. Thus, let us hope, and let us do what reason tells us to, and the rest will be bestowed on us in addition—as the Scriptures tell us.

Now for some home news: I am sorry to say that life is not rosy. At present half of our country goes hungry, which in turn naturally affects us by a rise in the cost of living. It seems to me that this calamity has been purposely inflated by those interested in obtaining specially favourable treatment; and the attitude of the Government —which for the first time has shown some concern in the matter before and not after the event—has, as usually happens, contributed a great deal towards an exaggerated estimate of the situation, leading in turn to excessive panic. We shall see what events will bring about. . . .

Up till now the winter has been very mild—but this is only the beginning of the winter—the second half of it may be more severe, and the hopes for the next harvest are not too good. The most important piece of family news is that Kazimierz's widow has herself recognized the impracticability of living any longer in Radom and will probably move to Łowicz. Her daughters will remain in Radom. The sons-in-law are glad, and so is Stanisław for whom his stays in Radom had become real torture. Her removal will be in the spring. The youngest, Michaś, may be suffering from the same illness as you were—anyway he had a similar fit to yours in the autumn. The only difference is that the symptoms appeared much later than in your case and this makes one wonder if he will grow out of it by the age of fourteen, as you did?[1] Mrs. Koprowska is still in Dziadkiewicze and as always is complaining—I can't help her, for I can't change people and she is seventy-two and her son fifty-one.

Tomorrow, my dear lad, you begin the thirty-fifth year of your life and although—or possibly because—your past thirty-four years have not been very successful, I now send you my best wishes for the next thirty-four. Up till now, I have loved you with all my heart, and I vow to do the same in the years to come.

Your Uncle,
T. BOBROWSKI.

[1] The only possible explanation of this remark—taken in the context of other allusions to Conrad's bad health and nervousness, and to fears that Michaś would be mentally retarded—is that Conrad suffered from epilepsy as a child (cf. Introduction).

64

My Dear Boy!

I can't think of a better and more pleasant way of spending the lonely moments of Christmas than by thinking of and talking to you. For although it will be some time before you read this letter—you will see for yourself then how in these moments that remind me agreeably of the past, of my childhood and my parents' home, of youth, of my own home and of those who were its consolation—my thoughts, orphaned and battered by the trials of life, are directed towards you and your destiny, seeking in them a vital centre for my own life which is gradually drawing towards its end. Hence, my dear lad, according to the custom of our ancestors, I embrace you, bless you, and wish you all happiness at Christmas and the New Year, which you will already have celebrated and the arrival of which we are awaiting. What these wishes are—you may complete the song yourself! Secondly, in order to disperse any tinge of sadness which may have been suggested by the above introduction, I am happy to inform you and to assure you that my health is quite good and that since October I have had no attack of dizziness—such an 'échappée' of sad thoughts usually assails me during our national festivities, sanctified as they are by our customs, for formerly on these occasions there was more gaiety and bustle around me and I myself felt stronger and more active than today. It is nothing in fact but the result of thinking of the past, which one usually finds more beautiful than the present! Pushkin, the Russian national poet, expressed it very successfully in his poem: 'a czto proszło—to budiet miło' (what has passed will always be pleasant).[2] We are having here not the winter which is due according to the calendar, but early autumn weather. True, since October we have had slight frosts, but so far it has never been below −7°C. whereas usually at this time of the year we have −20°C. or less! This relatively mild weather does not augur well for the spring, and makes one expect possible ground-frosts in May which ruin our gardens and often, as was the case last year, even the crops. However, our farmers, who are well tried by the relatively bad harvests—we don't suffer from

---

[1] From Europe.

[2] Slightly distorted quotation from a well-known short lyrical poem beginning : 'Если жизнь тебя обманет'. Actual words: 'что пройдет, то будет мило', i.e. 'what will pass—will be pleasant'.

hunger here—and high prices, are hoping now that the year to come will be prosperous. This is not an impossibility—as the present winter has this advantage over the last, that if the snow should come it will cover the ground already frozen. We had sledge-roads only for a few days—now we skid on ice—the horses are falling down, but communications are not too bad.

I have no fresh family news to pass on to you. Mrs. K. B. is quarrelling with her sons-in-law, or rather, is at war with two of them and hates the third, The Right Hon. Dąbrowski, but she became so exhausted by it that now she intends to leave Radom and to settle down in Łowicz where there are schools. God alone knows if and when Michaś will be able to attend one of them, for he is still ill—possibly threatened by a mental illness. Naturally, as the lady-cousins side with their husbands, their relations with the mother become cooler. It is a source of great pain to Stanisław for Mother is not always in the right—and this is where the bitterness originated. Possibly Tadzio is the only one in a better position, being away and having only himself to look after—he learns well, his health is good, and he enjoys relative peace. It goes without saying that from the very first I have been in accord with Mrs. B.'s change of abode, and this is to happen in the spring. In my part of the world, your young cousin Miss Stanisława Nikorowicz is to link up with Tadeusz Florkowski. I don't know if you remember this, but we have been to see him at Skała; he is my ex-pupil and he will be the executor of my will. The girl is the younger one of the two handsome lassies that you have met and probably remember.

Poor Mrs. Zaleska is spending the winter in Warsaw. I have not seen her since last (1890) summer. The Montresors have gone somewhere south but I know not where as they have not written. Things do not go badly for Staś Zaleski, and of the people whom you met at my place, Mr. Darowski died recently. He was still quite a young man, very honourable and pleasant—he is deeply mourned by us all. It is a great loss.

Well, that is all till our next chat—now I embrace and bless you,

Your Uncle,
T. BOBROWSKI.

65

2/14 May, 1892
Kazimierówka

My Dear Boy!

I am sending this letter on the off chance to St. Helena—it might still find you there and provide you with a pleasant diversion which will be a gain to us both: for you a surprise, for me—a joy to have caused it.

Up till now I have received from you two letters from Adelaide dated the 4th and 24th March. I am now expecting the third, which you were to write on your departure and which, as usual in a case like this, I expect to be laconic and purely informative.

In my present letter, I am going to give prominence to the news of my health, in order to appease the anxiety of my dear boy. Thus, I am going to tell you that since February till the first days of April, in spite of constantly taking medicine for it—I suffered daily from dizziness, which has greatly tired and worried me. Just before the Easter Holidays and after having taken four lots of medicine, I made a pause, following the instructions of the doctors. As a result of this the dizziness stopped and I have not gone back to the medicine which originally I put aside only for a limited time. I am quite happy without it and I am waiting now to be seen by one of the three consultants (who were at Kiev—Dr. Fritschel—professor at the clinic; Dr. Orlikowski and Dr. Dynowski, whom you know) to ask them for further instructions and to find out if the present relief is due to the medicine or is the result of having stopped it. Meantime I am keeping reasonably well and thank the Lord for it, leaving to the worthy Aesculapiuses, two of whom are my friends, to solve the above problem.

Things with us don't look too good. We have had hardly any rain since the spring—the winter corn withers away and the seed sown in the spring doesn't sprout—the greenfly has got at the beets. Things are bad for us but they could be still worse! What is the solution? Patience.

Having informed you about myself I shall now point my pen in your direction and in the direction of your future plans. Firstly, I can't be overjoyed at the news of your indisposition and weariness at the age of thirty-five—which is not yet old by any means— and I hope that you will get over it. As to your intention to stay on the *Torrens* another year—you are the judge and the master in this matter—common sense certainly should not let you give up a tolerable occupation which you have for an unknown and uncertain one which you have to seek and possibly in vain. Let me add in order to strengthen you further in your decision, that I hope to survive somehow this year and the next one and to see you and embrace you in 1894—the Lord may grant it—let's hope so! Let me add this as well: should you wish to visit me this year I wouldn't be able to cover your expenses, for apart from the lack of success of the lease-holders, to whom I had to offer certain reliefs, I have also to bear the costs resulting from Stanisław's imprisonment as his Mother has been in Warsaw since January. I can't recollect if I had already mentioned to you that the poor lad got arrested on the 3/15 January this year, and accused of some political or rather social propaganda. He is still under lock and key in the Warsaw citadel. It seems to me to be nothing more than simply a case of unauthorized teaching of artisans—but as there is about it a tint of nationalism, it becomes complicated.[1] The exceptional ad hoc procedure is carried out in secrecy and an exceptional penalty may be imposed on the poor devil, ruining his present life—for he was just about to finish the University—and possibly even his whole future. Mrs. B. said in her letter that the investigation is over and the case is being transferred to Petersburg—perhaps it will be all over by May, but God alone knows how it will turn out.

On your return to London you will certainly find my letter— perhaps a couple—I shall inform you about everything and every-body, and now keep well, my Dear Boy.

I embrace and bless you a hundredfold.

Your Uncle,
T. BOBROWSKI.

[PS. at the top of the letter.]
Iodine mixture which could have over-saturated me—according to someone competent.

66

2/14 July, 1892
Kazimierówka

My Dear Boy!

The time of your arrival at London is drawing near and I wish my letter to greet you—may God grant, a healthy you—and add to

---

[1] Teaching without official permission was strictly forbidden in the Russian part of Poland. Unauthorized teaching would certainly be given in Polish, while Russian was the official language in schools. Moreover, any unregistered assembly of individuals was re-garded as leading to subversive conspiracy.

your high spirits and good disposition. Undeterred by the distance, both my thoughts and my heart have been frequently with you, following carefully your steps or rather your movements. As a proof of my mental participation in your life, you were to get my letters on the way, in Cape Town and at St. Helena. That is where I addressed my letters after having received the details of the proposed voyage of the *Torrens*. Did you receive them?

As I know that your first concern when getting back on land will be my health I shall inform you first of all about it: after having struggled through March with the almost daily fits of dizziness—I have been quite well since Easter—I even move about a little—but this satisfactory state depends on the most regular observance of hygiene in daily life.—The lightest insomnia or overfilling of the stomach immediately affects my general health—that is why I travel little and although I have a railway station at half an hour's distance I make little use of it—and what may seem surprising, I am visited now less frequently than in the past—however, to me it doesn't seem surprising for having now less strength to devote myself to people, I am less sought for by them—this is a simple, age-long practice in life! However, I am not too bad on the whole and I both hope and desire to see and embrace Captain Konrad in 1893. Let us hope for the best!!

I expect, then, by way of repayment for the good news, that you will send me similar news about yourself. I shall await this with impatience in August.

I can give you none—or at least very little favourable news about the family. If you received my letters addressed to Cap. and St. Helena, you already know that Stanisław was imprisoned in January and still remains under lock and key, thus bringing great sorrow to me and his Mother who is still in Warsaw. She had hoped that he would be freed on bail—I have sent her the sum required, but up till now no one has asked for it. Any day now they might call or this deposit—in any case this poor boy has spoiled his future, and knowing him, it is difficult to believe him to be as guilty as he seems. His reputation must have been tarnished by false appearances or friends. Tadeusz passed first in his class into the highest form—in a year's time he will finish school and has two years of higher professional studies ahead of him—this is due to him as he is an excellent pupil—the Government pays for it on condition of repayment by service. Kazimierz's widow, still at variance with her sons-in-law, has moved now to Łowicz (on the Bydgoszcz–Warsaw line) where there is a mathematical college which Michaś will attend. Each of your cousins has one child—the eldest ones of Zuzia and Marta died and Marylka has her first one. Jan Zagórski and Aunt Żanetta both died last year. Mrs. Gaba is not very well—she is paralysed. The Karols are still in Lublin. Marguerita has not written to me for a long time—she lives in Paris.

Things here are not good; primarily the harvest is very bad—for the fourth year in succession—which has brought ruin to hundreds of tenant farmers' families and to some of the less prosperous gentry. There are forebodings of plague coming from Persia—which (the plague) has already crossed the borders of Russia—it is already widespread in Baku, Tiflis, and Astrakhan. To add to everything, locusts have descended in our neighbourhood, beyond the Dnieper in the province of Czernihów. It appears to be some errant cloud brought by the wind, for one had heard nothing of this impending disaster. However, for a man who in his life has gone through all sorts of disasters, nothing seems very terrifying—common sense says that each one must affect somebody—egoism whispers 'it won't be me'—this brings temporary appeasement, but sometimes misleads one!

Keep well, my dear lad, I embrace you a hundredfold and bless you.

Your Uncle,
T. BOBROWSKI.

67

6/18 September, 1892
Kazimierówka

My Dear Boy!

Thank God you are in Europe! I had begun to worry quite seriously about you and in fact the same messenger who took to the post a letter to Mr. Krieger brought me your epistle which has appeased me a little in spite of a grey cloud of misgiving and dissatisfaction which emerges from beneath the surface. I believe and share your longings for a command, but one cannot expect everything to happen at once. Possibly had you decided to stay for some time in Australia you might have got a command but this would have kept you for a long time or even for ever away from Europe, from me, from your friends—and being endowed with such gifts from heaven 'à la portée de votre main', speaking in metaphors—you have to wait a bit longer for the realization of your professional hopes. This, Panie Bracie, is the natural course of human affairs—

one compensates for the other and there is no complete satisfaction to be found in this 'vale of tears'. You say that my letters give you encouragement; well, here you have the key to my philosophy of life: one has to wait patiently till fortune shows the bright part of her face and then grab it with grace—meantime doing one's duty. All the better for you and myself if you can find encouragement in this theory.

Knowing that of all the local news my health interests you most, I hereby inform you that from March up till this day I have been feeling quite well and not once since Easter have I suffered from dizziness. I think that I have already reported this to you in a letter sent to London to greet you on your arrival—and which you never mentioned. Since April the 7th—that is since the day when you sent your letter from Port Adelaide—I wrote to you as follows: once to Cape Town, the second time to St. Helena, the third time to London, the fourth time a few days ago to good old Krieger, and this is the fifth.

I have been besieged as well by Mme Marguerita's voluminous letters which to top it all have been so illegible that I had to read them through a magnifying glass—but I answered every one of them—now she has somewhat cooled down in her fervour as she has not written, I think, since April. The little darling is a 'bas bleu'; it would be better if she changed this title for that of Mme La Bourgmestre Buls—I tried to talk her into it, but she would not listen. She is as romantic as a girl of sixteen. I cannot tell you anything either new or better about poor Stanisław—in spite of his mother's efforts to bring about the opening of the trial sooner. He is being accused of giving unauthorized instruction to the workers, which is punished lightly when practised individually but entails a severe penalty when practised by an association. It seems that the former has been proved, but they wish now to prove the latter and this is the reason for delay. His health will suffer, not to speak of his career or of the fact that his maintenance in prison costs a lot. A ruined future! Tadeusz is a rather nice boy, develops well and has a sober outlook on life—he is lucky with people—not in vain is he my namesake and was a seven months baby. The sons-in-law have now 'un moment de répit' with Kazimierz's widow as she is preoccupied with her son—but the woman comes from a family of jurists both on the distaff and her father's side. Her grandparents were jurists 'portés à la chicane'—'elle chasse de race' and can't remain quiet— thank the Lord she is not too near to me! Mrs. Koprowska, Gaba, and Karol inquire in a most solicitous way after you as always. My part of the world is still free from cholera and will possibly remain so but we have cholerine and diarrhoea—not deadly as yet, thank God. I embrace you a hundredfold, write to me—

Your Uncle,
T. BOBROWSKI.

68

20 September/2 October, 1892
Kazimierówka

My Dear Boy!

The day before yesterday, I received your letter of the 11/23 instant which gave me much pleasure by its gaiety and the news of your good health and I rejoice wholeheartedly in this change in your personal state—and as you announce a new departure about the 8/20 October, I hasten with my reply to find you still in London, hoping that as usual on your departure you will give me your itinerary so that I may follow you on your voyage with my letters. . . .

As for today I have nothing new to say—I think I shall repeat the old news: I am quite well; since Easter I have not suffered from vertigo—but I feel apprehensive when thinking of what is going to happen when the real autumn weather begins. At present it is very warm and beautiful—alas too beautiful—no sign of rain and the seeds don't grow! My lease-holder may flee, which wouldn't surprise me, this being the fourth year of loss to him—nevertheless this possibility makes me sigh heavily as this would mean great trouble to me and a decrease in my income—made all the more painful by the fact that next year Tadzio is due to leave school and you are to come here. All this means extra expenditure which I am prepared to meet provided that the usual income will flow into my pocket—otherwise I shall be in trouble. We shall see what the future will bring.

As a rule I feel worse in autumn because I am less active and the skies are overcast (in my health and disposition the sun plays a very important part)—I might therefore go and spend a few weeks in Kiev to refresh myself a bit with movement and amid social activity. But this is just a project—I shall see if it can become reality.

Not only do I know nothing new about Stanisław, but I know nothing at all as Mrs. Bobrowska has not written to me for about a month. She usually becomes more animated towards the end of a quarter when it is time to send her money. She even occasionally postpones the acknowledgement of its receipt—considering me to be a bank obliged to supply her with 'filthy lucre'. It is certain that poor Stanisław will pay with his health for all he goes through. His father suffered from a bad heart and it wouldn't be at all surprising if under the present circumstances he developed the same trouble. 'Tu l'as voulu Georges Dandin'—Mais Moi non!!—and yet it affects me as well—such is the justice in life that the innocent has to answer for the faults of others. I thank you for answering Tadzio and Marylka—you will do good by writing to Karol Zagórski. Young Miss Ołdakowska is near here as a governess at the Rakowskis—she is rather a nice girl. I was afraid that she might be lightheaded as she seemed inclined to be—but she became a bit more serious and presented herself well. Keep well my dear boy—go—write and stay cheerful—thinking about our meeting next year. I embrace you a hundredfold and bless you.

Your Uncle,
T. Bobrowski.

[PS. at the top of the letter.]
You didn't say how Mr. Krieger is! Do write and give him my regards.

69

5/17 October, 1892

My Dear Boy!

Yesterday I received your letter of the 6th instant and as you announce your departure for the 13/25 instant there is still a whole week for my present letter addressed directly to the docks to reach you in London and to convey to you my blessing and best wishes for a successful voyage and for a safe return which is so important for both of us because of your visit which is to follow. Now, Panie Bracie, the main task is for you to stay healthy and for me to stay alive till you return! I say this not because I feel unwell or worse than in March but because when one is over the age of fifty—and even more so when over sixty—each new day is a gift—at my age one shouldn't plan too far ahead, but one is allowed to have hope and one should not lose it. . . .

Although you complain at being 'torn from the bosom of your friends' (a poem by Wąż[1] written before 1831)—I do not complain at all, as the sooner you depart the sooner you will return and the

---

[1] Mikołaj Wąż, a little-known poet, active at the beginning of the nineteenth century.

sooner I shall see you in Kazimierówka. As your voyages last, as a rule, from eight to nine months, by leaving now you may be back just about June or July—and I would wish you to see our country at a time of year when it is really beautiful, as it is in the early autumn. Then, people also make a better impression, being busy working and gathering the fruits of their labour. The awakened intellect presents itself in a more favourable light. And so, with all my hopes, I bid you farewell and I embrace and bless you, my dear boy, with the old Polish wish 'Deus te ducat, perducat et reducat'—in addition I embrace you heartily.

You wish and expect before your departure to have some definite news of Stanisław. Alas, it is not as easy as it seems. The procedure in his case is exceptional—according to judicial as well as administrative ordinances—the gendarmerie decides and, to tell the truth, they are as a rule no worse than other functionaries, but the conducting of the case is devoid of the elementary principles of defence—the presence of the public and verbal defence. Kazimierz's widow has just written that the Court's Prosecutor (up till now the case has been in the hands of the Inquiry Judge—a gendarme) in Warsaw firmly refused to let him out on bail and announced that the case has been forwarded to St. Petersburg where the H.Q. of the gendarmerie could pass sentence on him without a trial—or else may hand the case over to the Court Martial, as for the past twelve years Warsaw has been under the so-called 'state of protection'; or else they may hand the case over to the Court of Peace for trial. Most probably the first will be the case and he will be sent to Siberia for a period. Whichever way it goes he is a lost man—especially as he has studied law—he could never become either a government official, a solicitor, or a notary—not even in Kamchatka!! His whole life has gone off the rails—together with all the hopes and confidence I had placed in him. There is nothing to be done! His poor Mother would like to go to Petersburg but I try to dissuade her, saying that not having the right contacts she won't achieve anything—and whatever can be done, Mr. Spasowicz will do. Up till now the case has cost me several hundred roubles; the bail is unfortunately being returned to me—I would have willingly sacrificed it to get Stanisław out—if not of trouble then at least out into the fresh air. I am certain that he will emerge from his sentence with heart disease; 'Tu l'as voulu Georges Dandin', but it is no comfort that he is responsible for what is happening, since one suffers as well as he does. Well that is enough, recriminations will not help! Otherwise there is nothing new—we have had a little rain—the corn has begun to sprout—now we are having cold weather, which is bad, for it can freeze the weak fresh growth. I embrace you a hundredfold—please write.

Your Uncle,
T. BOBROWSKI.

70

10/22 May, 1893
Kazimierówka

My Dear Boy!

I recently received your third and last letter from Adelaide dated the 19th March and although you named Cape Town and St. Helena as your stopping places, I am sending my present letter directly to London having calculated that if I sent it to St. Helena it would arrive after your departure. I wrote to the Cape immediately on receipt of your second letter from Adelaide, dated the 9th March —that is six weeks from the latter date, but I am not at all certain if the letter will have found you in Cape Town. Our post fails frequently when localities little known to it beyond the Atlantic are concerned and sends mails frequently in the wrong direction. However, I recollect that last year you found a letter from me awaiting you at St. Helena? Nevertheless I certainly dislike taking chances with the letters I send, and so I prefer to address this present one to London in the hope that, though later, you will receive it with greater certainty. . . .

I would like to welcome you on your return to Europe (God grant in good health and spirits) and I would like, as soon as possible, to discuss with you our three-year-old project: our meeting— or rather your coming to me, for I myself have no strength for an excursion to London!

The present year has been an awful one for us—the winter corn and wheat were completely frozen and hardly a quarter of it has survived. I have to be prepared for the bankruptcy of my tenant farmer, who will be unable to pay this year's rent, with the result that there will be a great hole in this year's income. But I am rather fearing another type of bankruptcy—which would be caused by having to give up hope of seeing you—for I do not want to forgo this pleasure, which might be my last one, whatever the reason might be for the failure of our dream of meeting, so, as always, I wish for and await your visit, my dear lad—for at my age any postponement might mean final defeat!! Doubtless you yourself will

Bobrowski's Letters to Conrad

agree with my point of view in this matter although for a different reason, for though it is natural at my age to fear that a happiness may pass me by, it is natural for your part that you should be impatient for its coming: why is it not yet here? So then, if your prospects in your job and career do not stand in the way—come, Panie Bracie! and if after my death there should be left a few hundred roubles less, I shall have had one more joy, that's all there is to say about it. To simplify matters, I am not sending you any money for the voyage now—use your own, or if you have none, as on the last occasion, borrow some from good old Mörring. I shall repay the expenses of the journey either to you or to him as the case may be. Probably, as on the previous occasion, you will travel through abominable Berlin, and then take a fast train via Białystok, by-passing Warsaw which is already empty and will be even more so during the summer, and then via Brześć to Koziatyń where after waiting a few hours you will have to change on to a modest, partly goods, partly passenger train, which will bring you at 11.30 a.m. to the station of 'Oratów', which is seven versts from Kazimierówka. From Brześć telegraph for horses, but in Russian, for Oratów doesn't receive or accept messages in an 'alien' language.[1] As you can see, existence along our part of the line is 'dans l'enfance de l'art', with no fast trains, in fact with only one train a day each way —but it connects with the fast trains. However, if for some reason you had to wait in Koziatyń for half a day or more, take a carriage and make for the manor of Mr. Wasiutyński, a friend of your parents, who was disappointed last time because of your not having visited him. On your way back, if you wish, you can travel again through Lublin and Łowicz. Anyhow, go any way you wish—you know the country now and the season is more favourable for travelling than it was three years ago. Tadzio passes his examinations most successfully and is to go to Chicago in the suite of the Heir to the Throne—he is full of jubilation—otherwise there is nothing new—my health is not bad—and on seeing you it will improve. I embrace and bless you.

Your Uncle,
T. BOBROWSKI.

[1] This seems to suggest that Conrad must have known some Russian. That he could read the Russian alphabet we gather from Bobrowski's letter of 26 Oct./7 Nov. 1879.

71

1/13 July, 1893
Kazimierówka

My Dear Boy!

Your letter dated the 17th May from Cape Town reached my home some weeks ago but because of my absence it lay on my desk till the day before yesterday. I have been first in Nałęczów from the 7/19th June, where Mrs. Cecylia Zaleska is spending the summer, then to Warsaw where some of my widowed clients live, then to Łowicz where Kazimierz's widow has been residing since last year, and finally to Żagławice near Lublin where my ex-wards, the older Florkowskis, live. In Lublin I visited the Zagórskis; in all it took three weeks, but I returned from my expedition in good health, although tired.

I have received three letters from you dated the 29th February, the 9th and the 19th March—but the fourth one which you mention, written on your departure from Adelaide, has never reached me. My particular letter, addressed to Cape Town, which you say gave you great pleasure, was the only one I sent there. Since then I have written to you to London and that letter I expect you will find waiting for you, together with this one, on your arrival. In my previous letter, not being well acquainted with the situation, I pressed you to carry out our project of meeting this year in Kazimierówka, 'quand-même', in spite of the 'bad times' we are passing through and the threat of a bad harvest and the expectation of my being faced with a deficit, but today after having read your letter of the 17th May and after having considered the possible consequences of this visit, 'quand-même', I have nevertheless to soften my appeal somewhat. . . . Consider, my dear lad, at what cost, and I am thinking solely of the cost to you, this visit would take place?—your giving up your present post on the *Torrens*, which you like, and possibly even the chance of obtaining the command of this ship in the event of Capt. Cope succeeding in his endeavours to get the command of a steamship in the future. Obviously, the command of the *Torrens* should then not go to anybody but her 1st Officer. Please consider this possibility coolly and then decide. I do not want to take blindly upon myself, for my own pleasure, a decision in a matter which may entail—even if it is only to some small extent—any sacrifice connected with your future career! Judge for yourself, Panie Bracie, the whole question from the point of view of your future career and I shall accept your decision as an indispensable conclusion which concerns both of us and as a professional necessity which is good and well justified—however unpleasant from our personal point of view.

I suppose that the best route for you to take would be by a fast train to Koziatyń via Vlissingen, Berlin and Białystok and from then onwards by an ordinary train. From Eitkunen send a telegram—but remember that it must be in Russian for there is no international service at the station at Oratów. I am not sending you any money—take some from Krieger as you did the first time—that is the simplest procedure, or else use your own if you have any saved up and I shall reimburse you on your arrival—that is if you come—but think first about leaving your employment—it is easy to give it up but difficult to get it back—as you have seen for yourself.

On your way back, si le cœur vous en dit, you can visit the Zagórskis and even one of your female cousins, who have been asking not less often than Kazimierz's widow herself—will you visit them?—I treat all their inquiries 'évasivement', not wishing to tie you down with my promises. On the 8/20th May, Stanisław was taken to St. Petersburg to serve his sentence—a year and a half in prison—which period starts on the 5/17th February this year. Otherwise there is nothing new in the family. Marta and Maria came to Łowicz to see me. Zuzia was not there, probably one of her children—she has got two—or her husband, was unwell.

I await your return and your decision as to your visit or its postponement, and I specially beg that your decision should be guided by a sober awareness of your interests and not by sentimental considerations by which our lives must not be guided!

I embrace you a hundredfold and bless you.

Your Uncle,
T. BOBROWSKI.

TWO LETTERS FROM TADEUSZ BOBROWSKI TO STEFAN BUSZCZYŃSKI

Tadeusz Bobrowski to Stefan Buszczyński[1]

12/24 March, 1879
Kazimierówka

Dear and gracious Sir!

I am grateful beyond expression for your solicitude as to the fortunes of Konrad, who, I gather, has quite forgotten about the gratitude due to you for all your kindness to him. In this matter I have nothing to reproach myself with, for each time I have appealed to him to keep up his correspondence at least with his paternal and his maternal uncle, I put your honoured name next to theirs and informed him of your as well as of their address. He always excused himself for not writing to his Uncles on the ground that not knowing them he had nothing to write about. He assured me, however, that he was writing to you. And so it appears that I was the only one honoured with his correspondence—which more or less amounts to feeding the hen which lays the golden eggs, as the fable goes. His negligence provoked me on one occasion to point out an explanation that I could see for this 'favour'—but this also produced no result, and his paternal Uncle died (in Tomsk, January 1878) without ever having received a letter from him. My brother was always grieved by this behaviour and now you also are beginning to complain about it! My conscience is clear as I not only never attempted to win Konrad's feelings exclusively for myself—as guardians often do—but on the contrary constantly brought to his attention his duties towards the people who were closest to his father, among whom you, dear Sir, occupy a prominent place.

The news that has reached you about my journey to Marseilles and possibly about the reason for it is, alas, quite true!—however, since you have been out of touch with the events in Konrad's life for a long time, I must make a short recapitulation of what has happened. During the years 1875–76 and '77 Konrad made four voyages on French merchant vessels to Guadeloupe—Martinique —the Island of St. Thomas—Haiti—New Orleans—always from Marseilles, always for the same shipowner although under various captains, and always for an annual premium of between 2,000 and 2,400 fr. In 1876 he played a trick upon me for, after having withdrawn from the Bank his half-yearly allowance all at once, he said he lent it all to friends; in which young Chodźko, his co-protector, participated. I had no reason to doubt that this was the

---

[1] Bobrowski's letters to Buszczyński are preserved in Cracow, Polish Academy of Sciences (PAN) Library, MS. 2064, vol. ii.

case, and to this day I do not doubt it—and I filled the gap, gave him a good scolding—and again he departed;—I may add that both the shipowner and the captain gave the most favourable testimonials possible about his application to work and his conduct. At the beginning of 1877, just before departing on another voyage, he fell ill with an anal abscess—which lasted four weeks. The ship sailed, much to the regret of Captain Escarras, who even wrote to me about this, leaving Konrad behind, who, not wishing to sign on under another captain, remained in Marseilles pursuing his theoretical studies and awaiting the return of his chief with whom he was to make a voyage round the world. In October 1877, in answer to his urgent demands and since his voyage was to last a year and a half to two years, I sent him with my blessing a further 2,000 fr. over and above his allowance. I was absolutely certain that he was already somewhere in the Antipodes, when suddenly, amidst all the business at the Kiev Fair in 1878, I received a telegram: 'Conrad blessé envoyez argent—arrivez.' Naturally I could not fly to him straight away like a bird; but having settled my business and having received a reply that Konrad was already better I set off at once from Kiev on the 24 February (old style), and arrived at Marseilles on the 27th. I found Konrad already out of bed and after having had a previous talk with his friend Mr. Richard Fecht, a most prudent and worthy young man, I saw the victim in person. And this is what I discovered. Although Konrad had been absolutely certain of accompanying Captain Escarras on his next voyage, the Bureau de l'Inscription forbade him to go on the grounds of his being a 21-year-old alien who was under the obligation of doing his military service in his own country. Then it was discovered that he had never had a permit from his Consul—the ex-Inspector of the Port of Marseilles was summoned who in the register had acknowledged the existence of such a permit—he was severely reprimanded and nearly lost his job—which was undoubtedly very unpleasant for Konrad. The whole affair became far too widely known and all endeavours by the Captain and the shipowner proved fruitless (the shipowner, Mr. Délestang, himself told me all this) and Konrad was forced to stay behind with no hope of serving on French vessels. However, before all this happened another catastrophe—this time financial—befell him. While still in possession of the 3,000 fr. sent to him for the voyage, he met his former Captain, Mr. Duteil, who persuaded him to participate in some enterprise on the coasts of Spain—some kind of contraband! He invested 1,000 fr. in it and made over 400 which pleased them greatly so that on the second occasion he put in all he had—and lost the lot. This Mr. Duteil consoled him with a kiss and then went off to Buenos Aires. He, Konrad, was left behind, unable to sign on for a ship—poor as a church mouse and, moreover, heavily in debt—for while speculating he had lived on credit, had ordered the things necessary for his voyage, and so forth. Faced with this situation, he borrows 800 fr. from his friend Mr. Fecht and sets off for Villa Franca where an American squadron was anchored, with the intention of joining the American service. He achieves nothing there and, wishing to improve his finances, tries his luck in Monte Carlo and loses the 800 fr. he had borrowed. Having managed his affairs so excellently he returns to Marseilles and one fine evening invites his friend the creditor to tea, and before his arrival attempts to take his life with a revolver. (Let this detail remain between us, as I have been telling everyone that he was wounded in a duel. From you I neither wish to nor should keep it a secret.) The bullet goes durch und durch near his heart without damaging any vital organ. Luckily, all his addresses were left on top of his things so that this worthy Mr. Fecht could instantly let me know, and even my brother, who in his turn bombarded me. Well, that is the whole story!

I spent a fortnight in Marseilles, at first investigating the whole affair and then the Individual himself. Apart from the 3,000 fr. which he had lost, I had to pay as much again to settle his debts. Had he been my own son I wouldn't have done it but—I must avow— in the case of my beloved sister's son, I had the weakness to act against the principles I had hitherto held. Nevertheless, I swore that even if I knew that he would shoot himself a second time— there would be no repetition of the same weakness on my part. To some extent also I was influenced by considerations of our national honour, so that it should not be said that one of us had exploited the affection, which Konrad undoubtedly enjoyed, of all those with whom he came into contact. He is lucky with people.

My study of the Individual has convinced me that he is not a bad boy, only one who is extremely sensitive, conceited, reserved, and in addition excitable. In short I found in him all the defects of the Nałęcz family. He is able and eloquent—he has forgotten nothing of his Polish although since he left Cracow I was the first person he conversed with in his native tongue. He appears to know his profession well and to like it. I suggested to him that he should return to Galicia,[1] get naturalized, and look for a career there, but he refused this, maintaining that he loves his profession, does not want to and will not change it. In spite of watching him carefully I didn't detect any of the bad habits common among sailors—

[1] The southern part of Poland, then under Austrian occupation, was so called.

he drinks hardly anything except red wine—does not gamble (he said that himself and Mr. Fecht confirmed never having seen him gambling—the unfortunate incident in Monte Carlo sprang from the thought 'first time lucky'). His manners are very good, as if he had never left drawing-rooms—he was very popular with his captains and also with the sailors—more than once have I witnessed scenes of cordial greetings with sailors who call him M. Georges. During my stay in Marseilles he was twice called for to bring vessels into the port, for which service he was paid 100 fr. a time. I must therefore regard him as a man who knows his profession. My studies of the Individual have not deprived me of the hope that a real man might still be made of him—as used to be said—certainly the temperament of the Nałęcz family is predominant in him—and I may be mistaken but I think that unfortunately he has taken after his paternal Uncle rather than after his father. In his face he rather resembles his Mother and is quite a handsome boy; in his build he is more like his Father and is quite robust. In his ideas and discussions he is ardent and original. We Poles, particularly when young, have an innate liking for the French and for the Republic—he, however, does not like them at all and is an imperialist. De gustibus non est disputandum—but several times I couldn't control myself and rebuked him.

Finally, it was decided that he should join the English Merchant Marine where there are no such formalities as in France—and so, directly after my departure from Marseilles, in the first days of May of last year, his friend Fecht (from Wittenberg) sent him off on his way to England to Lowestoft where until October he stayed with a coastal vessel learning all about steamships and perfecting his English which had been rather weak (he had another friend, Mr. Grand, an Englishman). In October he entered the service of an English Company in London, with whom he deposited £20 as security—he is to serve there for three years: the first year he must pay for; the second year he serves for nothing; the third year he gets a small salary, and after that he is to take an examination and be naturalized. He left for Australia, for Sydney, and is not due back till August—however, I haven't had a word from him since his departure, although not only did I write to him to Sydney but I have even sent him some money. He writes to no one, as recently I received a letter from this Mr. Fecht inquiring for news of Konrad—I have even written myself to Lowestoft but there also nothing was known of him nor of the ship. I am beginning to feel worried and will write again to Lowestoft—I shall inform you as soon as I know something.

It may be that my description of Konrad's Odyssey has been too detailed—if so, please accept my apologies but all I want you to know is that I have not and will not desert him unless he does something extraordinary, which I don't expect will happen.

Thank you very much for inquiring after me. Nothing has changed in my way of life except that I have aged greatly, so they say, and I feel it myself. I have made my will and have left Konrad 15,000 roubles and now I am quietly waiting for my 'Assumption'. Before that happens, however, God may allow me to see you again, and to assure you personally of my high esteem and deep affection.

—T. BOBROWSKI.

I am very sorry that last year in Warsaw I missed Konstanty—I send him my best regards. Thank you for Dr. Pulman's address—I shall write to him.

Tadeusz Bobrowski to Stefan Buszczyński

18/30 May, 1879
Kazimierówka

Dear Sir!

By way of gratifying your friendly concern about Konrad's fortunes—something which I couldn't do at the time of getting your letter—I hasten to inform you that in the course of the last few days I have received from Konrad two letters from Sydney, dated the 4th and 16th of February. Letters take two months and six days to reach England—and from London another seven days, thus two and a half months are needed for a letter to arrive and therein lies the secret of Konrad's silence. He is in good health but complains of the uncomfortable conditions on English ships where no one is in the least concerned with the crew's comfort. This fate is shared by all the junior officers who, however, being well aware of the situation knew how to deal with it, while Konrad, having counted on finding the same comfort as he had had on French vessels, did not think about his convenience and consequently had to put up with all the discomfort for 109 days—for such was the duration of the voyage from London to Sydney. To crown it all, the poor boy didn't find on his arrival in Sydney the money he had asked me to send him—but which, however, arrived 10 days later. In spite of all this, Konrad's letters are satisfactory—a liking for his profession and hope of a better future shines through them. He expects to be back in England by September and, not wasting much time, to set off in October again on a voyage to Australia—but this time in order to stay there several years—or at least two. He has it in mind to devote himself to the investigation of trading arrangements on the Archipelago of the Sunda Isles, the beauty and wealth of which he describes with the greatest enthusiasm. In Sydney he became acquainted with some captain famous for his knowledge of the trade with that Archipelago and for his contacts there and well known both in geographical and trading circles.[1] In fact that captain, who is at the same time a shipowner, took a fancy to Konrad and offered him a job—to start with £5 a month, that is £60 a year—and an officer's keep on the ship—and as I am giving Konrad 2,400 fr., which comes to approximately £100, he would be receiving £150 per annum plus upkeep, which would not be at all bad. His prospects would be: naturalization in England and experience of a trade which he considers profitable—and who knows, maybe in time he would try his luck in this branch of activity? Obviously, not having myself any special views on this matter, I do not feel that I can oppose this project. My only objection is the distance, but as in any case I am not seeing him, it's all the same to me whether he is in London or in Sydney, and if he sees his future there, let him look for it! Here I should add—not so much a credit to him as to his gift for languages—that the Polish in Konrad's letters is as good as if he had never left Poland, when in fact, since his departure from Cracow (1874) he has spoken Polish only once—with me in Marseilles.

Well, Dear Sir, for the time being this is all I have to tell you. Convinced as I am of your interest in my nephew's fortunes I shall inform you about him from time to time—possibly I might even have an opportunity to talk to you in person about our wanderer and to express the esteem and respect that I feel for you, Dear Sir.

Yours sincerely,
T. BOBROWSKI.

[1] We do not know the name of this captain, and although one is tempted to identify him with Tom Lingard (the living prototype of the hero of *Almayer's Folly*, *An Outcast*, and *The Rescue*), the hypothesis is rather improbable.

TADEUSZ BOBROWSKI'S
'DOCUMENT'

THE DOCUMENT

For the information of my beloved Nephew
Konrad Korzeniowski

On your reaching maturity, I want you to know all about the relations of your Parents with the other members of your Family—I want you to know how the small fund was established which is designed to serve you in your future work and independence.

In undertaking to relate this story, I am not doing so in order to glorify my own merits in the matter for, as you will see for yourself, your other relatives, in proportion to their means, have done more than I for your Parents and yourself—but I am undertaking it mainly so that you should know that we all loved your Mother and through her both you and your Father.

Uncle Tadeusz B.

1st December, 1869
Nowofastów.

Your Parents were united in marriage on the 28th April 1856 in Oratów, the family estate of your late Grandfather Józef Bobrowski, in the Oratów parish church, and the marriage was celebrated by the Rev. Jan Szymański. According to the last will and testament of our late Father, your Mother's share in his estate was to have been equal to those of her Brothers. Since after the death of our Sister Teofila, four brothers were left: Stanisław, Tadeusz, Kazimierz, and Stefan, and our Sister and your best Grandmother—our Mother—your Mother was entitled to one sixth of the bequest.

After the estate had been divided up by our cousin the late Józef Poradowski and our friend the late Seweryn Syroczyński, and after the sale of part of the village of Oratów, where your Mother's inheritance was located—your Mother got as her dowry *eight thousand roubles*. In addition, by her Mother's wish she received a double share of the silver lbs.: 12 ł 13,[1] a beautiful pine-marten fur, and a beautiful big carpet—from us brothers she received 1,000 roubles towards her dowry which we didn't want to deduct when dividing the estate, and various household requisites such as a couch, a dinner-service, trays, etc., which if divided would have had no great value but if offered to one person were adequate equipment towards a household. At the time of his marriage your

---

[1] A Polish pound (no longer in use), equal to 32 *luts*, is 405 grams; Ewa received then about 11 lb. 10 oz. of silver.

father did not own any capital; he was administering the estate of Mrs. Melania Sobańska, the Łuczyniec demesne in Podolia—and that is where they spent their first year together. In 1857 after the sale of Oratów and on receipt of his wife's dowry, your father took a lease of a farm at Debreczynka in the Mohilew district. Economic difficulties and possibly some lack of caution resulted by 1860 in your parents losing their capital and even some of your mother's capital, a third part of which was invested in the lease, so they moved to Żytomierz where your father intended to devote himself to literary work. Your father was always secretive so far as his financial situation was concerned, and therefore not only we, his brothers, but even our Mother was not acquainted with your parents' means and later on I found out that your Mother also was not fully aware of what financial means her husband had at his disposal. *In the spring of 1862* your Father went to Warsaw—in the autumn of the same year your Mother followed him. The purpose of this departure was the establishment of a literary magazine, the title of which was to have been 'Dwutygodnik'—however, within two weeks of your Mother's arrival in Warsaw your Father was arrested and taken to the Citadel. On hearing this news, your Grandmother went at once to Warsaw and remained with your Mother till *the departure of your parents and you to exile in Vologda.*[1] *I forgot to mention that you came into this world on the 21st November 1857 in Berdyczów, where you were christened with water, and your christening was confirmed with oil in 1862 in Żytomierz, by the Rev. Szczeniowski. In 1863, your parents* got permission to settle in Chernikhov, and in August of that year your Mother and you came to me to Nowofastów; it was then that I noticed the first signs of the disease which eventually sent this Being beloved by us all, prematurely to the grave! During her stay in Vologda your Mother always assured me, whenever I wanted to help them, that they had the means of subsistence—which I believed to be true. Only later it came out that they owed this means to your Uncle Kazimierz, who at that time collected from me an instalment of our Father's bequest and sent a single sum of 2,000 r. to your Father—your Mother never learned of that to her dying day. After her return to Chernikhov in the autumn of 1863 she continued to pay no attention to her bad state of health, which was steadily deteriorating and in spite of the insistence of her Mother, who came to you in the summer of 1863, she refused to undergo treatment. On my arrival

---

[1] It seems that since, contrary to Bobrowski's assertion, Ewa Korzeniowska as well was accused, tried, and sentenced to exile (and therefore almost certainly arrested), her Mother went to Warsaw to look after young Conrad.

at your parents' home for the New Year of 1865, I became alarmed at your Mother's condition and I extorted from her a promise to seek the advice of Mr. Romański, whom I brought from Żytomierz and who at first expressed some hope of saving her. Subsequently he visited her once again, in February, only to inform us of the inevitable loss of this most beloved sister. Thus, together with your beloved Grandmother, we left on the 1st March 1865 for Chernikhov and remained there with all of you till your Mother's last breath *on the 6th April of that year*. According to the law, the small inheritance left by our Brother and your Uncle should have been divided between the remaining Brothers. However, both your Uncle Kazimierz and I wished your beloved Mother and our Sister to take part in it and, therefore, in spite of her resistance to it and without her knowledge, your Father accepted this inheritance *amounting to 1,954 r. 94 kop.* While your Mother was still alive, and during her last illness, I remitted to your Father 954 r. out of this sum. *One thousand roubles* remained with me as your property, bearing interest. After the death of your beloved and ever lamented Mother, your Father admitted to me that he had no funds or means of support and requested me to pay on his behalf, 600 r. out of the 1,000 r. that I had to the Hon. Lubowidzki to whom he had been in debt since 1864. This I did—and so out of your Mother's 1,000 r. 400 r. was left for you. I undertook to

	Capital Expenditure	
	R. Kop.	R. Kop.
give 400 r. regularly each year for your maintenance. Thus during the year 1865, I sent your Father in April, July, and October, the quarterly remittance apart from 60 r. by way of interest . .	300	–
In January, March, June, and September of 1866, apart from the 24% interest on the remaining 400 . .	400	–

Doubtless you recollect having been taken in May 1866 from Chernikhov to Nowofastów where you spent the summer and then returned to Chernikhov with your Granny. In October because of ill-health you were taken for a cure to Kiev where you remained till the spring of 1867. You returned to Nowofastów in a better state of health, then went down with measles and were again taken to Żytomierz.

| Carried forward | 700 | – |

	Capital	Expenditure
	R. Kop.	R. Kop.
Brought forward		700 –
The cost to me of your treatment in		
roubles		485 –

Your dear Grandmother, who with the greatest devotion and disregarding her own strength and health watched constantly over you, must have spent the same amount again, for she accepted help from me only when her own resources were exhausted. From the moment of your arrival in this world your inestimable Grandmother bore constantly and unflinchingly all kinds of sacrifices. Our paternal Uncle, the late Mikołaj Bobrowski, died in 1866 leaving some small capital. Your Uncle Kazimierz insisted that this legacy should be equally divided into three parts, one of which was to be for you. In fact, you had no right as a descendant from the sister's side to inherit anything. I objected to it since your Uncle already had three children and I insisted on a division between the two of us, assuring him that I would leave you half of my share. I had two reasons for this, firstly I always wished you to have a share, but not in the form of a legacy, but as a gift from me, ensuring that it was I as the donor who would administer your money and not your father (who with the best possible character could never keep any money—especially as he was then both ill and heartbroken), whose sensitiveness was very well known to me and I felt sure that he would not interfere with the little donation remaining under my care. Thus, I decided to put aside for you half of my share as it gradually accrued from our paternal Uncle's estate and to secure it on my own property.

Carried forward		1,185 –

	Capital	Expenditure
	R. Kop.	R. Kop.
Brought forward		1,885

For the first time in January 1867, 5,000 r. was released—my share in it being 2,500 r.—therefore your account was credited with . . . . 1,250 —

In *January, March, July, and October 1867* I sent your father in roubles . . 425 —
for his maintenence, apart from 100 r. of the interest from the small capital deposited for you—may it become the basis of your independence, with God's help and the blessings of worthy people and in the memory of the deceased relation whose honest work it represents. This is my most sincere wish for you. From the 400 r. left from your Mother's estate, a further 150 r. was drawn by your father to cover a debt in Chernikhov—which means that only 250 r. was left . . 250 —

After having added it all, I drew up on the 4th March 1868 a formal deed of gift for *1,500 r.*, which is to be found among other deposits kept by me.

In January 1868 you and your father set off happily for Lvov—in January you both left Nowofastów where you— almost recovered—had been collected by your father. To cover the costs of the journey and the allowance for the first quarter, I supplied him with 200 r. Subsequently, in *April, July, and September* I sent him 100 r.—in addition to 100 r. being the interest for the year 1868; it all together amounted in that year to . . . . . . 500 —

In January of the same year we collected from the late paternal Uncle's inheritance from Countess Działyńska 1,000 r. and in September—1,500 r. In

Carried forward 1,500 — 2,110 —

	Capital R. Kop.	Expenditure R. Kop.

Brought forward

accordance with my decision, I entered for your credit in my books out of the half of the sum due to me. . . . **1,500 –** **2,110 –**

625 –

In 1869 at the beginning of January and in March I sent again to your father a further 200 r. Subsequently, during your father's illness in May, I sent c/o S. Buszczyński 100 r. I repaid Mr. Wł. Mniszek the funeral expenses incurred by him, amounting to 120 r. The total . **420 –**

After your father's death, your most beloved Grandmother took you at her own expense to the waters at Wartemberg —on her way back she was to leave you with Mr. Georgeon, with whom I have agreed on the terms for your education and lodging to the amount of 480 r.— appointing for your personal needs and clothing additionally 120 r. I sent to Mr. Georgeon to meet these expenses a half-yearly sum . . . . . **300 –**

In September having once again received from the paternal Uncle's bequest from Countess Działyńska 2,000 r. I deducted 500 r. for you from the 1,000 due to me . . . . . **500 –**

This will carry interest from the 10th January 1870, while for the year 1869 you are due to receive the interest on the sum of 2,125 r., that is 127 r. 50 kop. I have therefore decided in this matter that while your maintenance and education are costing more per annum than the 500 r. assigned by me—the 6% interest due will cover the extra expenditure. As soon, on the other hand, as the 500 r. from me meets your needs—the interest will be added to the capital. *In September*

Carried forward **2,625 –** **2,830 –**

188

	Capital R Kop.	Expenditure R. Kop.
Brought forward	2,625 –	2,830 –

of the same year, your cousin Miss Katarzyna Korzeniowska made you a present of a promissory note for 500 r. owed to her by Mrs. Johanna née de l'Arbron Bratkowska. The sum when received will be added to your capital. In November as you were living with your Grandmother in Cracow I sent her . over and above the 300 r. handed to her by Mr. Georgeon.

    100 –

In January 1870 because of personal misunderstandings with your relation Miss Katarzyna Korzeniowska and not wishing the promissory note for 500 r. to be deposited with me—I returned it to her. In March I sent 300 r. for your maintenance to Mr. Georgeon and I paid back 300 r. to Mrs. Pruszyńska, a friend of your parents. This money was borrowed back in 1864 from her grand-daughter, the late Mrs. Mniszkowa, by your father who had never mentioned this debt to me. .   .   .   .

    600 –

As I was certain of a new instalment coming from Countess Działyńska, I prepared a second deed of gift, again for 1,500 r., before departing abroad; this deed will also be found amongst my papers—it was formally drawn up in the presence of the *Public Notary* at Skwira. In June of that year, on my way through Cracow, I sent you to Krynica together with Mr. Pulman, using thus the remaining 50 gulden collected from the bookseller Igl out of the money previously sent by me to which I added another .

    150 –

In September on my instructions   . was again sent for your maintenance and

    300 –

| Carried forward | 2,625 – | 3,980 – |

| | Capital | Expenditure |
| | R. Kop. | R. Kop. |

Brought forward 2,625 –   3,980 –

as during this month the instalment of
1,000 r. arrived for me from Countess
Działyńska I have, therefore, added to
the balance in your favour . . .   500 –

In November, when your beloved
Grandmother returned from Italy, where
we were together, to Cracow, the widow
of your relation the late Onufry Korzeniowski brought to your Grandmother
a gift for you of 500 r. This sum was lent
by your Grandmother to your late
Father's friend, Mr. Stefan Buszczyński.
As your dear Grandmother had expressed
her wish to live with you in Cracow, I
declared that I would make an annual
addition for this purpose of 200 r. to the
600 r. given to you.

In March 1871 400 r. was sent for the
half-year's maintenance of you both—
out of this, for yourself . . .   300 –

In May I forwarded to Mr. Pulman   150 –
for the purpose of sending you to Krynica.

In September, on my return journey
home I paid Mr. Pulman for half a year's
maintenance for you and for half a year
in advance, as he needed it. In all I gave
him 500 r., of which 300 r. for you and
100 r. for P. . . . . .   400 –
During the same month I added to your
credit out of the Countess Działyńska's
payment . . . . . .   500 –

In October your relation Miss Katarzyna
Korzeniowska, carrying out the gift of
500 r. she had made earlier, brought this
sum to your Grandmother. The money
was used to buy securities. Consequently
you have *one thousand roubles* as a result
of the generosity of your father's relatives

Carried forward 3,625 –   4,830 –

	Capital R. Kop.	Expenditure R. Kop.
Brought forward	3,625 –	4,830 –

which I have left under the management of your most worthy Grandmother, and for the sake of order I shall record here its fluctuations.

In February 1872 I forwarded to your Grandmother 400 r., of which for your half-year's maintenance . . .   300 –

In May, out of the 500 r. deposited with Mr. Buszczyński, 150 r. was withdrawn for your journey to Krynica.

In September, out of the last instalment from Countess Działyńska I added on my balance sheet to your credit to round off the sum of 4,000 roubles (i.e. 250 r. left by your mother and 3,750 r. being half of   375 – the inheritance left by my late paternal Uncle and your Grandfather Mikołaj Bobrowski).

In September that year I forwarded 500 r. to your Grandmother, out of this for you and Mr. Pul. . . .   400 –
But this proved insufficient. On my arrival in Cracow, I discovered that your beloved Grandmother had got into debt partly in connexion with her own cure and partly because of the needs of both of you, so in order to cover these debts I disbursed 300 r., of which I am charging to your account . . . .   100 –

In February 1873 I sent your Grandmother 500 r. for a half-year's maintenance of which, according to our new expenses plan, I debited you with .   400 –
In May on doctor's orders it was decided to send you to Switzerland. Mr. Pulman accompanied you—you were to spend 6 weeks at the most—the estimated cost was to be 300 r.—for this purpose

| Carried forward | 4,000 – | 6,030 – |

	Capital R. Kop.	Expenditure R. Kop.
Brought forward	4,000 –	6,030 –

your Grandmother drew 200 r. out of the
sum deposited with Mr. Buszczyński—
moreover I sent her for the same purpose .... 100 –

But, because of the cholera which was
prevailing in Cracow, you remained away
from home nearly twice as long as was
intended and your Grandmother drew
the remaining 150 r. of the sum deposited
with Mr. B.—thus out of the 1,000 you
had had you were left with only 500 r.,
with which your Grandmother had already in 1871 purchased securities, yielding 5 % to the value of 1,000 Austrian
gulden. We decided that your Grandmother should take up her residence in
Warsaw, and that you should be put in
the care of your relation Mr. Antoni
Syroczyński and that is what was done.
Then I went to Cracow to establish you
there and to see Mother off to Warsaw.

In September, I sent you off to Lvov to
Uncle Antoni. To cover the costs of your
naturalization in Austria, I paid a solicitor
20 r. and your equipment cost 70 r. ...... 90 –

For half a year's maintenance and education I sent through you to Uncle Antoni ...... 350 –

From now on, nothing but your needs
and expenses will be entered here, as you
have parted from your dear Grandmother
and you have left her immediate care in
order to go out into the world—God
grant that you may be as happy there as
when your beloved Grandmother kept
her eye on you and you were so close to
her heart—this will certainly not be so
but what happens to you will give you a
truer picture of what is awaiting you in
life. The worthy guardianship to which

Carried forward	4,000 –	6,570 –

	Capital R. Kop.	Expenditure R. Kop.
Brought forward	4,000 –	6,570 –

I have entrusted you will help to harden you, which is something that every man needs in this life.

In February 1874 to cover your education and other needs I sent your Uncle Antoni . . . . . .   350 –

In September on my arrival in Cracow and Lvov in order to send you off to the Merchant Marine which you had been continually badgering me about for two years, *I repaid* Mr. Antoni and Mr. Leon Syroczyński the 190 Austrian gulden for your maintenance during the vacation. On your clothing and various other items, I spent 119 gulden. To the solicitor who, unsuccessfully, occupied himself with your naturalization in Austria— 80·50 gulden. Your twenty-five days' stay in Cracow cost 43 gulden. Finally, your journey to Marseilles cost 137·75 gulden and as I couldn't afford more than 450 roubles for your maintenance for that half-year, I was obliged to sell for 841 gulden the 1,000 gulden in securities (purchase of which is mentioned above) —so that part of this money would cover the difference between the actual expenses and the sum appointed for your maintenance, as can be seen from the detailed account under the date of 3/15 October 1874. I had to spend out of your money 341 gulden. *Thus you were left with 500 gulden*—which were deposited on my account in the Bank of Trade and Industry of Galicia . . . .   G. 500 –

I paid part of the cost of equipping you and sending you to the Merchant Marine;   150 –

| Carried forward | 4,000
500 gulden | 7,070 – |

193   o

	Capital		Expenditure	
	R.	Kop.	R.	Kop.
Brought forward	4,000	–	7,070	–
	500 gulden			

Likewise I have deposited in the same
Bank (in Cracow) your half-yearly allowance from the 3/15 October 1874. . .   300   –

On the *14th December* I sent to
Marseilles as reimbursement of the addi-
tional money spent by Messrs. Chodźko
and Solary, also through the Cracow
Bank and the House of Frayssinet in
Marseilles, 250 fr., i.e. . . .   75   –

At about the same time I was informed
by Mrs. Justyna Syroczyńska that Miss
Katarzyna Korzeniowska had given instructions to deposit in the Savings Bank
in Lvov one thousand Rhenish 1,000—
thus for the second time your kind relative
has given you . . . . .   G. 1,000 –

In 1875 I sent to Cracow to the Bank
of Trade and Industry of Galicia 300
roubles   300   –
to cover your half-yearly allowance from
the 3/15 April 1875.

Likewise *in July* I sent through the
same channel to Mr. Wiktor Chodźko
for looking after you   60   –

In September again through the B. of
T. and I. of G. your half-yearly allowance until 3/15 April 1876 . .   300   –

In November, at your request, for the
return journey from Havre to Marseilles
I dispatched directly through the Post
Office to Havre   100   –

On the 23rd March 1876 via the B. of
T. and I. of G. for your allowance from
15th March until 3/15 August 1876.   300   –

Carried forward   4,000 roubles
1,500 gulden
8505   –

	Capital		Expenditure	
	R.	Kop.	R.	Kop.
Brought forward	4,000	–	8505	–
	1,500 gulden			

I learned from Mr. Wiktor Chodźko's letter of 5th April that you had drawn from the Bank in one sum your allowance for the eight months from January till October of that year, and having lent it (or possibly squandered it) you are in need. Subsequently, in May, you wrote to me apologizing but not offering any clear explanation. At last on the 21st May you sent a telegram requesting an order for *700 fr.* which was paid out to you on the 2nd July; again in answer to another telegraphic request I ordered 400 fr. to be paid out to you, and on departing from Marseilles you wrote asking me to pay 165 fr. to a friend of yours—Mr. Bonnard, who had lent you this sum and so I did. Thus in the course of three months you *spent over and above* your allowance 1,265 fr. that is 664 gulden. As it is only fair that everyone should be made to pay for his own follies out of his own pocket and as I lack an extraordinary income for covering the extraordinary expenditure of my nephew, therefore for this purpose *your own 500 gulden* (out of the gift of Miss Korzeniowska) deposited in the Bank of Galicia (see the previous page) were used for this purpose, and I took responsibility for the remaining 166 g. The bill amounted to .   .   .   .   . 150 –

After your youthful escapade you were left with only 1,000 gulden out of your own money .   .   .   . G. 1,000

On the 16th October I sent to Cracow

Carried forward	4,000	8,655	–
	1,000 gulden		

	Capital	Expenditure
	R. Kop.	R. Kop.
Brought forward	4000 –	8,655 –
	1,000 gulden	

to the Bank of Trade and Industry of
Galicia, to cover your half-yearly allowance from 3/15 October . . .   300 –

On the 22nd March 1877 to the same
Bank for the same purpose, for your
allowance from March till October .   300 –

In September 1877 I sent you via Mr.
Antoni Syroczyński your half-yearly
allowance (from 15th October till 15th
April 1878) of 1,000 fr. equal to.   400 –

Informed by you of your intention to
set off with Capt. d'Escarras on a voyage
round the world lasting a year and a half
or two years, I asked Mr. A. S. to forward
to you 1,000 fr. out of the 1,000 gulden
deposited in the Savings Bank. Subsequently, as a result of your insistence
that this 2,000 fr. was insufficient, I asked
in December for another 1,000 fr. to be
forwarded to you from the same source,
intending to cover this sum out of the allowance due to you during your absence.

In February 1878 in Kiev I received a
request from Mr. Bonnard to meet your
bill of exchange for 1,000 fr., and almost
simultaneously I got news from Mr.
Fecht that you had shot yourself. Thus at
the end of February I hastened direct
from Kiev to Marseilles where I found
you already out of bed and learned that
for reasons beyond your control you had
been unable to go with Mr. Escarras and
that the 2,000 fr. sent to you via Mr.
A. S. had been lost in speculation, as you
maintained, the truth of which I saw no
need to investigate—and that you had

Carried forward	4,000	9,655 –
	1,000 gulden	

| | Capital | Expenditure |
| | R. Kop. | R. Kop. |

Brought forward 4,000 – 9,655 –
1,000 gulden

got into debt. I paid your debts for you as
follows: *Mr. Al. de Toussaint* (Fecht,
Richard) 1,706 fr., *Mr. Bonnard* 1,000
fr., *Mrs. Tagor* the housekeeper 233 fr.
and the *doctor* 700 fr.—in all 3,009 fr.
equal in roubles to .   .   .   .   1,228 –

Apart from this the cost of my journey
to Marseilles and the fortnight I stayed
there amounted to .   .   .   .   328 –

Taking your needs into consideration,
I decided to keep up your allowance of
2,400 fr. per annum and therefore
handed to Mr. Fecht 1,200 fr. to cover
the first half of the year, from the 15th
April till the 15th October .   .   .   468 –

Apart from this I gave you 110 fr.,
the balance of the 1,000 gulden belonging to you of which already 2,000 fr. had
been sent to you and squandered irretrie-
vably and, what was worse, quite unpro-
ductively.[1] This is the nice position you
got yourself into. I trust it will serve you
as a lesson for the future. If not—it will
be all the worse for you.

Carried forward 4,000 – 11,679 –

[1] The following receipt was published in *Echo Tygodnia*, Cracow, 1929, No 31:

Dated 12th/24th March 1878,
Marseilles

I hereby declare that from the bequest of my relation Katarzyna Nałęcz Korzeniowska made in December 1875 and deposited in the Savings Bank in the City of Lvov amounting in Austrian currency One Thousand Gulden I have received from Mr. Antoni Syroczyń-ski to whom the above-named bequest was entrusted at the request of my Uncle and Guardian Tadeusz Bobrowski:

in June 1877 200 francs, i.e. 98 gulden
in November 1877 1,000 francs, i.e. 488 gulden
in December 1877 1,000 francs, i.e. 500 gulden
on today's date 111 francs, i.e. 54 gulden

The total capital together with the interest in Austrian currency *One thousand One hundred and Forty gulden.*

Konrad Korzeniowsk

Tadeusz Bobrowski, Guardian.

	Capital R. Kop.	Expenditure R. Kop.
Brought forward	4,000 –	11,679 –

Having collected your allowance from Mr. Fecht you set off on an English ship for Lowestoft and there again you committed another absurdity—having quarrelled with the Captain, which you might have been justified in doing, you then went to London and there frittered away prematurely the remainder of your allowance. As a consequence, in answer to your and Mr. Fecht's renewed appeal for help, I sent via Warsaw and Mr. Fecht *600 fr.* . . . . . — 240 –

In September, as it was due, I sent through Kiev your half-yearly allowance of *1,200 fr.* till 1/15 April 1879 . — 476 –
This money, after all your necessities for the long voyage had been paid for, proved to be insufficient and therefore I again sent through Mr. Fecht £5, which you had asked for, to be forwarded to you to Sydney. . . . . . . — 50 –

1879 Because of your sailing for Australia the allowance due to you on the 1/15 April was not dispatched to Mr. Fecht (the firm of Toussaint) until *July.* The sum amounted to *1,200 fr.* and was sent through Odessa which cost . . . — 479 –

On your return in October you found almost the entire half-yearly allowance saved and you therefore wrote to me yourself that you would be able to manage if I sent you £20 so I sent you again via Odessa 500 fr. which amounted to — 194 –

Thus I was able to recover for myself the 725 fr. spent over and above your allowance last year.

1880 in March your allowance of *1,200 fr.* which was due on the 3/15

Carried forward	4,000 –	13,118 –

198

	Capital		Expenditure	
	R.	Kop.	R.	Kop.
Brought forward	4,000	–	13,118	–

April was dispatched via Odessa and
Marseilles (Mr. Fecht) . . .   457 –
—and in September via Odessa and
Marseilles (Mr. Fecht) your allowance
of *1,200 fr.* due on 3/15 October .   467 –
1881 in March via Odessa and
Marseilles (Mr. Fecht) allowance of
1,200 fr. due for the 3/15 April . .   467
was sent together with an intimation that
starting on the 3/15 October I should be
giving you only half of the present
allowance, i.e. 600 fr. twice a year, the
reason for this being that I had helped to
a point where you could stand on your
own feet and that you would be 24 years
old on November 21st which is old
enough to support oneself. I undertook
to keep up this reduced allowance for
another three years.—In August having
learned about the shipwreck of *Anna
Frost* £10 . . . . .   100 –
—in October from Montreux the reduced half-yearly allowance from the
3/15 October 1881 to the 3/15 [April]
1882 which I rounded off to £25 half-
yearly, sent to Mr. W. Ward in London   260 –
In April 1882 £25 as your allowance
from the 3/15 March 1882 sent to Mr.
Ward via Odessa to London . .   250 –
—in November £25 as your allowance
from 3/15 October 1882 sent to Mr.
Krieger via Odessa to London . .   260 –
In April *1883* £25 as your allowance
from 3/15 April sent to Mr. Krieger in
London via Odessa . . . .   256 –
During July and August we saw each
other a month in Marienbad and Teplitz,
this being for both of us a mutual pleasure.

| Carried forward | 4,000 | – | 15,635 | – |

	Capital	Expenditure
	R. Kop.	R. Kop.
Brought forward	4,000 –	15,635 –

At that time we discussed at great length
your plans for the future. We talked
about a partnership with Messrs. Krieger
and Möring. I promised to advance in
the course of the following year between
£300 and £350—considering this money
as part of the sum which I shall leave you
in my will. Meantime I gave you £25 for
your naturalization, £10 for the cost of
your voyage, and £5 for presents . .   400 –

The cost of your month's stay in
Marienbad and Teplitz was 181 gulden   150 –

1884—in February, in accordance
with my promise, I dispatched via Odessa
£350 c/o Mr. Adolf Krieger, your
partner and plenipotentiary. The cost of
it was . . . . . .   3,600 –

Consequently you were left with only
400 r. out of the capital left to you by my
late paternal uncle. May this sum serve
you for building up your future. I know
men who started with less than this and
yet scrambled through. As I had informed
you that after this payment I must curtail
your allowance accordingly—I shall give
you henceforth only £30 a year. Likewise in July I sent via Odessa c/o Mr.
Krieger £30 . . . . .   305 –

1885—in September I sent £30 c/o
Barr Möring & Cie, London . .   311 –

1886 in October again to the same
address I sent £30 for the year 1886 .   315 –

In the same month Konrad passed his
examination for a master's certificate and
his name was entered on the Captain
Register[1]—proof of which is shown both
by a letter and by a newspaper cutting.

Carried forward	7,600 –	17,454·70

[1] Two words in English in the original.

| | Capital | Expenditure |
| | R. Kop. | R. Kop. |

Brought forward 7,600 –   17,454 –

1887—in September I sent via Odessa
to the above address £30 the cost of which
was 338 70

In view of the fact that in November
you will reach the age of thirty, by which
time everyone ought to be self-supporting,
and moreover because the education of
the late Kazimierz's children is costing
more, I told you that I must discontinue
a regular allowance. This I intend to do
and must do. *Thus the making of a man out
of Mr. Konrad has cost*—apart from the
3,600 given you as capital   .   .   .   17,454 –

1889 In May in the 49th issue of
Peterburgskye Senatskye Vyedomosti[1]
your release from subjection of the
Russian Empire was published.

In June you returned after three years
sailing the Indian Sea and as you had to
increase your share in the partnership
Barr Möring et Cie, I sent you on the
4th May via Odessa the remainder of the
capital intended by me for you. This
amounted to   .   .   .   .   .   400 –
for which a sum of £42. 6. 6 was obtained.

8,000 –   17,454 –

1890—on the 4th February you
visited me at Kazimierówka and I am
availing myself of this opportunity to
hand over to you this statement together
with my cordial blessing for your future.

Your loving Uncle,
T. BOBROWSKI.

Information which might be useful to you.

Your parents were married in Oratów in 1856.
Your were born on the 21st November 1857, at Berdyczów.

[1] Senate's News of Petersburg.

Your baptism took place in Żytomierz in 1860.
Your birth certificate can be found at Żytomierz in the Rom. Cath.
Consistory.
The Korzeniowski family—nobility of Podolia. Their family
documents can be found in the Noblemen Association of the
Province of Podolia in the district of Winnica where your Grand-
father Teodor Korzeniowski owned the village of Pieńkówka
brought to him as a dowry by his wife.
Your father was born in 1820, but I do not know either his birth-
place or the parish where he was baptized.

Addresses of the Executors of my Will:

Stanisław Syroczyński: Province of Kiev, Station Ilińce, village of
Jurkowce.
Tadeusz Florkowski : Province of Kiev, Station Lipowiec, village of
Skała.
Stanisław Zaleski with whom your title to 15,000 roubles is
deposited—Province of Kiev, Station Skwira, village of Śnieżna.

Konrad's property to be found in my house:

1. 17th-century antique clock, 'Ave Maria'.
2. A black canteen with table silver for 12 people marked with the
   family crest; spoons, knives, forks twelve of each. One ladle, one
   serving spoon, nine small spoons. That is how I received it on the
   death of Konrad's parents.
3. Large silver-plated trays (Fraget).
4. Various small family souvenirs contained in an antique chest.
5. Table linen.

CONRAD'S LETTERS

1. *To Apollo Korzeniowski*[1]

[Terechowa, 23 May 1861]

Daddy,

I am fine here, I run about the garden—but I don't like it much when the mosquitos bite. As soon as the rain stops I will come to you. Olutek has sent me a beautiful little whip. Please Daddy dear lend me a few pennies and buy something for Olutek in Warsaw.

Have you been to see this Bozia,[2] which Granny?

KONRAD.

2. *To Stefan Buszczyński*[3]

Teplitz.
14th August, 1883.

Dear and Honourable Sir,

We had hoped—Uncle Tadeusz and I—that we would be able to meet you here, in Teplitz; but we have learned upon our arrival of your departure.

Therefore, being unable personally to remind you of myself and to obtain your indulgence for all my faults, I hasten to do it in writing, enclosing my photograph, in the hopes that in memory of the friendship for the father the son will find a friendly remembrance, and for his letter—even after such a long silence—a kind reception.

Although I have been long away from my country and apparently forgetful of those whose favour I once experienced, I have never, in fact, forgotten either the country, the family, or those who were so kind to me—amongst whom I number you, dear Sir, my guardian when I was orphaned, and who amongst them must take the first place.

I, therefore, permit myself to ask you to remember me to dear Kostuś[4]—if I may venture to call him thus. True! I have given him every reason to forget the friendly relations between us in Cracow:—I shall never forget them although they seem so long ago! Perhaps he too will be good enough to remember those old

[1] This letter, probably Conrad's first written piece, is part of Ewa Korzeniowska's letter to her husband. Conrad's hand was guided by his mother. Text in *Kobieta Współczesna*, Lwów 1931, No. 17.

[2] 'Bozia' [literally 'little God'] is the name used by Polish children for God and for the effigies of God. The boy had most probably in mind the celebrated crucifix in Warsaw cathedral.

[3] The original is in the Library of the Polish Academy of Sciences, Cracow, sign. 2064 t. iii k. 433–4. Paper with a monogram of superimposed letters 'C' and 'K' pressed on.

[4] Stefan's son Konstanty (1856–1921).

205

days, and will accept from me my heartfelt good wishes and a friendly embrace.

I am leaving here for London in a few days; from there I do not know where fate will take me. During the last few years—that is since my first examination, I have not been too happy in my journeyings. I was nearly drowned, nearly got burned, but generally my health is good, I am not short of courage or of the will to work or of love for my profession; and I always remember what you said when I was leaving Cracow: 'Remember'—you said—'wherever you may sail you are sailing towards Poland!'

That I have never forgotten, and never will forget!

In the hope that my sins will be forgiven me, and commending myself to your kind memory, I remain, with affection, gratitude, and the highest regards,

Your humble servant,
KONRAD N. KORZENIOWSKI.

3. *To Aleksander Poradowski*[1]

16th January, 1890

My dear Uncle.

I have just had a letter from Kazimierówka, in which, in reply to my inquiry, Uncle Tadeusz tells me that you are living in Brussels and gives me your address. I am terribly sorry that I did not know this earlier, as I was in Brussels in October last year. It is possible, however, that before long I shall have to visit Brussels again. The object of this scrawl to you is to remember myself to the relation whose great kindness to me in Cracow I have certainly not forgotten. I do not ask whether you will permit me to visit you—for I permit myself not to doubt it; but I would very much like to be certain that you are in Brussels and that I shall be able to find you there in the course of the next month.

I returned to London six months ago after a three years' absence. Of these three years I spent one among the islands of the Malay Archipelago, after which I spent two years as master of an Australian vessel in the Pacific and Indian Oceans.[2] I am now more or less under contract to the 'Société Belge pour le Commerce du Haut Congo' to be master of one of its river steamers. I have not signed

---

[1] This, as well as the two subsequent letters to A. Poradowski, is preserved in the Rare Book Room of Yale University Library. All three are written on paper with printed letterhead: The British and Foreign Transit Agency. Barr, Moering & Co., Shipping and Custom House Agents, 36, Camomile Street, London, E.C.

[2] Actually Conrad left London in February 1887 and came back in June 1889; he commanded the barque *Otago* between January 1888 and April 1889.

any agreement, but Mr. A. Thys, the director of that Company, has promised me the post. Whether he will keep his promise and when he will send me to Africa, I do not yet know; it will probably be in May.

I intend to visit Uncle Tadeusz soon; that is to say I want to, and he also wants me to; but he says that it is difficult during the winter. I am expecting a letter from him in a few days' time, which will decide the matter. If I do go home it will be via Hamburg— returning via Brussels. If, however, my visit is postponed I shall nevertheless be going to Brussels in March in connexion with the post in the Congo. Therefore in any case I shall have the pleasure of seeing you, my dear Uncle, and of making myself known to Aunt Poradowska whom I only know from that portrait of her which you had with you in Cracow.

In the meantime, my dear Uncle, a most cordial embrace from your affectionate relation and servant,

KONRAD KORZENIOWSKI.

A letter care of Messrs. Barr Moering will always find me.

4. *To Aleksander Poradowski*

[London] 20 January, 1890.

Dear Uncle,

My most affectionate thanks to you and to Aunt for the kind expressions contained in your letter. The sight of your handwriting gave me inexpressible pleasure, but, alas, my joy was short-lived! The news of your poor state of health has grieved me greatly. Please, do not trouble to answer this letter. I hasten to inform you that in view of the state of your health, I have decided to come home via Brussels. I realize that after the operation you will need not visits but a complete rest. This morning I received, simultaneously with your letter, one from Uncle Tadeusz that says 'come'. However, those villains in the Russian Consulate do not want to grant me a visa—which means further delay, inconvenience, and visits to the Embassy, perhaps to no avail.

I shall let you know how I am getting on as soon as I settle matters with these pirates. And so, au revoir to you, my dearest Uncle. I kiss the hands of dear Aunt.

Your loving and devoted nephew and servant.

KONRAD.

My apologies for the scrawl, but I have barely time to catch the post.

5. *To Aleksander Poradowski*

[London] 31 January, 1890.

My dearest Uncle.

I am already in possession of all the necessary documents and intend to leave London next Tuesday or, at the latest, Wednesday, but not later, via Brussels of course. I shall, therefore, arrive at your place on Wednesday or Thursday and if you allow me I shall stay there 24 hours. I would not like to cause any embarrassment to dear Aunt—especially as you are not well. I could spend the night at an hotel and the day with you both 's'il n'y a pas d'empêchement'. When I leave you we shall say to each other 'see you soon', for I shall come back again shortly, via Brussels of course. A thousand embraces.

I shall come to you directly from the station.

Your loving,
K. N. KORZENIOWSKI.

6. *To Gustaw Sobotkiewicz*[1]

17/29 March, 1890
Kazimierówka

Dear and Honourable Sir,

I thank you heartily a thousand times for the kind and friendly words addressed to me in your letter to my Uncle. That I have not forgotten those who in their kindness remembered me may be witnessed by my letters to Uncle, in which I frequently asked after you and your daughter—not out of good manners—a quality which my way of life has not done much to develop—but out of a yearning from my heart which has not forgotten the good old times. And were they really so long ago? My later life has been so different, so unlike the life that I began, that those earlier impressions, feelings and memories have in no way been erased. And now, reading your letter, they are revived more clearly than ever.

I am extremely sorry that circumstances do not permit me to

---

[1] *Tygodnik Powszechny*, Cracow, 1959, No. 13. The original is in the possession of Miss M. Korniłowicz, Zakopane. Gustaw Sobotkiewicz was a distant relation of the Korzeniowskis.

return through Cracow. I came here through Warsaw in order to reach my Uncle as soon as possible, and now I must go back the same way, so as to see the family in Radom, and to get back to London in time.

Although I am sorry to hear you speak of your journey to the last port of call in this life—a port from which there is no return, I have seen so many people living long years on the edge of eternity; indeed I myself have so often seen, as I thought, its portals, that I well know how illusory those presentiments are.

Your health will surely mend, and you will stay fit! Please allow me—as I set out on a long journey, with your blessing—to go away in the hope that in the near future—a year or two—I shall have the joy of seeing you and of thanking you personally for your kindness—which is so dear to me.

I thank Mrs. Dębowska[1]—whom I remember so well as Miss Marya sitting in a highlander's carriage together with you, somewhere on the Hungarian frontier—with all my heart for remembering me so kindly. Of our comrade on that excursion—Pulman—who so determinedly ran from mountain hut to mountain hut asking the way—I have news only from my Uncle, who refuses to accept the tragic story of his death in the flames of the burning Vienna theatre as not being in accordance with the documents in the archives of Kazimierówka. Probably he is living at Sambir,[2] but I do not know how he is getting on.

Hoping that both you, honoured Sir, and your daughter will continue to remember me, I am,

> Your grateful and humble servant,
> K. N. KORZENIOWSKI.

7. To Maria Tyszkowa[3]

London, 2nd May, 1890.

My dear Maryleczka.

I could not write any sooner. I have been extremely busy and in fact still am so. In four days' time I am sailing to the Congo, and

[1] Sobotkiewicz's daughter; the correct spelling of her name is Dembowska.
[2] An interesting *lapsus linguæ*. Adam Pulman, Conrad's tutor in his Cracow days (cf. footnote to Bobrowski's letter of 30 August/10 September 1881), lived for some time in Sambor (Galicia). At the time of writing this letter Conrad was busy composing the first chapters of *Almayer's Folly*, set in 'Sambir' (actually Berouw) in Borneo.
[3] Conrad's letters to Maria Tyszkowa (born Bobrowska, daughter of Kazimierz Bobrowski) were published in *Ruch Literacki*, Warsaw 1927, No. 5.

I have to prepare myself for a three years' stay in Central Africa. You can, therefore, imagine how precious each minute is to me. I hope that your Mother is better now and that you, my dear, will soon be writing to me. Probably your letter will be too late to find me in Europe, but it is certain to be forwarded to me. Do not be surprised by the delay in getting a reply; no one can tell where your letter will eventually catch up with me.

Please explain to Zunia[1] and Marcia[2] my reasons for not writing to them. I am sorry indeed! My photographs will not be ready till after my departure. I am leaving addressed envelopes ready for posting them. That is why you will find the photographs unsigned and no letter enclosed. So you see, my dear Maryleczka, how sad the situation is. I doubt even if I shall have time to write a few words to Stanis.[3] and Tadzio.[4] Please act as my intermediary with the family. Embrace them all on my behalf and ask for kind remembrances of the wanderer.

My best regards for Mr. and Mrs. Meresch, Mr. and Mrs. Dąbrowski, and Mr. Tyszka.[5] I kiss my Aunt's hands and embrace you a thousandfold, commending myself to your heart.

Your loving,
K. N. KORZENIOWSKI.

8. *To Maria Tyszkowa*

London, 6th May, 1890.

Maryleczka dear,

I am sailing in an hour. As soon as the photographs are ready I shall send a letter.

The second photograph is for dear Marcia. I shall send a separate one for Aunt. Embraces and best regards for all,

Your loving,
K. N. KORZENIOWSKI.

I am sending one separately for Zunia as well.

---

[1] Zuzanna Meresch, née Bobrowska, addressee's sister.
[2] Marta Dąbrowska, née Bobrowska, addressee's sister.
[3] Stanisław Bobrowski, addressee's brother.
[4] Tadeusz Bobrowski, addressee's brother.
[5] Teodor Tyszka, addressee's fiancée.

9. *To Karol Zagórski*[1]

Freetown, Sierra Leone,
22nd May, 1890.

My dearest Karol!

It is just a month today since you were scandalized by my hurried departure from Lublin.[2] From the date and address of this letter you will see that I have had to be pretty quick, and I am only just beginning to breathe a little more calmly. If you only knew the devilish haste I had to make! From London to Brussels, and back again to London! And then again I dashed full tilt to Brussels! If you had ony seen lall the tin boxes and revolvers, the high boots and the tender farewells; just another handshake and just another pair of trousers!—and if you knew all the bottles of medicine and all the affectionate wishes I took away with me, you would understand in what a typhoon, cyclone, hurricane, earthquake—no!—in what a universal cataclysm, in what a fantastic atmosphere of mixed shopping, business, and affecting scenes, I passed two whole weeks. But the fortnight spent at sea has allowed me to rest and I am impatiently waiting for the end of this trip. I am due to reach Boma on the 7th of next month and then leave with my caravan to go to Leopoldville.[3] As far as I can make out from my 'lettre d'instruction' I am destined to the command of a steamboat, belonging to M. Delcommune's exploring party, which is being got ready. I like this prospect very much, but I know nothing for certain as everything is supposed to be kept secret. What makes me rather uneasy is the information that 60 per cent. of our Company's employés return to Europe before they have completed even six months' service. Fever and dysentery! There are others who are sent home in a hurry at the end of a year, so that they shouldn't die in the Congo. God forbid! It would spoil the statistics which are excellent, you see! In a word, there are only 7 per cent. who can do their three years' service. It's a fact! To tell the truth, they are French! Des nevrosés! (C'est très chic d'être nevrosé—one winks and speaks through the nose.) Yes! But a Polish nobleman, cased in British tar! What a concoction! Nous verrons! In any case I shall console myself by

[1] Out of 13 existing Conrad letters to the Zagórskis 3 only had been published in the original Polish before they perished during the Warsaw rising in 1944. Jean-Aubry published all these letters in an English translation in his *Joseph Conrad: Life & Letters*, Heinemann 1927, vol. i, but with numerous mistakes and omissions. The present text is based on the collation of the published English translation and a manuscript of a French translation (fuller and more precise), preserved in Jean-Aubry's archives, now in Yale University Library.

[2] Conrad spent two days in Lublin on his way back from Kazimierówka.

[3] He arrived at Boma on 12 June and left for Leopoldville (from Matadi) on the 28th.

remembering—faithful to our national traditions—that I looked for this trouble myself.[1]

When you see—with the help of a microscope, no doubt—the hieroglyphics of my handwriting, you will, I expect, wonder why I am writing to you? First, because it is a pleasure to talk to you; next, because, considering the distinguished personage who is penning this autograph, it ought to be a pleasure to you too. You can bequeath it to your children. Future generations will read it with admiration (and I hope with profit). In the meantime, trêve de bêtises!

I kiss my dear uncle's and aunt's[2] hands, and your wife's too. I forget none of you, but can't write the whole list because this abominable lamp is going out.

Yours very affectionately
K. N. KORZENIOWSKI.

10. *To Maria Tyszkowa*

Kinchassa,
Stanley Pool,
Congo.
24th September, 1890.

My dear Maryleczka,

Your letter and the photograph reached me today and I hasten to write and explain to you the long interruption in our correspondence.

I have been on the river Congo, some 2,000 versts from the coast where the post office is, so I could neither send nor get news from Europe. I was pleased to get your letter although at the same time it saddened me slightly. I have lived long enough to realize that life is full of griefs and sorrows which no one can escape, nevertheless I cannot help feeling sad at the thought that people whom I love must suffer, and are suffering. It is nonetheless pleasing to get a proof of the trust you place in me by writing openly about your worries. Indeed, I do not deserve to have a place in your hearts—for I am practically a stranger to you—nevertheless the affectionate words you have written are most precious to me. I shall carefully preserve them in my heart, and the photograph will be in my album so that I can glance each day at my dear little sister.

---

[1] A Polish proverb in the original.
[2] Addressee's parents: Jan Zagórski and Gabriela (Gabrynia, Gaba), née Poradowska.

To Maria Tyszkowa (24 September 1890)

Now that you are married[1] and your desires fulfilled my wish for you both is that your lives will be nothing but sunshine with no clouds in the sky. Please, assure your husband of my deep esteem, and of the very friendly feelings I have for him. I accept your invitation with gratitude and I promise to devote as much time as possible to my good lady sister. I trust that Aunt's health will improve steadily now that all the unpleasant contacts are left behind. I have a letter from Uncle Tadeusz, who intended to visit you in August. He is probably back home by now.

I am very busy with all the preparations for a new expedition to the River Kassai. In a few days I shall probably be leaving Kinchassa again for a few months, possibly even for a year or longer. Thus you must not be surprised if you get no sign of life from me for a long time.

My love to dear Zuzia and my apologies for not having written to her. Please send me her exact address—and your new one as well. I kiss dear Aunt's hands. I commend myself to your thoughts and especially to your heart, dear Maryleczka.

Do not forget about me amidst all the new events in your life. I embrace you most warmly.

Your always loving brother,
K. N. KORZENIOWSKI.

11. *To Maria Tyszkowa*

London,
15th April, 1891.

My dearest Maryleczka!

Your letter of the 24th February found me ill, and that sickness of mine lasted so long that it has been impossible for me to answer you sooner. Do not suspect me of indifference—or even of laziness. I was in bed for two months. I got up not long ago and for three weeks my hands were so swollen that I only managed with the greatest difficulty to write a few words to my Uncle. Thank God, you yourself are well again, my dear sister! You say that you will be leaving Elżbiecin, but you do not say why,—I hope that you will let me know the reason—that is if I may be permitted to know it. I thought that you intended to stay there permanently. As to troubles—who has not got them? But you, surrounded as you are

---

[1] Maria Bobrowka married Teodor Tyszka on 15 July 1890.

with the loving care of good and kind Teodor, can bear them more easily than those who have to struggle through life alone.

With my whole heart I congratulate dear Zunia and Marcia on the birth of their children. From afar I participate in their joy, commending myself to the kind thoughts of both their households.

A warm handshake for dear Teodor, and I kiss both your hands. I embrace you a thousandfold.

Your loving brother,
K. N. KORZENIOWSKI.

I kiss Aunt's hand and commend myself to her heart.

12. *To Maria Tyszkowa*

London, 8th September, 1892.

Dear Maryleczka,

Thank you for your very kind letter which I found here on my return. I can't imagine why they did not forward it to me to Australia,—anyway that is what has happened and so through no fault of mine the reply is delayed.

I am sad to learn of your troubles and worries. From Uncle's letters I already knew of Stanisław's unhappy case and I can well imagine your anxiety and sorrow.[1] Generally the news from home is far from cheerful.

I congratulate you both on the arrival of your daughter, and I shall endeavour to come as soon as possible in order to have the joy of making her acquaintance. I am afraid, however, that it will not be possible until next year. You did not say what name you have given to the young lady?

I am myself, dear Marylcia, such a bad correspondent that I would never dream of blaming anyone for not writing. But I am always glad to receive a token that I am not forgotten and I value it all the more because I feel myself unworthy of it.

I returned from Australia on the 3rd of this month and I am going back there again on the same ship, on the 20th October. At the end of July I shall probably return from that voyage and shall then take 6 weeks' leave to visit Uncle and all of you. Till then I shall live in the hope of finding you all healthy and happier than you have been this year. My own health is not at all bad, but still rather uncertain, and the less we say about my happiness, the better. From the worthy Tadeusz I have also received a letter written in

[1] Cf. Bobrowski's letters to Conrad of 2/14 July and 6/18 September 1892.

May like yours. I am answering it today. I thank your husband for remembering me so kindly and I send him a warm handshake— My brotherly embraces to you and many kisses for Miss Tyszka.

Your brother,
KONRAD KORZENIOWSKI.

Kiss Zunia for me and give my regards to Mr. Meresch.

13. *To Karol Zagórski*[1]

17, Gillingham Street,
London, S.W.
10th March, 1896.

My dear Karol,

Once again I am posting to you my masterpiece[2] (this time the second one). Last year I sent three copies of my novel to Poland. Two of them reached their destinations. The third one, destined for you and your wife—presumably did not. I am trying again, hoping that this time both the book and the letter will reach you.

At the same time, I announce solemnly (as the occasion demands) to dear Aunt Gabrynia and to you both that I am getting married. No one can be more surprised at it than myself. However, I am not frightened at all, for as you know, I am accustomed to an adventurous life and to facing terrible dangers. Moreover, I have to avow that my betrothed does not give the impression of being at all dangerous. Jessie is her name; George her surname. She is a small, not at all striking-looking person (to tell the truth alas—rather plain!) who nevertheless is very dear to me. When I met her a year and a half ago she was earning her living in the City as a 'Typewriter' in an American business office of the 'Caligraph' company. Her father died three years ago. There are nine children in the family. The mother is a very decent woman (and I do not doubt very virtuous as well). However, I must confess that it is all the same to me, as vous comprenez?—I am not marrying the whole family. The wedding will take place on the 24th of this month and we shall leave London immediately so as to conceal from people's eyes our happiness (or our stupidity) amidst the wilderness and beauty of the coast of Brittany where I intend to rent a small house in some fishing village—probably in Plouaret or Pervengan (near St. Malo). There I shall start working on my third opus, for one

---

[1] *Pion*, Warsaw, 1934, No. 50.
[2] *An Outcast of the Islands*, published by Fisher Unwin.

has to write in order to live. A few days ago I was offered the command of a sailing vessel—the idea had pleased my Jessie (who likes the sea) but the terms were so unsatisfactory that in the end I refused. The literary profession is therefore my sole means of support. You will understand, my dear Karol, that if I have ventured into this field it is with the determination to achieve a reputation —in that sense I do not doubt my success. I know what I can do. It is therefore only a question of earning money—'Qui est une chose tout à fait à part du mérite littéraire'. That I do not feel too certain about—but as I need very little I am prepared to wait for it. I feel fairly confident about the future.

I hope that on the day of my wedding all of you—who are my whole family—will join me in your thoughts. I kiss the hands of my dear Aunt and ask for her blessing. I commend myself to your heart and to that of your wife.

Your loving
KONRAD KORZENIOWSKI.

14. *To Mrs. Aniela Zagórska*[1]

12.6.1896.
Ile-Grande — par Lannion

My dear Cousin,

Forgive my long silence: I have been ill. I had an attack of rheumatism in my hand and foot. This attack not only kept me in bed for two weeks, but it has so shaken me that I still feel giddy. What's more my hand is swollen, which doesn't make writing easy.

I cannot express to you, my dearest Aniela, what a great pleasure your letter has given me—seeing the news you sent me of you all and your so very artistic appreciation of my book.[2] The expressions in your letter inspire me with confidence and the desire to continue my work. I again read your letter today and it is with a fresh sense of gratitude that I send you my thanks.

Please forgive me for not being able to write a longer letter today. I am not yet recovered either in body or in mind. Fortunately before I was taken ill I was able to finish the first part of my new novel.[3] Naturally my illness has made my wife very tired, but otherwise she is well. As for me, I feel better and better every day.

[1] Jean-Aubry, English and French translations (cf. note to the letter of 22 May 1890).
[2] *An Outcast of the Islands*.
[3] *The Rescue*, at that time called *The Rescuer* and soon abandoned for *The Nigger of the 'Narcissus'*.

To Mrs. Aniela Zagórska (12 June 1896)

My dearest—I wish to be remembered to you all. I hope that you will find a moment to write to me. We shall stay here for three months longer.

Your very affectionate brother and servant,
K. N. KORZENIOWSKI.

15. To Karol and Aniela Zagórski[1]

Stanford-le-Hope, Essex
20th December, 1896

My dear Karol and Aniela,

The first Christmas is approaching which I am or shall be spending in the married state. And now, no longer singly so to speak, but jointly we send you our heartfelt wishes for your happiness, peace, and successes both great and small—for the latter constitute the essence of the joy of life. And we both beg our most gracious and dear Aunt that at this moment when families are united—if only for a moment, if only in thought—she should graciously remember us in her heart, which has known those whose memory guides our lives.

I planned to come to Poland[2] for the holidays—by Poland I mean you. It was a vague and timid plan although the desire behind it was warm enough. I did not write about it—I scarcely allowed myself the thought that perhaps it might be possible. Nevertheless the disappointment is acute. There will be no holiday for me this year, but I console myself with the thought that there is next year and will be other years—and wishes sometimes (although not often) are fulfilled. In the meantime I must work, for praise does not feed a man (not to speak of a man's wife!). Therefore I have been writing, writing endlessly—and now the sight of an inkwell and of a pen fill me with anger and horror;—but I go on writing! Do not be angry at the long periods of silence. The above is a sample of my state of mind,—and why should I fill your ears with the sound of my complaints? You can be sure that if there was any reason for self-congratulation I should at once come running to wag my tail!

Confidently, but I hope not brazenly, I commend myself to your hearts.

From the depth of my soul, your brother and servant.

KONRAD KORZENIOWSKI.

[1] *Droga*, Warsaw, 1928, No. 6.
[2] In the original 'kraj', i.e. home country.

217

16. *To Janina de Brunnow*[1]

Ivy Walls Farm,
Stanford-le-Hope,
Essex.
9th August, 97.

Chère Madame,

The gallant Fisher Unwin has just sent your letter on to me—as according to him his principles do not allow him to give the address of his authors to anyone at all! Anyhow it is I in person who am replying to the sign you have given me of your kind recollection.[2] My own is also very much alive! The sight of your signature has reawakened in me all the images of the past, the most happy moments of which were those I owe to your mother's kindness and to the childhood friendships—the delight of which is the better appreciated the further one has journeyed on the pilgrimage of life. Thus, once again I thank you for your kind thought!

Time that passes so gently is extremely cruel in its silence, and I hardly dare ask all I wish to know. Nevertheless I do wish to know! So, hoping that you will write me a long letter, I am, chère Madame, always your humble and devoted servant.

JPH CONRAD KORZENIOWSKI.

17. *To Janina de Brunnow*[3]

Ivy Walls Farm,
2nd October, 1897.

Chère Madame,

Please accept my most humble apologies for my apparent neglect in not answering your kind and charming letter from Krynica. It

[1] Conrad's letters to Janina de Brunnow, all written in French, were published by G. Jean-Aubry in *Joseph Conrad: Lettres françaises*, Gallimard, Paris, 1929. Address on the envelope of this letter: 'Madame la Baronne Jeanne de Brunnov, à Rudawa, poste Berestowica, Govt de Grodno, Russia'.

[2] Baroness Janina de Brunnow, born Taube, was Conrad's friend in Cracow in the early seventies. The Taube family consisted of four brothers (Aleksander, Artur, Roman, and Gustaw) and two sisters (Karolina and Janina). They lived in the same building as Conrad. After the death of their father Tadeusz Bobrowski became their guardian. Some writers assume that young Conrad was in love with Janina Taube and that she is the person mentioned as his first love in the Author's Note to *Nostromo* and in a cancelled opening to *The Arrow of Gold* (see J. Baines, *Joseph Conrad*, pp. 28–29), but there is little documentary evidence to support this hypothesis. On the other hand, according to the family tradition of the Taubes, Janina played a very important role in Conrad's emotional life—and not only in his youth.

[3] Envelope addressed: Madame la Baronne J. de Brunnow, Krynica, Galicie, Austria. Poste Restante.

To Janina de Brunnow (2 October 1897)

is only appearances however that make it seem a negligence, for I have never ceased to think of you; but, in fact, I was finishing one thing[1] and at the same time correcting another for publication,[2] while Blackwood, whom I promised a story for his November number, bombarded me with letter after letter asking for the manuscript. As you can see, I was really very busy and on top of all my wife's health was giving me anxiety—for which, happily, there is no longer any reason. It was not till today that I could find a free moment for correspondence—and you are the first person I am writing to. If only you could see the pile of letters on my table waiting to be answered, you would realize how close to my heart is my correspondence with you. For although I have little or no contacts at all in society, I correspond, firstly with a lot of people whom I do not know personally, then with others whom I like very much and also with some whom I must treat tactfully in order to keep to the path of my existence. But they can all wait till tomorrow and some of them have waited for months! But what can one do?

I married about 18 months ago[3] and since then I have worked without interruption. I have acquired a certain reputation—a literary one—but the future is still uncertain because I am not a popular author and I shall probably never become one. That does not depress me in the least as I have never had any ambition to write for the all-powerful masses. I have no liking for democracy and democracy has no liking for me! I have gained the appreciation of a few chosen spirits and I do not doubt that I shall eventually create my own public—limited of course, but large enough for me to earn my living. I do not dream of making a fortune and anyway it is not something to be found in an ink-well. However, I must confess that I dream of peace, of a little recognition and of devoting to Art the rest of a life that would be free from financial worries. Here you have, chère Madame, the secret of my life.

I thank you with my whole heart for all the news you have given me. Will you please convey my most respectful regards to your mother, for whom I have had for many years feelings of gratitude and affection. Please remember me to your brothers who are, in fact, my only friends from childhood.

How distant all that is! And yet how alive it is in my heart. The last time I saw my Uncle Bobrowski he spoke a lot of Aleksander. He was the eldest among us and, certainly, the most sensible. I think of you all very often. I saw Gustaw seven years ago, and then I sent

---

[1] 'The Return', included in *Tales of Unrest*, published in 1898.
[2] *The Nigger of the 'Narcissus'*, published by Heinemann on 5 December 1897.
[3] On 24 March 1896.

him my first book, to his club. I wonder if he ever received it? Your sister and Artur have always been very kind to me. Please, assure them that they are constantly in my memory. And then, dear Roman, I am certain that he has still kept the charm of his vivacity. It is difficult for me to imagine him otherwise than as he was when I saw him last in 1874. Oh! Tempi passati! but life moves inexorably on!

Please believe me, chère Madame, to be always your obedient and faithful servant and friend.

J. C. KORZENIOWSKI.

PS.—My best regards to your husband whom I remember very clearly although I saw him only for five minutes that evening in Warsaw. If you will permit me I shall send you in November a copy of the *Blackwood Magazine* with my story[1] in it.

18. *To Mrs. Aniela Zagórska*[2]

20.12.1897.
Stanford-le-Hope

My dearest Aniela,

I know that you do not forget my existence and I know also that this is not due to my merit, but to your goodness. Silence may be a sin, but it is not always a mortal one; there are circumstances when one may obtain pardon. Naturally, I think that my sins deserve forgiveness. Du reste tout le monde pense de même, au point de vue personnel bien entendu. In all sincerity I may add earnestly that there is in me so much of the Englishman, the sailor, and the adventurer, that I do not care to write—even to my nearest and dearest relatives—when things do not go well. This is the reason for my long silence. I do not want to count the months. I prefer to ask you to forget them. We have lived another year. Autant de gagné! Therefore we must wish one another happiness—ce bonheur dont personne ne connait le premier mot—and wish it sincerely with all our hearts: we must try to forget that man's wishes are seldom fulfilled.

I write here words of affection, words that vanish when once spoken—but the feeling remains. May the next year bring you health, peace, and the realization of your dreams—without dis-

---

[1] 'Karain: a Memory.'
[2] Jean-Aubry, English and French translations (cf. note to the letter of 22 May 1890).

enchantment. And if you think that this is not possible—I shall tell you that my wishes do not reflect the possibility, but my feelings for you all.

My wife joins me in my wishes. She knows you all—comme les enfants connaissent les personnages de Contes de Fées, and like children eager for stories, she is always ready to listen, and I (un vrai conteur) am always ready to relate. In this way you live two lives. Over there, at Lublin, where life is hard, no doubt—and here in Stanford, Essex, on the banks of the Thames—under the spell of my words: for the one you have never seen, vous avez la douceur des Ombres et la splendeur de l'Inconnu!

I have worked during the whole year. I have finished two books.[1] One came out a fortnight ago and the other is ready for the press. Voilà. And while waiting I live in a state of uncertainty. I enjoy a good reputation but not popularity. And as to money I have none, either. Triste. But things are going better at present. That I shall some day attain material success there is no reason to doubt. But that requires time and meanwhile???

The worst is that my health is not good. Les nerfs, les nerfs! Uncertainty torments me. It is very foolish, no doubt—mais que voulez-vous? l'homme est bête.

And this is how I battle with time. At my age ce n'est pas drôle. I fear that 'Before the sun rises, the dew will have destroyed the eyes'.[2]

Enough wailings. A few days ago I had news from good Margot.[3] Her life is not very easy either. I do not know if she has written to you that we expect a baby here. Jessie is very happy with this expected event, which will take place in about a week—si le diable ne s'en mêle pas. Moi je suis plus calme. As a matter of fact, not very 'calm' as, possessing a certain amount of imagination—je m'imagine toutes sortes de désastres. As I have already had the honour to inform you, l'homme est bête. I must close, it is already late. I only hear the bells of the ships on the river, which remind me how far I am from you all. Do not forget me malgré tout! I kiss the hands of Aunt Gabriela and yours, dear Aniela. I embrace Karol, whose photo stands on the mantelpiece in the room where I work at my chefs-d'œuvre.

Yours very affectionately
K. KORZENIOWSKI.

---

[1] *The Nigger of the 'Narcissus'* appeared on 2 December; *Tales of Unrest* were published in March 1898.
[2] Polish proverb.
[3] Mrs. Marguerite Poradowska, widow of Aleksander Poradowski.

19. *To Janina de Brunnow*[1]

Stanford-le-Hope
Essex.
31st December 1897.

Chère Madame,

The year here is drawing to a close and I am ending it by devoting the final moments of its last month to writing to you. I am sending you my most sincere wishes for your happiness and for the happiness of those who are dear to you and I hope that on the days of your Christmas[2] and New Year you will give a moment's thought to me.

I wonder if you received the copy of the *Blackwood Magazine* which I sent you almost a month ago? I am rather afraid that you did not. Anyway, your loss would not be great; I shall, in any case, make up for it by giving myself both the pleasure and the honour of sending you a volume of five stories which will be published next March.[3]

I hope you will be good enough to remember me to your Mother and to all the family as well as to your husband, to whom I take the liberty of sending a warm greeting.

I remain, chère Madame, your devoted and obedient servant and friend.

JPH CONRAD KORZENIOWSKI.

PS.—I hear twelve strike on our village church clock. Midnight! May you have many, very many happy years.[4]

[1] Envelope addressed: Madame la Baronne Jeanne de Brunnow, à Rudawa, par Grodno, Russia.
[2] Falling on 5 January, due to the 12 days difference between the Julian and the Gregorian calendars. See note to the first letter of T. Bobrowski to Conrad.
[3] *Tales of Unrest*, published by T. Fisher Unwin in April 1898.
[4] The postscript is in English in the original.

21 January 1898

20. *To Mrs. Aniela Zagórska*[1]

Stanford-le-Hope,
Essex.
21st January, 1898.

Chère Cousine,

I have received the wafer[2]—accompanied by a bitter complaint that was not quite deserved. Les apparences mentent quelquefois. But that does not altogether excuse me.

The baby was born on the 17th of this month and I particularly waited these three days in order to be able to inform you definitely that tout va bien. The doctor reports that it is a magnificent boy. He has dark hair, enormous eyes—and looks like a monkey. What upsets me is that my wife maintains that he is also very much like me. Enfin! Please do not draw hasty conclusions from this surprising coincidence. My wife must be wrong.

He will be christened in the Chapel of the Cloister of the Carmelites in Southwark (London).[3] The principle on which his name was chosen is the following: that the rights of the two nations must be respected. Thus, my wife representing the Anglo-Saxons chose the Saxon name Alfred. I found myself in an embarrassing situation. I wanted to have a purely Slavonic name, but one which could not be distorted either in speech or in writing—and at the same time one which was not too difficult for foreigners (non-Slavonic). I had, therefore, to reject names such as Władysław, Bogusław, Wienczysław etc., I do not like Bohdan: so I decided on Borys, remembering that my friend Stanisław Zaleski gave this name to his eldest son, so that apparently a Pole may use it.[4] Unless, Aniela dear, you care to suggest a nicer name (and there is still time) please remember that there is a certain Alfred Borys Konrad Korzeniowski, whom I commend to your heart in the name of God and of those who, after a life full of trouble and suffering, remain in your and my memory.

I kiss your hands. A warm embrace for Karol.

Your loving,
KONRAD KORZENIOWSKI.

---

[1] *Wiadomości Literackie*, Warsaw, 1929, No. 51.

[2] It is a Polish Christmas custom to break the wafer with those present at the Christmas Eve supper; customarily, pieces of the wafer are sent to the absent members of the family.

[3] There has never been a Cloister (or Convent) of Carmelites in the borough of Southwark and there are no documents concerning Borys Conrad in the baptismal records of St. George's Cathedral.

[4] The name is typically Russian and only occasionally encountered in the Ukraine.

21. *To Mrs. Aniela Zagórska*[1]

6.2.98.
Stanford-le-Hope

My dearest Aniela,

It is still more painful and hard to think of you than to realize my loss;[2] if it was not so, I would pass in silence and darkness these first moments of suffering. Neither you, nor he, know—can know —what place you occupy in my life—how my feelings, my thoughts and my remembrances have been centred round you both and your children.[3] And perhaps I myself did not know until now how much I depended on his memory, his heart, and his personality—who, even when seen only once, could arouse such feelings of devotion and confidence. He had the gift of drawing all hearts to him and from the moment when I saw him for the first time, fourteen years ago,[4] I was overcome with affection for him, as the man most akin to me in thought and by blood—after my ¸Uncle, who took the place of my parents. Not a single day passed but I found myself thinking of you both—et dans les moments pénibles l'idée qu'il y aurait un jour où je pourrais lui confesser ma vie toute entière et être compris de lui: cette pensée était ma plus grande consolation. Et voilà que cet espoir—le plus précieux de tous—s'est éteint pour toujours.[5]

The sound of human words does not bring consolation—there is no consolation on this earth. Time can soften but not efface sorrow. I have never felt so near to you and your little girls until this moment when we feel together the injustice of Fate which has loaded you with the burden of life without any support. In the presence of your grief I dare not speak of mine. I only ask you to believe in my attachment to you and in my memory of the mourned husband and father who, with you, was my whole family.

My wife said to me with tears in her eyes: 'I felt as if I knew him'—and seeing her tears, it seemed to me that never had I cared for him so much as now. Unfortunately she never knew him— although she had often heard me speak of him—for I was not capable of appreciating the worth of such a man. I did not know

---

[1] Jean-Aubry, English and French translations (see note to the letter of 22 May 1890).
[2] Karol Zagórski died on 19 January.
[3] Daughters (Aniela 1881–1943) and Karola (1885–1955). Aniela, letters to whom are included in this book, was to become the best-known translator of Conrad into Polish.
[4] In Marienbad in the summer of 1883.
[5] 'During the painful moments the thought that a day would come when I would be able to confess to him my whole life and to be understood—this thought was for me the greatest consolation. And now this hope—the most precious of all—has vanished for ever.'

him thoroughly; but I believe that I understood him. I had a profound affection for him, I always went to him in my thoughts. And now I feel quite alone—even as you.

I kiss your hands, my poor Aniela, I also kiss your little daughters, for whose sake you must be courageous. Be sure of my affection and devotion to you.

K. KORZENIOWSKI.

22. *To Mrs. Aniela Zagórska*[1]

12.4.98.
Stanford-le-Hope

My dear Aniela,

Forgive my long silence. The bad state of my health is the reason why the news of our terrible bereavement has put me in such a state of nervous excitement that I am quite unable to follow my thoughts or to write a couple of lines.[2]

I am filled with admiration for your courage and the strength of mind with which you bear this awful blow inflicted by Fate. I have not written, but I can tell you that every day I have been with you in my thoughts.

The exigencies of life do not bring relief[3]—they only drive back the outward show of grief. The day before yesterday I returned to my work; it could not be otherwise. And it is thus, with poignant grief in my heart, that I write novels to amuse the English!

I thank you for your letter which I read with much sadness and which brings me nearer to your grief; in sharing your feelings and your sorrow, I do not feel so much alone! I feel as if in sorrow, at least, I were near you. Alas! it is impossible to remove the consciousness of the distance which separates us. There is a wish to take the hand and to hear the sound of the voice, but it cannot be. My wife and child are well, thanks be to God. As for me, I am not ill, but I am not well either. And then the uncertainty of our destiny oppresses me. We live with difficulty, from day to day—et c'est tout! My reputation grows, but popularity remains behind. The work is not easy and every day seems more difficult to me. Que la vie est cruelle et bête! But enough for today.[4]

[1] Jean-Aubry, English and French translations (see note to the letter of 22 May 1890).
[2] That this was not an exaggeration is shown by other of Conrad's letters of this time, especially by a desperate one to Edward Garnett (29 March).
[3] English word in the original.
[4] No ending preserved.

23. *To Mrs. Aniela Zagórska*[1]

Pent Farm, Stanford.
18.12.1898.

My dear Aniela,

If I did not believe in the constancy of your sentiments towards me I would not dare write to you after so long a silence. As a matter of fact, my dear, I have been in a sad state of health—miserable rather than bad—and I preferred not to weary or tire you with the sadness of my letters. And also I was ashamed to display before you —who are so brave among the difficulties and sufferings of life— my foolish and not very praiseworthy pessimism.

This is how the days, weeks, and months have gone by; I waited —always thinking of you, with my pen ready to write—I waited for a moment of lucidity, of calmness, of hope. It is hard to attain. And here come Christmas and the end of the year. One has to ask for pardon, express one's feelings—promise to amend for the hundredth or thousandth time, as all sinners do.

As you will see, we have come to live here; this is also a farmhouse,[2] somewhat smaller but more convenient and, what is most important, it is situated on higher ground. I found that I could not work in our old place. It is better here although I have nothing to boast about. We are only five kilometres from the sea. The railway station[3] is 3 kilometres and Canterbury 1¼[4] kilometres away. Before my window I can see the buildings of the farm, and on leaning out and looking to the right, I see the valley of the Stour, the source of which is so to speak behind the third hedge from the farmyard. Behind the house are the hills (Kentish Downs)[5] which slope in zigzag fashion down to the sea, like the battlements of a big fortress. A road runs along the foot of the hills near the house—a very lonely and straight road, and along which (so it is whispered) old Lord Roxby—he died 80 years ago—rides sometimes at night in a four-in-hand driven by himself. What is rather strange, however, is that he has no head. Why he should leave his head at home while he takes a ride, nobody can explain. But I must tell you that during the two months we have lived here, we have not yet heard the noise of any wheels and although I sometimes walk along this road near midnight, I have never met a four-in-hand. On the other side of the

[1] Jean-Aubry, English and French translations (see note to the letter of 22 May 1890).
[2] English word in the original.
[3] Westenhanger Station.
[4] Probably an error in the copy; Canterbury is about 14 miles (21½ kilometres) from Stanford.
[5] English word in the original.

To Mrs. Aniela Zagórska (18 December 1898)

little garden stretches out quiet and waste land intersected by hedges and here and there stands an oak or a group of young ash trees. Three little villages are hidden among the hillocks and only the steeples of their churches can be seen. The colouring of the country presents brown and pale yellow tints—and in between, in the distance one can see the meadows, as green as emeralds. And not a sound is to be heard but the laboured panting of the engines of the London–Dover express trains.

We live like a family of anchorites. From time to time a pious pilgrim belonging to la grande fraternité des lettres comes to pay a visit to the celebrated Joseph Conrad—and to obtain his blessing. Sometimes he gets it and sometimes he does not, for the hermit is severe and dyspeptic et n'entend pas la plaisanterie en matière d'Art! At all events, the pilgrim receives an acceptable dinner, a Spartan bed—and he vanishes. I am just expecting one today, the author of *Jocelyn*,[1] which is dedicated to me! The novel is not remarkable, but the man is very pleasant and kind—and rich, que diable fait-il dans cette galère—where we are navigating whilst using pens by way of oars—on an ocean of ink—pour n'arriver nulle part, hélas!

Jessie is dreaming of a visit to Poland—which to her means a visit to you. And I am dreaming the same. Pourquoi pas? It costs nothing to journey in thought to those we love. It costs nothing— only a little heartache when we find how far the dream is from reality.

Now Christmas is drawing near.[2]

24. To Mrs. Aniela Zagórska[3]

Christmas 1898.

My dear Aniela,

I have just received your letter and I am replying to it at once. The news that you give me distresses me. La vie est dure—très dure, for me also, my dearest.

I shall send you some cuttings (in envelopes, like letters) from the *Saturday Review* and other periodicals which deal with litera-ture—and I shall add occasionally some notes taken by myself.

[1] John Galsworthy; *Jocelyn* was published in 1898 under the pseudonym of John Sinjohn.
[2] Here the preserved text ends.
[3] Jean-Aubry, English (with many omissions) and French translations (see note to the letter of 22 May 1890).

Grant Allen's *Woman Who Did*,[1] c'est un livre mort. Gr. Allen
is a man of inferior intelligence and his work is not art in any sense.
The *Woman Who Did* had a kind of success, of curiosity mostly
and that only among the philistines—the sort of people who read
Marie Corelli and Hall Caine. Neither of these writers belongs to
literature. All three are very popular with the public—and they are
also puffed in the press. There are no lasting qualities in their work.
The thought is commonplace and the style(?) without any distinction. They are popular because they express the common thought,
and the common man is delighted to find himself in accord with
people he supposes distinguished. This is the secret of many popu-
larities.[2] (You can develop this idea as an explanation of the enthusiasm of the public for books which are of no value.) Grant Allen
is considered a man of letters among scholars and a scholar among
men of letters. He writes popular scientific manuals equally well.
En somme—un imbécile. Marie Corelli is *not* noticed critically by
the serious reviews. She is simply ignored. Her books sell largely.
Hall Caine is a kind of male Marie Corelli. He is the great master
of the art of self-advertising. He is always being interviewed by
reporters and is simply mad with vanity. He is a megalomaniac,
who thinks himself the greatest man of the century, quite a prodigy.
He maintains that the lower part of his face is like Shakespeare and
the upper like Jesus Christ.[3] (This gives you an idea about the man.)
Du reste aucune valeur, as you will see reading that book. Besides,
one should say that he certainly made more than 60 thousand
roubles on this book. His publisher is my publisher too—and I know
it from this source. For the American edition he got almost another
60,000 roubles.

Among the writers who deserve attention the first is Rudyard
Kipling (his last book *The Day's Work*, a novel). J. M. Barrie—
a Scotsman. His last book *Sentimental Tommy* (last year). George
Meredith did not bring out anything this year. The last volumes
of the charming translation of Turgenev came out a fortnight ago.
The translation is by Mrs. Constance Garnett. George Moore has
published the novel *Evelyn Innes*—un succès d'estime. He is supposed to belong to the naturalistic school and Zola is his prophet.
Tout ça, c'est très vieux jeu. A certain Mr. T. Watts-Dunton
published the novel *Aylwin*, a curiosity success, as this Watts-

[1] A novel, published in 1895, which caused a considerable sensation by its bold—for
that time—treatment of sexual matters. Grant Allen (1848-99) was in fact a quite
intelligent and sometimes original writer, popularizing and developing recent scientific
ideas (e.g. his *Physiological Aesthetics*, 1877).
[2] English in the original from 'Gr. Allen is. . .'.
[3] English in the original from 'Marie Corelli is. . .'.

To Mrs. Aniela Zagórska (Christmas 1898)

Dunton (who is a barrister) is apparently a friend of different celebrities in the world of Fine Arts (especially in the pre-Raphaelite School). He has crammed them all into his book. H. G. Wells published this year *The War of the Worlds* and *The Invisible Man*. He is a very original writer, romancier du fantastique, with a very individualistic judgement in all things and an astonishing imagination.

But, my dearest, really I read nothing and I *never* look at the papers, so I know nothing of politics and literature. I have barely time to write, for I find work very hard and it is only with difficulty that I can earn a little bread. This is the whole truth.

I shall see Mr. Wells in a few days and I will ask him on your behalf for permission to translate *The Invisible Man* into Polish. If I can arrange this I will send you the book. The language is easy —the story very interesting; it would make a very good serial for a paper. If you undertook this work and if you would send me the sheets as and when you finish them, I shall put notes in the margin which may help you. But you certainly know English as well as I do—and I do not speak of your Polish!

For the moment I am not writing anything. Since the month of January! I have been in such a state that I have been unable to write anything.[1] It was not until November that I started to work. The novel[2] which was ordered from me is 10 months behind. This is catastrophe! and even now I am not at all well.

I kiss your hands. I embrace my little cousins.

Yours with all my heart,
K. KORZENIOWSKI.

PS. With what I have written you and two books to review, on peut faire un article,—pas une chose profonde, mais du bon journalisme. Try. I shall send you, at the same time as the cuttings, a few notes about the authors—if I know anything about them. This is what the papers need. A chat, an appreciation, something light and interesting. Du journalisme tout pur. If you begin writing, try to do it. It always pays.

[1] Apart from three reviews, in 1898 he wrote only *Youth*.
[2] *The Rescue*, abandoned in December for *Heart of Darkness*.

25. *To Janina de Brunnow*

Pent Farm.
Stanford. near Hythe. Kent.
6th Jan. 1899

Chère Madame,

Just a word immediately to let you know how grieved I am by the news of the terrible accident that has befallen you.[1] Above all, I also wish to tell you how happy it makes me to know that I still have a little corner in your memory.

This is just a word in great haste as I am extremely busy, being in the middle of some work[2] which is waiting and which is being waited for with great impatience because it was due to be finished in November and is still here—on my table.

My best wishes to you and your family. They come straight from my heart which is not eloquent at all. The more genuine the feeling, the less one is able to express it.

So I finish—for the time being—with a thousand thanks and with the assurance of my deep and sincere friendship.

Always your devoted servant
CONRAD KORZENIOWSKI.

PS. I shall give myself the pleasure soon of writing a long letter to you. My regards and a thousand good wishes to your husband.

26. *To Mrs. Aniela Zagórska*[3]

Pent Farm, 7.2.'99.

My dear Aniela,

Just a few lines in answer to your letter, for which I thank you. I have seen Mr. Wells, who considers it an honour that his works should be translated into Polish. You must know that the *Mercure de France* has finished the publication of his novel, *The Time-Machine*.

In two days I will send you the book. You can introduce the translation as being authorized by the author. If you plan to publish it in a newspaper, you could suggest a summary to the editor and an appreciation of the author—introduced to the Polish public, as

---

[1] The Baroness had lost one of her relatives.
[2] *Heart of Darkness*, finished in the first days of February.
[3] Jean-Aubry, English and French translations (see note to the letter of 22 May 1890).

it were—by myself—about 500–1,000 words. But only in the event of this being of any use to place the novel.

I am not sending you any cuttings, as there is nothing of any interest. I will send you soon a note on Miss Kingsley's book on Africa.[1] C'est un voyageur et un écrivain très remarquable. Her opinions on questions dealing with colonies are thought a great deal of.

Here is the photo of Mr. Borys, agé d'un an et deux jours. His mamma, who sends you 'lots of love',[2] is not well. She looks like a very stout old woman—which she is not yet.

Your card written in English is almost without a mistake. Evidently you have a practical knowledge of the language. Cela se voit.

Forgive this hasty letter, but I am awfully busy and surrounded with these wretched editors.

A thousand embraces
Your KONRAD KORZENIOWSKI.

27. *To Mrs. Aniela Zagórska*[3]

Pent Farm,
12th April, 1899.

My dear Aniela,

Excuse these few words. I am anxious about Karola. Please be so kind and let me know how she is—and how you all are. Since your last letter I have sent: 1.—the photo of the boy; 2.—3 packets of cuttings; 3.—a number of *Literature*; 4.—Wells's novel *The Invisible Man*. Let me know, my dearest, if you have received all this; especially the photo and the book. If the cuttings have gone astray, it will be necessary to send them in envelopes. If you have received *Literature* I will send it to you regularly. If the book has not reached you, I will send another copy at once.

I have been in bed for a whole week with gout. I do not feel at all well. But that does not matter. My wife and the youngster are

---

[1] Mary Henrietta Kingsley, *West African Studies*, Macmillan, London 1899. Miss Kingsley (1862–1900) was indeed very well known at that time, and after her death the African Society (now the Royal African Society) was formed in memory of her. She did not, however, travel in or write about the Belgian Congo and does not seem to have had any influence on Conrad's writings.

[2] English in the original.

[3] Jean-Aubry, English and French translations (see note to the letter of 22 May 1890).

both well. God grant that all may go well with you. A few lines will reassure me. I embrace you affectionately and kiss your hand.

Your K. KORZENIOWSKI

28. *To Mrs. Aniela Zagórska*[1]

Pent Farm, 25.12.1899.

My dearest Aniela,

Your letters, dearest, are very interesting; they give me courage and are very precious to me; my ingratitude is all the blacker—but it is only in appearance that I am ungrateful. In reality I am not—I am only a man with a weak will—and full of good intentions, with which—as they say—hell is paved. What would you have, my dear? The Malays say: 'The tiger cannot change his stripes'—and I—my ultra-Slav nature.

Much might be said about the war. My feelings are very complex —as you may guess. That they are struggling in good faith for their independence cannot be doubted; but it is also a fact that they have no idea of liberty, which can only be found under the English flag all over the world. C'est un peuple essentiellement despotique, like by the way all the Dutch. This war is not so much a war against the Transvaal as a struggle against the doings of German influence. It is the Germans who have forced the issue. There can be no doubt about it.

You are mistaken in saying that it is the Government who sends soldiers. The English Government has no right to make a single Englishman move, if he does not consent to it. Le pour et le contre of this issue have been weighed not only in the conscience of the people but of the whole race. Canada and Australia are taking part in this war, which could not influence their material interests. Why? Europe rejoices and is moved because Europe is jealous and here in England there is more real sympathy and regard for the Boers than on the whole Continent, which proclaims its compassion at the top of its voice. Quelle bourde![2]

[1] Jean-Aubry, English and French translations (see note to the letter of 22 May 1890).
[2] Here the preserved text ends.

27 *December* 1899

29. *To Janina de Brunnow*[1]

Pent Farm,
27th December, 1899.

Chère Madame,

To be honest, I must confess that your letter containing the announcement reached me some days ago but I did not dare to take pen in hand, but ever since getting the painful news, both you and your husband have been constantly in my thoughts.

What can I say! When one is faced with a loss like yours words appear to be devoid of any meaning. There is always the hope of a better life, and the consoling certainty that the bitterness of existence down here has been spared to the dear departed whose loss nevertheless tears our hearts.

You must derive consolation from the hearts of those who surround you, while I, distant and alone, can only send my deep and affectionate sympathy to the friend of my childhood for whom fate has reserved such a sore trial.

A thousand thanks for your letter which moved me deeply by its sincere friendship. Please give my warmest regards to your husband. If you will permit me, another letter will follow soon.

Please believe me to be with you in heart, always your devoted servant.

CONRAD N. KORZENIOWSKI.

30. *To Józef Korzeniowski*[2]

Pent Farm,
14th February, 1901.

Dear Sir,

I hasten to acknowledge the receipt of the Memoirs,[3] which reached me yesterday morning, and at the same time to thank you for your kindness in sending them.

Your so friendly letter, Sir, has given me the greatest pleasure. As we are bearers of the same name and have the same family crest there must surely be between us if not actual kinship at least an

---

[1] Envelope addressed : à Rudawa, poste Berestowica, Gouvernement de Grodno (Russie).

[2] Józef Korzeniowski (1863–1921; not to be confused with the writer of the same name, living 1797–1863) was a historian and the director of the Czartoryskis' Library in Cracow. Conrad's letter to him, discovered by Miss Barbara Kocówna in 1958, is in the National Library in Warsaw.

[3] Tadeusz Bobrowski, *Pamiętniki*, vols. i-ii, Lvov 1900.

affinity,—this is a great honour to me and its mention by you, dear Sir, has been most gratifying.

Incidentally, I heard from Mrs. Poradowska as well as from Mrs. A. Zagórska—a relation of mine from Lublin—that the Memoirs had met with a most unpleasant response.[1] It has upset me greatly, for that uproar (if it was such an uproar as they say) concerns the memory of a man for whose mind and heart I have always cherished the greatest admiration, to say nothing of my deep attachment to him as my Uncle, guardian, and benefactor!

It must only be due to the indulgent eyes of good Mrs. Poradowska, who has always been well disposed towards me, that she sees me as eminent in English literature. Apart from the fact that it is not easy for anyone to achieve a position of eminence, it is still a question whether my (and other peoples') mawkish romances can justifiably count at all as works of literature? However, I am not ashamed of my undertaking, as the path I have chosen is by no means an easy one—on the contrary, it is difficult and precarious—striving for recognition not by inventing plots, but by writing in a style which serves the truth as I see and feel it.

And please let me add, dear Sir (for you may still be hearing this and that said of me), that I have in no way disavowed either my nationality or the name we share for the sake of success. It is widely known that I am a Pole and that Józef Konrad are my two Christian names, the latter being used by me as a surname so that foreign mouths should not distort my real surname—a distortion which I cannot stand. It does not seem to me that I have been unfaithful to my country by having proved to the English that a gentleman from the Ukraine can be as good a sailor as they, and has something to tell them in their own language. I consider such recognition as I have won from this particular point of view, and offer it in silent homage where it is due.

With renewed thanks, I beg you, dear Sir, to accept my friendly expression of profound respect.

KONRAD KORZENIOWSKI.

[1] The Memoirs have been indeed strongly attacked, privately and in the press. The reason for it was that Bobrowski felt free to express his opinions, frequently quite spiteful, about his acquaintances. The Memoirs contain as well a great number of anecdotes and much gossip, compromising various families of Polish nobles and gentry.

31. *To Kazimierz Waliszewski*[1]

Pent Farm,
27th October 1903.

Dear Sir,

Pawling[2] has just sent me your letter, and I hasten to tell you that I am entirely at your disposal; however, I venture to ask you to give me an exact idea of the kind of information you desire. I cannot imagine how the details of my life 'before I had become a man of letters', if I can thus express myself, can possibly interest the élite public you mention. My life was eventful, but of a confused pattern and, apart from that, I must confess I do not like to appear as some kind of a phenomenon as a writer. My literary life began in 1895. I like to believe it has been honest, although difficult. Nevertheless, dear Sir and distinguished compatriot, please be assured that for your sake I shall conquer my slight repugnance where publicity is concerned. It is not, after all, much to sacrifice an unimportant whim when an article written by you is concerned.

Please accept, my dear Sir, the expression of the most sincere esteem that I have for you and of my admiration for your work.

JOSEPH CONRAD.
(Korzeniowski).

PS. I have opened the envelope again as I have just received your kind and obliging letter. I must explain that at the moment I am not at my own home (at the address above) but am staying with a friend to whose address your letter had been forwarded with a day's delay.

In the course of this week I shall send you some notes. As to the bibliography, the best way, if you allow it, would be for me to send you the volumes that you do not possess. I enclose a small list of grrreat! works. Send me back this list after having crossed out the titles of the books you are familiar with. Yes! Heinemann[3] is charming, and in their relationship towards me they have always been unusually nice, I am very pleased to say. Always yours.

J.C.K.

---

[1] Kazimierz Waliszewski (1849–1935), a Polish historian settled in France; specialized in seventeenth- and eighteenth-century Polish, Russian, and French history. Conrad would write to him either in French or in Polish. Letter in French, *Lettres françaises*, pp. 52–53.

[2] Sidney Pawling was a partner of the publisher William Heinemann.

[3] William Heinemann (1863–1920) established the well-known firm and introduced a broad international outlook into British publishing.

32. To Kazimierz Waliszewski[1]

Pent Farm,
8th November, 1903.

Dear Sir and confrère,

There are certain things that are difficult to explain, especially after they have happened. I consider *Romance*[2] as something of no importance; I collaborated on it at a time when it was impossible for me to do anything else. It was easy to relate a few events without being otherwise involved in the subject. The idea we had was purely aesthetic: to depict in an appropriate way certain scenes and certain situations. Also it did not displease us to be able to show that we could do something which was very much en vogue with the public at the moment. The heroic gospel of St. Henry, dear Sir, rules the entire world and, as you know, there is more than one way of laughing at it. There were moments when both Hueffer and I were very gay while working on this construction. Nevertheless we took pains with the technical side of the work. You will admit that it is well written. Flaubert (he was a real saint) applied himself well to achieve a spectacular success.

The press here gave full space to it. *The Times*, which condescended to write at length about my last two books (*Youth* and *Typhoon*—the others he does not know), giving them cautious and peevish support, now heaves a sigh of relief and gratitude. I say 'gratitude'. That's the word! An article in the *Daily News* (a special one—almost an entire column) begins with the sentence: 'This is the real thing!' and it goes on in the same vein.

Finally and a last reason. H. and I wanted to get started on a serious novel which we planned to write some day. As a pivot for the action we conceived a picture by an old and famous painter, and the base, wicked intrigues surrounding a great man who had been successful but just because he was a supreme artist remained misunderstood. A great deal can be made out of a subject such as this, expressing the thoughts on art which hover over us and on the materialism which creeps into life. H. has a well-founded knowledge of these problems thanks to a family tradition,[3] and also to his

---

[1] *Lettres françaises*, pp. 54–55.

[2] A novel on which Conrad collaborated with Ford Madox Hueffer (who later changed his name to Ford Madox Ford) between November 1898 and March 1902; published in 1903.

[3] F. M. Ford's father, Dr. Franz Hueffer, was a distinguished music critic. His maternal grandfather was Ford Madox Brown (1821–93), a painter and for some time teacher of Dante Gabriel Rossetti. Ford was, therefore, closely associated with the circle of the pre-Raphaelites.

own research, and also de visu for he had been a very close friend of Ford Madox Brown during the last six years of his life. I am telling you this, my dear Sir, under the seal of secrecy. Probably the book will never be written. I wanted to have no secrets from you.

A thousand regards, always yours,
J. CONRAD K.

33. *To Kazimierz Waliszewski*[1]

Pent Farm
15th November 1903.

Dear and Honourable Sir,

I am writing today to all my publishers, and as you have already procured the *Typhoon*, Heinemann will be sending you the *Inheritors* and the *Nigger*, while Blackwood will send *Lord Jim* and *Youth*. I am afraid it is not going to be easy to get my first book, *Almayer's Folly*, because the edition was not big and was sold out long ago. At home we have only one copy of it, and my wife—to whom I presented it, even before our marriage—naturally cannot part with it. I intend to try the publisher.[2] Du reste mes relations avec celui-là sont assez tendues.

I have pricks of conscience at showering my books on you in this way. However, a few pages of each volume will suffice to give you an idea of what I was aiming at and what I managed to achieve. At any rate, be so kind as to accept them as the only testimony that I can give you of my true admiration for your work—which unfortunately I do not know well and which I am certainly unable to appreciate as I should, but which I believe that I have been able sympathetically to understand.

I consider it a great happiness and honour to return to my home country under your guidance (if I may express myself thus). And if you are prepared to take my word for it and say that during the course of all my travels round the world I never, in mind or heart, separated myself from my country, then I may surely be accepted there as a compatriot, in spite of my writing in English.

Please accept, my dear Sir . . . etc.

KONRAD KORZENIOWSKI.

[1] Letter in Polish, apart from the postscript. *Ruch Literacki*, 1927, No. 6.
[2] T. Fisher Unwin, who published Conrad's first two novels, *Almayer's Folly* (1895) and *An Outcast of the Islands* (1896). Conrad fell out with him in October 1896 after being refused a bigger advance (cf. letters to Garnett of 16 and 25 Oct. 1896).

PS. Non! Non! Ne dites pas phénomène. Ça sent le Maxime Gorki à plein nez. Ils sont étonnants ces braves Russes: All their geese are swans.[1] Enfin, c'est leur affaire. Pour ma part, je n'ai jamais été ni vagabond ni aventurier de profession, ni une espèce de sauvage converti.[2]

Les notes et la photographie suivront dans peu de jours.

34. *To Kazimierz Waliszewski*[3]

Pent Farm,
20th Nov. 1903.

Dear Sir,

A thousand thanks for your kind letter. The book has also arrived. My wife is touched by your promptitude.

I have been extremely busy and still am, for although the year is drawing to its close, my miserable novel[4] is far from finished. The worst is that I am feeling discouraged and tired by all my efforts, which come to nothing in the end.

I began writing *Almayer's Folly*, just like that, not thinking much what I was doing, in order to occupy my mornings during a rather long stay in London after a three years' cruise in the South Seas.[5] That is the honest truth. I was 32 years old then. I knew nothing about anything. I do not know any more now!

I cannot tell you anything more for the moment. It is late. Sleep overcomes me. I feel more stupid than usual.

Do not doubt, dear Sir, that we shall take the opportunity of visiting you if we are in Paris next year, which is our intention. Please convey my respects to Madame Waliszewska, and believe me always, sincerely yours.

[1] English sentence in the original.
[2] 'No! No! Don't say phenomenon. That reeks of Maxim Gorki. These gallant Russians are astonishing: All their geese are swans. Oh well, that is their business. For my part, I have never been either a vagabond or an adventurer by profession, or a sort of converted savage.'
[3] *Lettres françaises*, pp. 57–58.
[4] *Nostromo*, finished only on 30 August 1904.
[5] In the summer of 1889 (cf. *A Personal Record*). He had spent 28 months in the South Seas (cf. note 2 to his letter to A. Poradowski of 16 Jan. 1890).

5 December 1903

35. *To Kazimierz Waliszewski*[1]

Pent Farm,
5th December, 1903.

Dear Sir,

A thousand thanks for the friendly letter which has just reached me. I shall begin by apologizing for the thin paper, which is what I am using for my manuscripts. It is late now and I have no other paper handy; so, removing the 567th page of the novel[2] I am now engaged on, I address myself to you.

The weekly *Kraj* to which you refer is probably the one that comes out in Petersburg. In this case you probably know Mr. Włodzimierz Spasowicz, a friend of my late Uncle Bobrowski, who wrote a preface to my Uncle's memoirs (published in 1900 in Lvov).

After his marriage, my Father, Apollo Korzeniowski (son of Teodor, a captain in the Polish Army), leased a farm on the estate of Mrs. Melania Sobańska. I was born in December 1857. Subsequently my parents moved to Warsaw. In 1862, my Father was imprisoned in the Warsaw fortress and after a few months was transported to Vologda. I accompanied my parents in their exile. Later they were moved to Chernikhov and there my Mother died. I can hardly remember her, but judging by what I heard about her and by the letters she wrote to her brothers—which I read later—she must have been a woman with uncommon qualities of mind and spirit. Her younger brother, Stefan Bobrowski, was a well-known personality in 1863. After my Mother's death, I stayed with my Uncle Tadeusz in the country. In 1867 my Father was released and he took me with him to Galicia. He died in Cracow in 1869. Mr. Stefan Buszczyński (a man of letters who was well known in his day) wrote a short biography of him entitled 'A little-known poet'. My Father's funeral was the occasion for a demonstration by the students of Cracow University. Cracow was also the place where I went to school, but in 1874 I left my country to go to sea.

I cannot write about Tadeusz Bobrowski, my Uncle, guardian and benefactor without emotion. Even now, after ten years, I still feel his loss. He was a man of great character and unusual qualities of mind. Although he did not understand my desire to join the mercantile marine, on principle, he never objected to it. I saw him four times during the thirty [sic] years of my wanderings (from 1874–1893) but even so I attribute to his devotion, care, and influence, whatever good qualities I may possess. The last two

---

[1] *Ruch Literacki*, 1927, No. 6.   [2] *Nostromo.*

occasions on which I visited him were in the Ukraine (as a British subject) in 1890 and 1893.

Everything about my life in the wide world can be found in my books. I never sought for a career, but possibly, unaware of it, I was looking for sensations. Now it is all over. With no connexions, contacts, or influential friends, I can nevertheless look upon the past with satisfaction. I managed somehow. During my life as a seaman, though mainly prompted by curiosity (as well as by a genuine liking for the profession), I was conscientious, passing all the necessary examinations, winning the respect of people (in my modest milieu) who, certainly not out of sheer affection, attested to my being a 'good sailor and a trustworthy ship's officer'. In what it seems to me were pretty difficult situations, I think I always remained faithful to the traditions of the profession I had chosen.

I received my first command of a ship at the age of 29, which, you must admit, was not bad for a foreigner without influence. That I never sought, and I have to give the English their due, they never made me feel a foreigner. I consider myself to be the last seaman of a sailing vessel. Anyway, no one will be writing any more about that old sea-life. As a work of fiction *The Nigger* puts a seal on that epoch of the greatest possible perfection which was at the same time the end of the sailing fleet. I feel that deeply each time I look at the British [*sic*] Channel where nothing but smoking chimneys are to be seen nowadays.

Both at sea and on land my point of view is English, from which the conclusion should not be drawn that I have become an Englishman. That is not the case. Homo duplex has in my case more than one meaning. You will understand me. I shall not dwell upon that subject.

Apparently, so far as writing is concerned, I have some sort of a talent. That is no merit of mine. You may judge if I make use of it conscientiously. All I know is that I am striving after a writer's honesty. But that is not a great merit either. Am I achieving anything? I do not know—or rather, I know I am not. It is difficult to depict faithfully in a work of imagination that innermost world as one apprehends it, and to express one's own real sense of that inner life (which is the soul of human activity). However, absolute sincerity is always possible—I mean sincerity of intention. One does what one can.

I shall finish now, apologizing for the alarming dimensions of this letter. Here are some dates. My wife, thanking you for your kind regards, expresses her readiness to lend you her copy of *Almayer's Folly*. I expect, however, to hear any day from the

publishers. *Almayer's Folly* was begun in 1889. It was written bit
by bit all round the world. It was finished in 1895. *Outcast of the
Islands* 1895.

Lagoon, Outpost of Progress, Idiots—1896; *Nigger of the 'Narcissus'*—September 1896–February 1897; *Karain, The Return*
1897.

Youth, Heart of Darkness 1898; *Lord Jim* October 1898–July
1899. Simultaneously with my collaboration in the writing of *The
Inheritors*.

The Inheritors and the beginning of the collaboration on *Romance*
1900, *Typhoon, Falk, Amy Foster* 1900–1.

To-morrow January 1902, *Romance* finished April 1902. *The
End of the Tether* November 1902.

Since that time I have not worked well. I was ill and lacked
inspiration. The circle of my readers is very small. Life has now
become much harder. I write with difficulty, slowly, crossing out
constantly. What a foul profession! 'This craft is exacting'—as dear
and good Henry James repeats, whenever we meet, throwing his
arms up to heaven. It is touching to hear that coming from the lips
of a man who is approaching sixty and who has to his credit forty
volumes practically free from imperfection.

PS. That is so, my dear Sir! A lot could be said and certainly there
wo uld be a lot for me to listen to. May it be granted to us that we
me et again soon. Do you ever visit England? I live only about 5
English miles from Folkestone. You could call on me on your way
from Paris to London—even if only for one night. Do not forget,
please!

36. *To Kazimierz Waliszewski*[1]

December, 1903.

Dear Sir,

Well, here it is, not like me at all! I am older, thinner, and not
so well turned out. And the fool took it into his head to retouch the
tip of my nose; hence its Israelitic appearance, which it does not
have in fact.

Herewith some reviews of my books. But you must not think me
a megalomaniac. I wished to give you an idea of what they say here
about me. The newspapers are stupid!

Yours ever.

[1] Letter in French, accompanying a photograph. *Lettres françaises*, p. 63.

37. *To Kazimierz Waliszewski*[1]

Pent Farm,
16th December, 1903.

Cher Maître,

A thousand thanks for the article you have devoted to me in the *Revue*.[2] I have read it with a lively interest, deep respect, and a great deal of gratitude.

You are kind and indulgent. It is justice that suffers by it, but it is not for me to complain. Anyway, I flatter myself that I have understood your article better than anyone else can do. Your words have penetrated deep into the recesses of the soul where a man tries to hide his failings from his own eyes.

After all one works as one can and not as one wishes to, especially when one is devoted without reservation to one's task. This is a reflection which excuses nothing, and so I put it to you in quite an unbiased manner, as if I were discussing with you in general terms the manner in which one practises one's art.

As to the question of 'inferiority of races',[3] I permit myself to protest—although evidently the fault is on my side for having given you a wrong idea of my intention. It is the *difference* between races that I wished to point out. If I say that the ship which bombarded the coast was French, it is simply because she was French. I remember her name: le Seignelay.[4] It happened during the war(!) in Dahomey. What follows could refer just as well to a ship of a different country. I pick my characters where I find them. Hermann[5] is a German but Stein[6] is one as well. I take great pains to give a cosmopolitan origin to Kurtz.[7] As to my two good fellows who were chasing after each other with revolvers in the *Outpost of Progress*—I rebel. Kayerts is not a French name. Carlier might

---

[1] *Lettres françaises*, pp. 63–65. Publishing a Polish translation of this letter in *Ruch Literacki*, 1927, No. 6, Waliszewski dated it '26th December 1903'.

[2] *Revue des revues*, 1904, No. 1 (appeared, according to Jean-Aubry, on 15 December 1903): 'Un cas de naturalisation littéraire'. A longer Polish version was published in *Kraj*, 1904, Nos. 3–7: 'Polski powieściopisarz w angielskiej literaturze' (A Polish Novelist in English Literature).

[3] Criticizing Conrad for a pro-English bias, Waliszewski pointed out that all his good seamen are English—and there is not a single Englishman among the colonialist exploiters described in his works.

[4] This refers to a scene in *Heart of Darkness*: 'There wasn't even a shed there, and she was shelling the bush. It appears the French had one of their wars going on thereabouts. . . . In the empty immensity of earth, sky, and water, there she was, incomprehensible, firing into a continent.'

[5] Captain and owner of the ship *Diana* in *Falk*, a simple-minded and slightly comic bourgeois.

[6] One of the main characters in *Lord Jim*, a romantic and ex-revolutionary of 1848.

[7] The hero of *Heart of Darkness*.

be, but as soon as I give his name I hastily add that he is an ex-non-commissioned cavalry officer of an army which is guaranteed against all dangers by several European powers. I took special pains to make a soldier out of this brute. They are brave Belgians. God bless them: they have been recognized as such here and in Brussels when the story appeared in 1898 in the Revue *Cosmopolis*[1] (which has ceased to exist). But enough of this nonsense. I shake your hand affectionately.

Yours ever.[2]

38. *To Kazimierz Waliszewski*[3]

17, Gordon Place,
Kensington,
London. W.
[March 1904]

Dear Sir,

A thousand thanks for the gift of your book,[4] which I am looking forward with much pleasure to reading.

For a month now we have been involved in all sorts of unpleasantnesses. My poor wife fell and dislocated her knee. And so doctor, surgeon, and masseur came into the picture. On top of this my bank[5] failed and I found myself without bank, without money, without even a cheque book—an excruciating experience which still makes me shudder when I think of it. Evidently, the proper thing for me to do was to write a drama in one act, which I hastened to do.[6] Merely reading it was enough to appal one of our managers, the others will doubtless be seized with terror in due course! Then I signed a contract for a series of sea sketches (for some paper).[7] My

[1] Actually in the June and July issues, 1897.

[2] The version published by Waliszewski in *Ruch Literacki* has a different ending, apparently Polish in the original: 'But that's enough of idle prattle! I send you a hearty hand-shake and the expression of my deep respect for Mrs. Waliszewska. I really must visit you soon in order to thank her personally and to apologize for having taken up so much of your time and thought.'

[3] *Lettres françaises*, pp. 65–66. Jean-Aubry dates this letter 'February 1904', but Conrad's letter to Sidney Colvin of 4 March that year, in which he mentions his waiting for H. B. Tree's opinion about the play *One Day More*, indicates that the letter to Waliszewski must have been written shortly afterwards.

[4] K. Waliszewski, *Ivan le Terrible*, Paris, 1904.

[5] Watson & Co.

[6] *One Day More*, based on the story 'Tomorrow' (from the volume *Typhoon; and Other Stories*), was performed by the Stage Society on 25 June 1905.

[7] It was to become *The Mirror of the Sea* (1906). Two first essays, 'The Grip of the Land' and 'Overdue and Missing' were published in the *Daily Mail* in 1904.

novel,[1] which has begun to be published in serial form, is not finished yet (there are still a dozen chapters to do) and in my free time I am looking for a naïve and kind-hearted banker who could provide me with a cheque book, one who is inspired by sheer love of his neighbour, as unfortunately I do not possess any money to offer. There you have it!

I hope, dear Sir, that you can envisage the situation. There is only one thing for me to add, which is that I have now read 24 pages of *Ivan the Terrible*, which means that I have been consoled 24 times by forgetfulness of all my troubles.

Anyway, my wife is making good progress with her recovery, although we have been very anxious about her. Today, in fact, she was able to cross the room, walking with the help of a stick. This little event accounts for the tone of my letter, which otherwise ought to have been mournful.

Kozakiewicz[2] is very kind to think of translating me—or is that perhaps due to your friendly initiative? As you have mentioned the possibility of your co-operation, I dare not think that any merit of mine is involved! And so *l'affaire* remains. Well, I am afraid that l'affaire will be bad! That is my candid opinion.

Please, be so kind as to convey to your wife my best regards, and believe me, dear sir, to be always yours.

39. *To Aleksander Marian Jasieński*[3]

Capri,
Italy.
25th April, 1905.

Dear Sir,

I was born on the 3rd December 1857 at Żytomierz. In no way am I related to Józef Korzeniowski.[4] Our coat of arms is that of Nałęcz. My Father, Apollo Korz., was a son of Teodor, a former colonel in the Polish Army and a landowner in Volhynia; for a time he was an administrator of one of Mrs. Melania Sobańska's estates. My Father was, however, also a man of letters; he was brought up first at Niemirów and then at Żytomierz. He graduated at the

---

[1] *Nostromo* (finished on 30 August 1904).
[2] Bronisław Kozakiewicz (d. 1924), well-known translator from Polish into French. He did not translate Conrad.
[3] *Ruch Literacki*, 1927, No. 5.
[4] Józef Korzeniowski (1797–1863) was a well-known novelist and dramatist, skilfully combining in his novels the influences of Jane Austen, Balzac, and Dickens.

To A. M. Jasieński (25 April 1905)

University of Petersburg. Together with Adam Pług[1] he translated *La Légende des siècles* (in 1852). Both his comedy in verse *Dla miłego grosza* and his translation of *Chatterton* (Alf. de Vigny) were published at Żytomierz in 1856–8. Later, when exiled, he translated comedies of Shakespeare and dramas by Victor Hugo; as well as *Les Travailleurs de la mer* by the latter. He was freed in 1868 and died in Cracow in 1869. Stefan Buszczyński, his closest friend, published a biographical pamphlet entitled *A Little-Known Poet*.

My Mother, née Bobrowska (from Oratów in the Ukraine), was the sister of Stefan Bobrowski who played a considerable rôle in Warsaw during the years 1862–3 as a member of the National Government; she died in exile.

I am writing all this not for publication but so as to acquaint you with my Polish origin.

I remain, dear Sir, respectfully yours,
KONRAD KORZENIOWSKI (JOSEPH CONRAD)

40. *To Zygmunt Szembek*[2]

Grand Hôtel de Genève,
Marseilles.
Tuesday, 16th May, 1905.

My very dear Sir,

As you can imagine I intended to write to you from Naples, but just when I was about to begin we were informed that the steamer was ready to leave at five instead of at seven o'clock as we had expected.

Our journey was not too pleasant; rain and high seas almost all the time. However, Borys has had a good time and my wife also apparently does not regret the adventure at all. Everyone was extremely charming to us. They were simple people but most obliging. As to myself, I was treated as a colleague—a man of the same profession—which certainly gave me pleasure.

We arrived this morning or rather during the night. We slept on board. Tomorrow morning we are leaving for Paris where we shall stay the night so as to arrive home on Thursday at 3.50. Otherwise we should be arriving either too late or too early.

[1] Pseudonym of Antoni Pietkiewicz (1824–1903), a novelist and Apollo Korzeniowski's fellow conspirator.

[2] Conrad's letters to Count Zygmunt Szembek—an elderly Polish nobleman he befriended during his stay on Capri between January and May 1905—all written in French, were published in *Lettres françaises*. Conrad's short story 'Il Conde' (1908, included in the volume *A Set of Six*, 1908) is based on an incident which happened to Szembek.

Here it is pouring with rain! What frightful weather we have had this year!

There is no need for me to tell you that the vivid recollection of your kind friendship will remain with us for the rest of our lives. The time of day when we used to have the pleasure of seeing you arrive to visit us in Capri has brought with it sorrow at your absence. Borys has been mentioning your name at least three times a day, and he was trying to explain to the officers on the boat the nature of his intimacy with 'my friend Count Szembek'! The child is very fond of you, as are his parents who are naturally more humble folk!

Rather late last Friday in Naples on a sudden impulse I went into a Banco Lotto which was just closing. As we left before the result of the draw was known, I take the liberty of sending you my ticket. One never knows what fortune may bring! Who knows! Perhaps I have won, in which case you will, no doubt, inform me by telegram. But what I would like most of all, however, would be a little note informing us of your health and of the moral state of Capri.

All best regards, cordially yours,
J. C. KORZENIOWSKI.

41. *To Zygmunt Szembek*

Pent Farm,
Monday, 21st May 1905.

My very dear Sir,

We arrived home on Thursday afternoon, really very tired after all but in good health. I was immediately overwhelmed by a mass of correspondence of all kinds, and even by callers who came to importune me in person. In addition, I found my political article,[1] which the *Fortnightly Review* had accepted enthusiastically but had asked for some corrections or rather changes to be made on one or two points. So I have been busy, as time was short.

I am telling you all this in order to explain why I did not send you sooner our most sincere thanks for the pleasure which your kind, good, and charming letter gave us on our arrival. My wife could not have been more touched by your kind thought, to say nothing of myself. You know that I have a great affection for you and that I regard any sign of your friendship as a most precious gift.

[1] 'Autocracy and War', published in July.

I finish now in great haste; in an hour we are leaving for London.

> Always yours most affectionately.
> J. C. KORZENIOWSKI.

42. *To Zygmunt Szembek*

> Pent Farm,
> 29th May 1905.

My very dear Sir,

Can you imagine, I am confined to bed by an attack of gout! We had gone to London and that is where it caught me. I arranged to be transported back here as quickly as possible for I could see that it would be a long business.

What bad luck! Anyhow, the only thing is to be patient, but I must confess it is unbearable to watch the days slip by while one is forced to remain lying on one's back.

A thousand and again a thousand thanks for the books, which to my great joy arrived just in time to help me to be patient and to forget the pain a little. He is a man of talent and of wit. He thinks well, and he knows how to express his thoughts in an interesting way. All that his imagination conceives he makes acutely alive and realistic for us and his opinions I find congenial as well.[1]

The weather is very fine here: it is even warm. From my bed I can see everything bathed in sunshine and I listen to the singing of the birds. But I myself am not very gay!

I do not want to sadden you with my mournful letter so I shall finish it now. My wife and Borys ask to be remembered warmly to you. Please, believe me, my dear Sir and friend, your always faithful

> J. C. KORZENIOWSKI.

PS. I have not even ordered the books yet which are due to you. Please forgive me. It will be my first care.

43. *To Zygmunt Szembek*

> Pent Farm,
> 21st June, 1905.

My very dear Count,

There is nothing to be said. I feel ill. I even had a relapse. This explains and I hope will make you forgive my long silence.

---

[1] It has been impossible to find out to whom this refers.

Your very warm letters have given me the greatest pleasure. As to myself, you can imagine I have been forced to neglect all my affairs and my obligations. But I have not forgotten any. I only have to ask of your kind friendship that you will spare a little patience for me.

My wife is preparing a small parcel to post to you. It will contain also a little matchbox for Luigi whom we esteem on account of his devotion to you. I have written to Paris for the book you mention. As to the copies of my works, they will be dispatched in a week's time at the latest.

If you should see Mr. Trower, would you please be so kind as to inform him of the misfortunes which have befallen me since my return and to convey to him my regards.

My wife, dear Sir, joins me in conveying to you the expression of our deep and lasting friendship. Please send us your news.

Always yours,

PS. Borys is asleep so I can say nothing on his behalf but I assure you that he often speaks of his 'friend the Count'.

My play[1] is being rehearsed! and I cannot go to see it! What bad luck! My visit to the highly placed person, you know whom, has not taken place either. Please convey my regards to Colonel Palms. Good-bye for the present!

44. *To Zygmunt Szembek*

14, Addison Road,
London. W.
2nd August, 1906.

Dearest Sir and friend,

Just a few words to announce to you the happy arrival of John Alexander Conrad Korzeniowski at 9.30 this morning. His mother is very well and commends herself to your kind thoughts.

Borys, who was greatly surprised, gave an excellent welcome to his little brother. Hence, perfect harmony reigns in the family.

Upon that, dear Sir, I send you a most affectionate handshake, for I still have a dozen letters to write and it is getting late.

Yours ever.

[1] One Day More,

8 December 1906

45. To Zygmunt Szembek

Pent Farm,
8th December, 1906.

Dearest Sir and friend,

I have no other excuse to offer for our long silence but, for my part, that of having been working desperately hard to finish a book,[1] and for my wife's part trouble with her eyes which rendered her incapable of reading or writing. Luckily, that is over or at least improved considerably for the past fortnight.

Since the birth of Jack I have been working, so to say, day and night. At last it is finished and we are on the point of going to Montpellier, because the two of us, or rather the four of us, are in need of sunshine.

I was surprised to receive a letter from Cerio,[2] asking me for a letter of introduction to Gorki. Why me? I replied that I had never met Gorki in my life! I did not even know that he was in Capri.

Nothing very interesting has happened in our secluded workaday existence. Days pass—time marches quickly on. That is all that I have to say! But rest assured, dear Sir, that we preserve carefully the memory of your kind friendship. Having said that, the truth of which I am sure you do not doubt, I shall now bid you good-bye for the present. I am crushed down under the burden of the arrears of my correspondence, because, to tell the truth, it will soon be three months since I wrote a letter.

Please believe me, dear Sir and friend, affectionately yours.

PS. My wife means to write to you soon. Borys sends his love.[3]

46. To Janina de Brunnow[4]

Someries,
Luton, Beds.
19th Feb. 1908.

Chère Madame,

Just a few words for the moment to thank you for your letter and to assure you of my participation in your grief.[5]

[1] *The Secret Agent*, finished at the beginning of November.
[2] Dr. Cerio, in whose library in Capri Conrad did some reading for a projected 'Mediterranean novel'.
[3] 'His love' in English in the original.
[4] Envelope addressed: Madame la Baronne de Brunnow, 22 rue Saint-Pierre, Fribourg.
[5] Mme de Brunnow's brother, Roman Taube, had just died.

This is not merely an expression of words, chère Madame. As the years pass, the memories of one's childhood grow all the more precious.

He was keen, lively, slightly scatter-brained but with a great charm and very open-minded. Of all your brothers, the companions of my youth (the only ones—I had no others, ever), he was the one, it seems to me, who most resembled his mother. And he is no more. I am saddened to the depth of my soul.

I shall give myself the honour, chère Madame, of sending you a copy of my latest book.[1] I am extremely touched by the interest which you are kind enough to show in my work; and I shall permit myself to send you also an older book—of sea sketches[2]—perhaps it is one without great interest but it is one I am very fond of, for it deals with events which happened long ago and with simple people whom I knew.

May I ask you to be so kind as to convey to your mother my sincerest wishes. The greying man who is now writing to you has retained an almost filial regard for her and a feeling of gratitude to her which the passage of time only enhances. And permit me, Madame, in the name of the precious memories which we have in common, to sign myself your very affectionate and very faithful servant.

47. *To Janina de Brunnow*[3]

Someries,
Luton, Beds.
24th March, 1908.

Chère Madame and Friend,

I am infinitely grateful to you for the interesting photographs. Really, your daughters are quite charming. That is quite obvious. You have given me the greatest possible pleasure. Your kind letter arrived this afternoon, and I have passed the evening in a world of memories.

Yes; the sofa was green. I remember it well,—and you were a quite small person with curly hair and of an exquisite charm.

As soon as the weather is a little better we shall get the best

---

[1] *A Set of Six.*
[2] *The Mirror of the Sea*, published in 1906.
[3] Envelope addressed: 22, rue Saint-Pierre, Fribourg.

photographer in Luton to take some photographs for you in the garden. At the moment I do not possess a photograph of myself to send you at once. It will be better if I send you some of all of us. We are four; our eldest boy, Borys, is ten years old; the second, Jack, is now 20 months old.

There has been a delay in sending you the books, as I wanted to send you first editions. Alas, they have been impossible to get. There are people who collect my books, and the editions were not very large. I am read by the élite and also by very ordinary folk. One of my friends tells me that my books are in request in the public and popular libraries. The great middle class knows my name, but not my books. The painters also—I mean the young ones, the independent ones—also like my prose very much. In the literary world I have quite a name. But I see very few people. We live a very quiet life, 40–50 minutes by train from London. And then it is a good 5 kilometres from the station to our house.

Am I right in thinking that your Mother is with you at Fribourg? In any case, chère Madame, please give her my most respectful regards, and believe me to be always your very faithful servant and friend.

48. *To Janina de Brunnow*[1]

Someries. Luton. Beds.
20th June, 1908.

Chère Madame,

At last I can send you the photographs promised long ago. They are very poor and I am infinitely sorry not to be able to send you better ones in exchange for your delightful and attractive snapshots.[2]

I trust that you are well, chère Madame, and also your husband and charming daughters. Please give my respectful regards to your mother.

Your for ever devoted servant and friend
J. CONRAD.

[1] Letter in French, never published. A copy in Jean-Aubry's papers, now in Yale University Library.
[2] Word in English in the original.

49. *To Mrs. Aniela Zagórska and Miss Aniela Zagórska*[1]

Cracow Railway Station
5 p.m. Friday
[9 October 1914]

Dear Aunt and Aniela,

Here we are, tired but in good health! The night journey was very comfortable but it was a bit cold. Mr. Z.[2] deserves admiration for having so ably conducted the convoy composed mainly of lame persons. He is now in town and we feel like children without their father—all squatting in a corner.

We still cannot believe that we shall not return to Konstantynówka.[3] Tonight at 7 or 9 o'clock we shall leave for Vienna.

We have sent back your fur coat via the coachman. Hot water bottles we are taking with us to Vienna, thanks to Mr. Kosch's kindness.

I feel ready to weep. As to my state of mind it is better not to speak about it. All I feel in my head is a black vacuum. Please remember us affectionately to all our friends—collectivement et nominalement—not forgetting young Jadwiga.[4] John is sad at having left you. Our dear love to you two.

Yours ever[5]
CONRAD.

[1] Conrad wrote quite a number of letters to the Zagórski sisters, Aniela and Karola, but only a few have been published. Although a conscientious translator of Conrad's works and deeply devoted to his memory, Miss Aniela Zagórska was rather careless as regards his letters, presenting them to her friends, etc. All originals of these letters seem to have been destroyed in the Second World War. The text of most of them has only been preserved in a French translation, made by Aniela Zagórska (daughter) for Jean-Aubry in the twenties. These translations, not very exact and frequently incomplete, are contained in a notebook, written in Miss Zagórska's hand, now in Yale University Library. The English text, as in the present edition, has been prepared on the basis of the French translation and of a reconstruction of the probable Polish original version. It was frequently possible to guess with a high degree of probability what had been the Polish original expression, rendered by Miss Zagórska in French; sometimes she would give the original word in parenthesis.

[2] Stanisław Zajączkowski.

[3] Name of the villa in Zakopane where the Conrads had stayed.

[4] Teodor Kosch's daughter.

[5] The last two sentences are in English.

50. *To Teodor Kosch*[1]

H. Mayreders
Hotel Matschakerhof
Wien.
Sunday, 18th October, 1914.

My dear Sir,

We arrived here on Saturday evening (the 10th), but the very same night I had an attack of gout which kept me in bed until Thursday!

Mr. Marian Biliński kindly visited me on Tuesday. I had the pleasure and profit of discussing with him the Polish question in general—in detail and exhaustively, for some hours, and how it might be put before a European Congress, and the hopes, fears, and possibilities connected with it. I was quite convinced by everything Mr. Biliński said, and he also won my heart for he proved to be not only intelligent but also friendly during our long and interesting conversation. Today I visited him and we talked again for an hour or more mainly about how the Polish question should be presented in England. It will be difficult in view of the course of events, but I can see that the way he proposes is the only one possible. He has a healthy judgement of things and of human sentiments; thus, having accepted his point of view, I shall endeavour to abide by it as far as the conditions I find on my return render it feasible. I have no idea of the mood which prevails there after the serious setbacks suffered in the west. It will be necessary to look around, sound the hearts and minds of influential people and only then start to act, if any action is possible in this question which is so close to our hearts.

Mr. and Mrs. Biliński asked a lot about you and your wife. With regard to the state of affairs in Konst.[2] I gave them an honest account which worried them somewhat. We, also, are anxious for news about you, your wife and Miss Jadwiga.[3] God grant that everything is well with you. My wife sends her great love to both mother and child, and her best regards to you. Please be good enough to convey to your wife my most esteemed regards, together with my best wishes for you both and for the youngest member of the family, who has come into this world in so stormy a time.

Mr. Zajączkowski took care of us in a most friendly way right up

[1] Dr. Teodor Kosch was a lawyer living in Cracow. Conrad befriended him and his family in Zakopane. Conrad's letters to Dr. Kosch, along with some letters by Jessie Conrad, are in the possession of the addressee's family in Cracow.

[2] Villa Konstantynówka, in Zakopane, where the Kosches were staying at that time.

[3] Teodor Kosch's daughter.

to the very moment of his departure. I only saw the Ambassador[1] on Thursday—i.e. as soon as I was able to get up and drag myself out of the room. I waited for about an hour in his waiting-room, because the Papal Nuncio was just then with him. Finally the Nuncio left and my turn came. The Ambassador kept me for a whole hour, discussing with me various subjects concerning the affairs of the whole world. He did not tell me much that was new. He said that His Imperial Majesty is not only well but that current events seem to have stimulated him both physically and mentally. Well, so much the better! America hopes to play the part of a mediator but, he thinks, the time for that is not yet near. Perhaps in the spring?

I have received enough to get to Milan, from where I shall be writing to you again. Yesterday I bade the Ambassador farewell, and tonight at 9.30 we are leaving for Italy via Pontebba. What is going to happen, and how, I do not know. In the Police Headquarters here they assure me that I shall have no difficulties at the frontier.

I conclude with sincere regards from us all (Jan[2] especially sends his greetings to the dear baby) and with a hearty handshake—not as a goodbye gesture but as 'au revoir' in happier times!

KONRAD KORZENIOWSKI

On the envelope:
H. Mayreder's Hotel Matschakerhof. Wien, L. S. Wien. 19. X. 1914. J. W. P. Dr. Teodor Kosch, Willa Konstantynówka, Zakopane, Galicja.

51. *To Stanisław Zajączkowski*[3]

S. Zajączkowski, Esq.   Sunday
Rynek, Zakopane, Galicia.   [Vienna, 19 October 1914]

My dear and honoured Sir,

Today at 9.30 we leave for Italy via Pontebba. I have not been given a permit to leave although I went myself to the Polizei-

---

[1] American Ambassador, Frederick C. Penfield (1855–1922).
[2] Conrad's son John (Jan is Polish for John).
[3] The original is in the possession of the addressee's daughter, Mrs. Albertyna Cichocka, Cracow. *Tygodnik Powszechny*, Cracow, 1959, No. 13.

To Stanisław Zajączkowski (19 October 1914)

Direktion to ask for one, presenting my British passport and my identity card issued in Nowy Targ. The Commissioner, Herr Brandl, assured me that I do not need an Austrian permit to cross the frontier, as owing to my age and the age of the boys I have the right to go. He merely recommended me to get a visa from the Italian Consul, and repeated that as far as the Austrians were concerned there would be no difficulties. I have not all that faith in him, but if we are detained in Pontebba[1] I shall telegraph to the Ambassador, and I am sure that in the end they will let us go. However, as I am afraid of being held up at the frontier, I am keeping all the money received here[2] and for that reason I am not sending you any part of the sum which I owe you. I will settle that in Milan.—We hope that you arrived safely at Zakopane and found everything there in good shape. I left your address in Cracow with Mr. Phillpotts, the British ex-Consul. Heartiest good wishes to you and all your family from us all. Borys asks to be remembered specially to Miss Tynia,[3] the companion of his excursions, to whom I also send greetings from myself. A handshake to Mr. Mieczysław.

[1] The Pontebba route was closed and they entered Italy through Cormons (letter to Galsworthy, 15 Nov. 1914).
[2] Conrad had borrowed some money from Frederick C. Penfield, American Ambassador to Vienna. Later he dedicated *The Rescue* to him. Below is a letter to him, written for Conrad in German by Dr. Teodor Kosch of Cracow (who still possesses the original) because of military censorship regulations. Only the heading, closing greetings, and signature are in Conrad's hand. The paper has a printed letterhead: Capel House, Orlestone, Nr. Ashford:

Zakopane, Galicia
Villa Konstantynówka
1st October 1914

My dear Mr. Penfield

Thank you very much for the five hundred Crowns you have so kindly sent me here to make possible my journey to Vienna.

My departure depends on receiving the permission of the military command in Nowy Targ (Neumarkt in Galicia). When I asked for such permission it was explained to me that it was impossible to give it to me without the authorization of the higher authorities in Vienna—since I am a British subject.

Now I have to ask you again for your kind help in obtaining this permission for me, my wife Jessie and my 15 and 8 years old sons Borys and John, from the appropriate authorities, perhaps the I. & R. Ministry of War.

I hope that the granting of this permission, especially in my case, will be considered as a simple formality and that the representative of the American Nation, to whom I think I am sufficiently well known, will not be caused too much trouble on this account.

Thanking you very much in advance for everything, I sign myself,

With kindest regards,
Yours faithfully,
J. CONRAD

PS. After having finished this letter I learned that the military command in Neumarkt requires the consent of the German Embassy as well.

[3] Zajączkowski's daughter Albertyna; Mieczysław and Ludwik were her brothers.

Ludwik must not forget about us, as we shall not forget about him.

Thanking you again for your kindness, I remain,

Always yours sincerely,
K. KORZENIOWSKI

52. *To Teodor Kosch*

Palace Hotel—Milan
Milan, 20th October, 1914.

My dear Sir!

Just a word immediately to let you know that we have arrived here in fairly good condition. I have already met a certain Mr. Enrico Ruberl, via Canova 36, who is an engineer and the agent here of Buszczyński. I have arranged with him to act as intermediary in the matter of my correspondence with Austria after my return to England. Thus I shall be writing to you, dear Sir, c/o Mr. Biliński, and also to all my friends in Poland. Please be so kind as to use this channel and send us from time to time news of yourself and your family.[1]

I sent a telegram to England this morning. It seems to me that all this will take some 6 days. I am being advised here to go via Northern Spain; from here by sea to Barcelona—thence by train to Bilbao and from there by sea again to Falmouth.

I am now concerned about my wife, who has somehow strained the ankle of her supposedly healthy foot and it is terribly swollen. She is still walking, and says that it is nothing, but I think we shall have to call a doctor. I myself and the boys feel well.

Kindest regards to you from us all.

Your faithful friend,
K. KORZENIOWSKI

53. *To Teodor Kosch*

Genova,
22nd October, 1914.

My dear Sir,

All of a sudden a boat has turned up and by tomorrow noon we shall be at sea.

[1] In his letter to T. Kosch (24 January 1915) Ruberl writes that he has not received any correspondence from Conrad. Letters to the Conrads, sent c/o Ruberl, were returned by the Austrian military censorship.

To Teodor Kosch (22 October 1914)

I have received from London just enough money for this unexpectedly precipitate departure. At the moment they could only send me 1,000 fr. . . . so, without waiting for more, I have decided not to let this opportunity (a Dutch boat) slip. I shall try to communicate with you, dear Sir, immediately after arriving—perhaps in 10 days' time. Signor Ing-re Enrico Ruberl, via Canova 36, Milan, will act as the intermediary in our correspondence. Through him I shall also be writing to Mr. Biliński. Mr. Ruberl is an Austrian subject and a very honest man. He is Konstanty Buszczyński's agent.

As far as I can judge, the islanders[1] understand our situation quite well. There is of course no grievance against Aus. But as for the others,[2] it is a different matter. Time will show what will happen, and in the meantime our situation is very difficult. I kiss your wife's hands. My wife sends her best love to Mrs. and Miss Kosch and asks to be remembered to you.

With a hearty handshake,

K. KORZENIOWSKI

54. *To Marian Biliński*[3]

Genova,
24th October, 1914.

Dear Sir,

Unexpectedly, an opportunity has turned up of leaving tomorrow on a Dutch boat. We expect to be back home in about twelve days. Soon after our return I shall be writing to you care of: Signor Ing-re Enrico Ruberl, via Canova 36, Milan. Mr. Ruberl is an Austrian subject and the commercial agent of Mr. Konst. Buszczyński. He is a trustworthy person.

I remain, dear Sir, sincerely yours,

K. KORZENIOWSKI

---

[1] i.e. the English; cf. Conrad's 'Political' Memorandum, pp. 303–4.

[2] The Germans.

[3] *Pion*, 1934, No. 31. Marian Biliński (mentioned in Conrad's letter to Dr. Kosch of 18 Oct. 1914) was the brother of Leon Biliński (1846–1923), at that time (1912–15) Austro-Hungarian Minister of Finance.

55. *To Stanisław Zajączkowski*[1]

24 Oct. 1914
Genova

S. Zajączkowski, Esq.
Rynek Zakopane Austria. (Galicia).

My dear and honoured Sir,

It so happens that a Dutch ship sails tomorrow. By noon we shall be at sea and in about ten days we expect to arrive at the end of our journey. Mr. Buszczyński[2] plans to be in Milan in about a week's time. I am leaving the money with Mr. Enrico Ruberl, via Canova 36, Milan, and Mr. Buszczyński will give it to you on his return to Zakopane.

Mr. Ruberl will also forward a few lines which perhaps you will be kind enough to write to us care of him.

Heartiest greetings from us all to you, to Miss Tynia, to Mr. Mieczysław and to Ludwik.

Your friend and servant,
K. KORZENIOWSKI

Please excuse this hurried scrawl—I am very tired, my leg still hurts.

56. *To Marian Biliński*[3]

9th November, 1914.
2 p.m.

Dear Sir,

In a few hours we shall land, and we shall immediately take a train for London. Tomorrow I shall straight away endeavour to meet some influential people in the world of journalism. We have had a very fine crossing but in spite of it, somehow, I am not feeling too good. My wife and the boys on the other hand look extremely well. I shall ask the steward on the ship to post this letter in Holland; I do not want you to think that I am treating the matter in any way

[1] *Tygodnik Powszechny*, Cracow, 1959, No. 13. The original is in the possession of Mrs. A. Cichocka.

[2] Konstanty Buszczyński; Conrad's meeting with him on his arrival in Cracow is described in Jessie Conrad's *Joseph Conrad and his Circle*, ch. xiii.

[3] *Pion*, 1934, No. 31.

To Marian Biliński (9 November 1914)

casually. We shall probably be staying in London a whole week so as to meet people, discuss things, and weigh up the situation.[1]

With expressions of my deepest esteem.

Yours sincerely
K. KORZENIOWSKI

57. To Gustaw Taube[2]

Capel House,
24th November, 1915.

My very dear friend,

I dare not! The doctors do not allow me to go out. I have not been allowed even to go to Potsmore to see our eldest son who is in the army and is on the point of leaving for France.[3]

To tell the truth, I have been ill almost the whole of this year, from the war.

I learned that you were staying in Paris, and I nursed the idea of going there soon in order to see you. But there's nothing to be done. A severe attack of gout put me to bed nearly a month ago. I am still confined to my room. I am getting better, but I am told that the slightest imprudence on my part could bring about complications.

I understand quite well that your occupations prevent you from venturing as far as here. But, my dear fellow, it is only a question of postponement. If God gives me life, I shall manage to see you soon. The memories which we have in common, the cordiality with which you received me in Warsaw,[4] render the friendship that Madame de Brunnow and you have been good enough to keep for me something that is very precious in my life.

I press your hands very tenderly, my dear Gustave, and I thank you for your very kind letter which really touched my heart.

Always yours,

[1] Conrad intended to fulfil the plan of political propaganda, as drawn up in his 'Political Memorandum' (q.v.). However, the only trace of his endeavours before 1916 I have found in Arnold Bennett's *Journal*. On 4 Nov. 1914 Bennett wrote that James B. Pinker (Conrad's literary agent) 'had seen Conrad that morning, just returned from Austrian Poland. C. had no opinion of Russian army, and had come to England to influence public opinion to get good terms for Austria! As if he could.' (Ed. by Newman Flower, London, 1932, vol. ii, p. 108.)

[2] In French; *Lettres françaises*, pp. 133-4. Gustaw Taube was at the time on a visit to England.

[3] Borys Conrad volunteered for the army and was commissioned in the Mechanical Transport Corps.

[4] In February 1890.

259

58. *To Józef Retinger*[1]

Capel House,
Orlestone,
Nr. Ashford.
21st August, 1916

Dear Józef,

If you want to know the impression made on me by our first meeting with Mr. Clark[2] of the Foreign Office regarding the memorandum on Polish affairs[3] (the plan for a protectorate)—here it is:

Because of his position in the Foreign Office and because the meeting was taking place in his office there, he could not say anything beyond what he did say. I remember that from the very beginning he gave you clearly to understand that it would be difficult for England to discuss Polish affairs anywhere else but in

---

[1] Letter in French, discovered by Mrs. Jadwiga Łuczak in the Library of the Polish Academy of Sciences in Kórnik (Signature: Zam. 195) and published, with an extensive commentary, by Bogusław Leśnodorski in *Twórczość*, 1957, No. 12.

Józef Retinger (Cracow 1888–London 1960; he changed the spelling of his name from 'Rettinger') was the most colourful and complex personality among all Conrad's Polish correspondents. Unfortunately, out of many letters to him, written in Polish and in French, only this one has so far been discovered. Retinger obtained his doctor's degree in law in Cracow and in humanities at the Sorbonne. His first major publication was *Histoire de la littérature française du romantisme à nos jours*, Paris, 1911. He early deserted literature for politics and in the same year published in London a study of Polish–Prussian relations (*The Poles and Prussia*), expounding Polish legal and ethnic rights to territories occupied by the Germans.

According to Retinger (J. H. Retinger, *Conrad and his Contemporaries*, New York, 1943, p. 65—incidentally, the book is not very reliable as a source of detailed information), he met Conrad for the first time in 1909, introduced by Arnold Bennett. However, the first mention of Retinger by Conrad, suggesting that they had not met before, is to be found in Conrad's letter to Bennett of 17 November 1912. Anyway, in a short time they apparently became close friends and it was on Retinger's mother's invitation that the Conrads went to Poland in 1914. Leaving the Conrads in Zakopane, in August 1914 Retinger hastened via France to England (on his experiences on the way there see Arnold Bennett's *Journal*, vol. ii, p. 108 : 5 Sept. 1914). In November he presented to the War Office a memorandum proposing the formation of a Polish Legion in America, which was to fight on the side of the Entente. The proposal was rejected, most probably because the British Government did not wish to get involved in Polish affairs behind the back of its Russian ally. Retinger spent Christmas 1914 with the Conrads and for some time he and Conrad met frequently. Conrad watched with somewhat dismayed admiration his friend's political activities. (See his letter to R. Curle of 20 August 1916.)

In 1915 Retinger published in Paris a well-documented memorandum, *La Pologne et l'équilibre européen*, arguing that to secure a permanent peace for Europe a strong Poland—under the protectorate of the Entente—should be re-established. Retinger's study provided a basis for Conrad's short memorandum, presented by Retinger (Conrad could not do it himself, being a British subject) to the Foreign Office. In the memorandum Conrad closely followed the argument of his friend.

[2] Spelling incorrect; the interlocutor was Sir George Russell Clerk (1874–1951), then a senior executive officer at the Foreign Office.

[3] Published in 1921 in *Notes on Life and Letters* as 'A Note on the Polish Problem'.

Petrograd, although the British would willingly draw inspiration from Polish desires.

To your concrete question whether the British Government (in agreement with France) would consent in general to the idea of a protectorate (tripartite) he replied: let the Poles first make a clearly defined request. This does not need to be over-enthusiastic—a properly argued request will suffice, supported by important personalities representative as far as possible of all political and social trends in Poland. *Only then* could the question of Poland's future be raised in the sense of the memorandum which you left him.

It seems to me that a reply like this (coming from a man whose high official position compels him to speak with the utmost reserve) makes it possible and advisable for us to proceed further. The problem that lies ahead of you is that of obtaining the agreement to this project of all Polish parties. For it is obviously better to receive the gift of national existence from one's friends than from one's enemies. An understanding on that issue would in no way restrict the freedom of action of all the political parties in the future.

Now, the main thing is to start to live, breathe, and put on flesh. Later on the battle of ideas will develop within the fundamental institutions, as it does in every free country.

> I send you my very best regards,
> JOSEPH CONRAD.

59. *To Miss Aniela Zagórska*[1]

> Oswalds,
> Bishopsbourne,
> Kent.

My dearest Aniela,   10th April 1920.

I don't know what you must think of me! I trust that you haven't given me up entirely. You will know from Karola[2] how things are in this house. They do not excuse me, but perhaps they will help you to forgive me.

I give you my best and completest authority and right to translate all my works into Polish. You are authorized to give or to refuse permission and to decide all matters concerned therewith, using your own judgement and taking decisions in my name.

---

[1] *Pion*, 1934, No. 50.
[2] Karola Zagórska, Aniela's sister, was at that time staying with the Conrads.

I should be happiest if you yourself had the wish and the time to translate at least those books which you like. I know from Karolcia that you worked on *Almayer's Folly*—possibly even too conscientiously! My dear, don't trouble to be too scrupulous about it. I may tell you (in French) that in my opinion 'il vaut mieux interpréter que traduire'. My English is not at all literary. I write idiomatically. Je me sers des phrases courantes qui, après tout, sont celles avec lesquelles on se garde le mieux contre 'le cliché'. Il s'agit donc de trouver les équivalents. Et là, ma chère, je vous prie laissez vous guider plutôt par votre tempérament que par une conscience sévère. Je vous connais. J'ai foi en vous. Et vraiment Conrad vu à travers Angèle, ça ne sera pas déjà si mauvais. Inspirez vous bien de cette idée qui pourra peut-être alléger un peu la tâche ingrate que vous pensez entreprendre—si j'ai bien compris Karola.[1]

I shall send you without delay my *Personal Record*, *Nostromo*, and *Arrow of Gold*[2]. With regard to titles, what do you think of 'Fantazja Almayera'? That is a possibility. In English the word Folly may also be used of a building. In Polish the word obłęd cannot be used in the same way. 'A's Folly' is a stupid title which can't exactly be translated into any other language.

Jessie embraces you warmly and sends you her best love. She is looking very well and I expect to have her home in a week or ten days. Thank you for the presents, and I kiss your hands for the two volumes si admirablement reliés—and also for the pleasure of having Prus[3] in my home. Everyone says that Jan is remarkably like his father; so one can expect that the time will come when he will write to you and thank you for the book and the drawing. Quel magnifique portrait![4]

Forgive this short letter after such a long silence, and do not judge my attachment to you either by the one or the other, but only selon la charité de votre cœur et la largeur de votre esprit. Sometimes, my dear, the thought itself takes the pen out of one's

---

[1] 'I use current expressions which, after all, are the best defence against "cliché". It is, then, a question of finding the equivalent expressions. And there, my dear Aniela, I beg you to let yourself be guided more by your temperament than by a strict conscience. I know you. I have faith in you. And indeed Conrad seen through the eyes of Aniela will by no means be so bad. Take heart from this idea which may perhaps lighten a little the thankless task that you think of undertaking—if I have understood Karola aright.'

[2] Titles in English in the original.

[3] Bolesław Prus was the pen-name of Aleksander Głowacki (1847–1912), a distinguished Polish novelist. According to Aniela Zagórska ('Kilka wspomnień o Conradzie' —'Some Reminiscences about Conrad', *Wiadomości Literackie*, 1929, No. 51), during his stay in Zakopane in the summer of 1914 Conrad read many of his works and became quite enthusiastic about this writer, who combined sober realism with romantic undertones.

[4] A portrait of Conrad painted in Zakopane by Dr. Kazimierz Górski, now in the possession of Mr. John Conrad.

hand. But why explain. I repeat, j'ai foi en vous — en toutes choses.

Your loving,
KONRAD

60. *To The National Committee Polish Government Loan*[1]

London, April 26, 1920.

For Poles the sense of duty and the imperishable feeling of nationality preserved in hearts and defended by the hands of their immediate ancestors in open struggles against the might of three powers and in indomitable defence of crushing oppression for more than a hundred years is sufficient inducement to assist in reconstructing the independent dignity and usefulness of the reborn republic, investing generously in honour of the unconquered dead in testimony of their own national faith and for the peace and happiness of future generations. To Americans one appeals for the recognition of the Polish Nation, of that patriotism not of the flesh but of the spirit which has sustained them so well in the critical hours of their own history in the name of common memories at the dawn of their own independent existence on the ground of rare humanity, and as to lovers of perseverance and courage. America cannot but feel sympathy for an idealism akin to her own in this instance of unselfish union of all hearts and all hands in the work of reconstruction. For the only sound ground of democracy is that unselfish toil in a common cause. Americans would wish help rebuilding that outpost of Western civilization, once overwhelmed by but never surrendered to the forces representing what they themselves detest in humanity, tyranny and moral lawlessness. Please edit as required. Salutations.

61. *To Józef Potocki*[2]

Oswalds
Bishopsbourne
3rd June, 1920.

I am very touched, dear Count, by the truly friendly idea that you have had to send me the page concerning my father.[3] I have

[1] Cable sent to Washington, in English. In Jean-Aubry, *Joseph Conrad: Life and Letters*, vol. ii, pp. 239–40.

[2] Letter in French; *Lettres françaises*, p. 155. Count Józef Potocki (1862–1922), at that time the secretary of the Polish Embassy in London, was a well-known traveller and politician.   [3] Some document concerning Apollo Korzeniowski.

only retained a vaguely sinister impression of those days. My childhood memories go back no further than a visit to the brother of my mother (Bobrowski) at Nowofastów between 1865 and 1869.[1] Those memories are also not too pleasant.

I have lived two lives since that time. It is all so long ago. Pulvis et Umbra!

Please accept my very sincere thanks, and the assurance of my high regard.

62. *To Karola Zagórska*[2]

Oswalds
16th November 1920

My dear Karola,

You have been through days of anguish but luckily your card which has just reached Jessie calmed us down. I am very happy to know that you are on the eve of departure to Italy. I beg you, my dear child, to let me have your address as soon as you get there.

Certainly, my dearest, I feel that life and work in Italy will do you good.[3] If I find a way of taking Jessie to the South this winter we might perhaps see each other. I don't know yet if that will be possible. Anyway, we shall see. She would like it very much. She is obviously in a much better state but at one point she was threatened with bronchitis—something that I dread for her.

I believe that in a few days' time Borys will establish himself in London where he will find work with one of my friends who has a considerable establishment for the production (experimental) of appliances for wireless telegraphy. John will sit next week for an exam at Tonbridge which is quite a distinguished 'public school'. I hope he will pass. As to myself, I haven't been well for the last three weeks and I even had to go to bed for 3 days. I haven't done anything worth while. Since the 10th September we have had good weather but lately I couldn't take any advantage of it as, in addition to my gout, I got an atrocious cough and dared not go out.

In the course of next week I shall write to Angela and send her the document.[4] Forgive me, my dear, for not having written. I have been thinking a great deal about you two—but I wasn't in a very

---

[1] Actually there were three visits: in summer 1863 (described in *A Personal Record*), in summer 1866, and between autumn 1866 and summer 1867.

[2] Letter in French. A copy by Aniela Zagórska is in Yale University Library.

[3] Karola Zagórska was threatened with tuberculosis.

[4] Transferring the copyright of Conrad's translations into Polish and Russian to Aniela Zagórska.

happy frame of mind and when I am in such a state it is impossible for me to touch the pen. I have a horror of it.

Jessie sends her love.[1] I kiss you both with all my heart.

CONRAD.

63. *To Miss Aniela Zagórska*[2]

Oswalds,
24.12.20.

My dear Aniela,

My thoughts are with you on this Christmas Eve and I wish you good health and a tranquil mind for the year to come; God alone knows how it may be achieved.

Mr. Śliwiński[3] (I don't know if you have met him) was here and told me about a Polish bookseller or publisher who, after having returned from England, was telling everybody that he had seen me and arranged with me for the publication of my books, etc. etc. I am quite annoyed because I have never seen any Polish publisher either at my home or anywhere else. Should anyone speak to you about it don't believe in it at all and just wave at him my previous letter which gives you all the copyrights in my works for Poland and Russia. In a fortnight I am going to send you the official document.

I have had news from Karola from Milan. I shall write to her today.

Jessie and the boys kiss you warmly and send you their best love.

Your devoted
KONRAD.

64. *To Miss Aniela Zagórska*[4]

Oswalds,
19.1.21

My dear Aniela,

I am sending you the document[5] endorsed by the Polish Consulate. . . .

---

[1] Sentence in English in the original.
[2] Miss Zagórska's French translation, in Yale University Library.
[3] Probably Artur Śliwiński (1877–1952), an historian.
[4] Miss Zagórska's French translation (with a passage deleted), in Yale University Library.
[5] Mentioned in Conrad's letter to Miss Zagórska of 24 December 1920.

I have received your letter. I embrace you tenderly for all you say. It is wonderful the way you write English! Jessie is going to write to you today. The day after tomorrow we are leaving for Corsica (Hôtel Continental, Ajaccio) for a two or three months' stay. I shall try to work there because it is already a year since I have done anything. The boys send their dear love to you.[1] I am asking you to forgive me the shortness of this letter but I am very busy with our Corsican expedition.

Yours with all my heart
KONRAD.

65. *To Karola Zagórska*[2]

6.3.21.
Gd Hôtel d'Ajaccio
Ajaccio

My dear,

I can assure you that on the day of our arrival here I gave a whole lot of postcards to the hotel door-keeper to post—among them was one for you. I cannot understand how it happened that it did not reach you. I must confess that since that day I have not written any letters, neither to you nor to anyone except Borys, about a matter concerning him.

I am quite ashamed of myself but I beg of you to forgive your Konrad who loves you, for this sin—as well as for all the others. Just before our departure I caught an atrocious cough and for about 10 days after we arrived here I did not feel at all well—it was something similar to asthma. You may add to it my moral depression which I cannot shake off. Je vous dis ça en confidence, because in public and with my wife I put a good face on things.

Jessie likes Corsica. She walks about with a stick and looks well. But she, too, has become lazy and neglects her correspondence. She sends you her dear love[3] and promises to write to you in a few days' time. We have good news from the boys. B. is working in London and John is at Tonbridge, the school where we sent him before leaving.

Please send me a line and say you have forgiven my long silence.

[1] Sentence in English in the original.
[2] French translation, with comments, by Aniela Zagórska; in Yale University Library.
[3] Three words in English in the original.

To Karola Zagórska (6 March 1921)

That is all for today. We are certain to stay here for about a fortnight and then perhaps we shall go to Bastia.

Always your loving
KONRAD.

66. To Bruno Winawer[1]

Oswalds,
Bishopsbourne,
Kent.
12.6.21.

Dear Sir,

Thank you very much for sending me the comedy,[2] I found it interesting and (pourquoi pas le dire) greatly entertaining, which however did not prevent me from taking your work quite seriously.

As far as the translation is concerned I do not have any connexions in the world where these things get done. So for the time being I can think of no one and it seems to me that if I looked for someone (which would be rather difficult as I seldom come to London) it would not be easy to find a suitable person.

At present I am very busy but I hope to be more free in some three weeks' time and I shall see then what can be done.

The translation, however, is not everything. What you probably have in mind is placing the play with a London theatre. I must explain that although I have a fairly wide reputation it is strictly confined to my own work. Personally I have no influence either in the world of publishers or in the theatre world. I do not know a single actor or actress, director or capitalist entrepreneur, nor in fact anything that is the theatre's. Furthermore, I must add that I have never met my publishers either socially or in business. All my affairs are in the hands of Mr. J. B. Pinker, my literary agent and

---

[1] The originals of Conrad's letters to Bruno Winawer (1883–1944) were destroyed in the Second World War. Winawer published eight of those letters in *Głos Prawdy*, 1926, Nos. 108 and 114; and Jean-Aubry included four—written in English—in *Joseph Conrad: Life and Letters*, vol. ii. In 1924 Winawer made, on Jean-Aubry's request, typewritten copies probably of all the letters (fifteen in number) that he had received from Conrad. These copies, with Winawer's comments in French, are now preserved in Yale University Library. Compared with the published letters, the text of the copies is much fuller and better (of the letter of 10 August 1921, for instance, Jean-Aubry published inexplicably only the first half; and three unpublished letters are included): therefore I have accepted the Yale typescript as the basis of the present version. The letters published here for the first time are those of 12 February 1922, 19 July 1922 and 9 September 1923. The letter above is the only one of which we have a draft (in Yale University Library), in Conrad's hand, dated 10.6.21. The draft differs very little from Winawer's copy.

[2] Bruno Winawer, *Księga Hioba* (The book of Job), Warsaw, 1921.

friend of 20 years' standing, who acts on my behalf and sends me contracts to be signed.

That is the position. Your comedy appeals to me so I shall try to do all that I can but please do not count on me. Anyway I shall write to you in 3 weeks' time.

Please accept my friendly greetings,

Yours sincerely,

JOSEPH CONRAD.

67. *To Bruno Winawer*

Oswalds,
Aug. 10th, 1921.

Dear Mr. Winawer,

I am writing to you in English this time, as I am confident that you know the language and it is easier for me to dictate.

I must begin by thanking you for the little book of satirical pieces[1] which I read with great enjoyment and in that sympathetic mood which your work arouses in me. As a matter of fact, I like all the pieces, both as point of view and as expression.

Now as to the play.[2] As I have anticipated I have not been able to find a translator. I did not even know very well how to begin to look for one. Of course there are translating and typewriting offices where they would translate from any language, but to deliver your play to that fate was not to be thought of. Therefore I took the matter in hand myself, notwithstanding the arrears of my own work in the way of preparing my Collected Edition, of which ten volumes have appeared by now, and the fact that I have a long novel in hand which causes me much labour and worry.[3]

The work now is finished[4] and I am sending you a copy by registered post. I don't for a moment suppose that you will be pleased with the translation. No author is ever pleased with a translation of his work. That cannot be expected. The first reading will no doubt exasperate you, but I am confident that after a time you will discover an amount of fidelity to your thought and even your expression which you could not have been able to find in any other translation more accurately verbal. You will notice no doubt that

---

[1] Bruno Winawer, *Groteski* ('Grotesques'), Warsaw, 1921.
[2] Winawer's *Księga Hioba*.
[3] *Suspense*, which was never finished.
[4] According to Jean-Aubry, on 25 June. The translation was published in 1931: *The Book of Job*, A Satirical Comedy, translated by J. Conrad.

it is strictly idiomatic and you may take it from me that the idioms are absolutely correct and employed in strict accordance with your artistic intention. My guiding idea was to make the work acceptable to a theatrical audience. In one or two places you will discover a certain shortening of speeches, but nothing material has been missed. I have also summarized rather than translated the preliminary descriptive matter, leaving just enough to guide the English actors. In one or two places I have altered the phrasing so as to make the thought more accessible to the English or American public, and I have taken the liberty to invent names for certain characters, in order to make them acceptable to the ears of the audience.[1]

This being done, I showed the play to several people capable of judging, not one of them being a dramatic author but any of them being possible as an intelligent member of the theatrical public. All the opinions were very favourable and indeed, I may say, very appreciative. Then I had down here my agent, Mr. J. B. Pinker, and we discussed the matter thoroughly. Personally he was very pleased. From a business point of view he said that the difficulty of getting it accepted would be great, but once accepted a success would be quite possible. He declared himself ready to take the matter in hand, both here and in America, not only on the ground that it is my translation but on the merits of the play itself. There are two courses now open before you. First, with the copy I am sending you, you may personally approach anybody here or in America by what ever means you can command. And in that case I can only wish you luck and beg you to submit the English text simply as a translation without mentioning my name. It is quite good enough to pass on its own merits. That is one alternative and in that case there can be no question of any financial transaction between you and me. I was very glad to do the translation for you, as a friendly act, and here is an end of it. The second alternative is that you should put the play in the hands of Mr. Pinker as a translation by Joseph Conrad, in which case the net proceeds, whatever they may be, would have to be divided as follows: 50 per cent. for you, 40 per cent. for me and 10 per cent. for Mr. Pinker, which is his usual charge for all the business he does for me and his other clients, such as A. Bennett, John Galsworthy and many others. In other words: we divide the proceeds but I pay the whole of the agent's commission; both our names appearing on the bills and in the advertisements. This seems to me a fair arrangement. Before

---

[1] Conrad made various rather important alterations in the text of the play, making it less specifically Polish in its social reference. Cf. Róża Jabłkowska, *Joseph Conrad*, Wrocław, 1961, pp. 349–51.

you decide you must thoroughly understand that the chances are very much against us, and that the placing of the play and (even if placed) its financial success are very doubtful indeed. Pray keep that well in mind. The success of a play, both with managers and the public, is mostly a matter of luck and in this particular case the foreignness of the play is bound to be an adverse element. I hope therefore you will not build any hopes on it and that you will regard the transaction as something in the nature of taking a lottery ticket.

However, should you select the second alternative you will have to write a letter, either in French or English, addressed to J. B. Pinker, Esqre., Talbot House, Arundel Street, London, W.C.2, empowering him to act on your behalf on conditions specified in this letter. This will be sufficient, and I do not think that a formal agreement as between you two is necessary, and as to me, of course Mr. Pinker will act under the general powers he has to treat on my behalf for all my work whatever kind it may be.

Yours faithfully
JOSEPH CONRAD[1]

Bruno Winawer, Esq.
Warsaw.

68. *To Miss Aniela Zagórska*[2]

Oswalds,
21.8.21.

My dear Angela,

I write in English because it is easier for me today. I ought to have told you long ago how deeply touched I was by your gifts to Jessie and myself on the occasion of our silver wedding.[3] My dear, I think you ought not to have deprived yourself of these mementos of the past. But you may be sure that at least with us they shall be cherished not only as coming from you two but also for the sake of your loved dead, to whom we too lay the claim of memory and affection.

I am truly glad at your news of the contract with a good pub-

---

[1] On the copy of this letter preserved in Yale University Library there is a note by Winawer saying that 'in a post-scriptum in Polish Conrad asks to keep everything a secret. He would not like to be asked to do other translations. "This one is an exception" —he says.'

[2] Miss Zagórska's copy of the letter, in Yale University Library.

[3] The sisters Zagórski sent the Conrads (who had been married on 24 March 1896) some old photographs and other family relics.

lishing house; and still more glad to hear that you, personally, are taking the translation in hand. I of course consent in advance to *all* changes and modifications you may find necessary to make in the course of your work. 'Almayer's Daughter' may be a very good title especially in point of view of the public.

A few days ago we had a letter from Karola. The treatment seems to have done her good. I am fairly well. Jessie is still in pain but improving slowly. We all here send you our dear love. Ever your faithful

CONRAD.

P.S. I am sending you *Notes on Life and Letters* by tomorrow's post. Many thanks for the books & newspapers. I shall remind Jessie about the photos. Je vous embrasse.

69. *To Tadeusz Marynowski*[1]

Oswalds,
Bishopsbourne,
Kent.
8th September, 1921.

Dear Sir,

Thank you very much for your letter informing me of the illness of my relation, Miss Karola Zagórska.

My health does not allow me to make the journey to Mil., and in addition it would be fatal for my work, which is my only source of income.

I feel certain that you will wish to exercise your care in a larger sense than a purely official one, when trying to organize a tolerable life for the invalid. It is, therefore, only a question of means.

The position is as follows: last year, before Miss Zagórska's departure from us, I assured her of an allowance of £120 (pounds sterling) annually for 3 years—that is £10 monthly, payable quarterly. I know that this is not a lot, but she assured me that she would be able to manage. The allowance for the current quarter was paid to her at the beginning of July (£30). Thus next quarter's will be due in October.

[1] In the possession of Mr. Mieczysław Zagayski in New York; a photographic copy was published by Aleksander Janta in the volume *Conrad żywy*, London 1957. Somebody, overzealously discreet, has crossed out all names mentioned in the letter; that it concerns Miss Karola Zagórska is made obvious by Conrad's letter to Richard Curle of 18 August 1920. Tadeusz Marynowski was the Polish consul in Milan.

Now, for the moment the following can be done: in the course of next week (probably on Monday) I shall send her £20*) (c/o xxx xxx[1]) with a letter in which I shall say that feeling somewhat anxious about her health I am sending her this additional £20 to enable her to make herself more comfortable, etc. and that I intend to raise her allowance from £30 to £50 per quarter until her health definitely improves. Thus your intervention in the matter will remain undisclosed; and I trust that you will be kind enough to let me know if £200 a year is enough to ensure a more or less tolerable life for Miss Zagórska in her present state of health. What happens later we shall see.

In any case, I take the liberty of asking you, in case of need, to advance Miss Zagórska any necessary sum, informing me of it by telegram or letter so that I can repay you immediately. Once again I thank you for your letter and I remain with great respect, your devoted servant.

JOSEPH CONRAD.

* for the current quarter July–September.

70. *To Bruno Winawer*

Oswalds,
Bishopsbourne,
Kent.
20.9.21.

Dear Sir,

I am pleased to learn that you liked my translation. My error in connexion with Okólnik[2] is amusing; but you know what—we could leave it like that. During the war, and even after, the English public has heard a lot about various government 'Circulars A/W 5087A' so it will be accepted at face value as something relating to a gentleman with two names and of a doubtful nationality.

Qu'en pensez-Vous?

Pinker was here at the end of last week. He has two copies of Job—one for England and the other for the United States, and you may rest assured that everything possible will be done to put the play on the stage. But it is a doubtful matter. Generally speaking

---

[1] Name crossed out.

[2] 'Okólnik' means in Polish 'a circular', but it is also the name of a street in Warsaw, where one of the characters in the play lives.

the circumstances are not favourable. My dramatized version of the novel *The Secret Agent* has been wandering around the world for the last 15 months. Recently Norman McKinnell paid £50 for the privilege of keeping it for consideration for a further 6 months. But I feel nothing will come of it.

That is the position. One cannot count on a success.

Bien à Vous
J. CONRAD.

71. *To Bruno Winawer*[1]

Oswalds,
Bishopsbourne.
Kent.
Oct. 23rd. 1921.

My dear Sir,

Thanks for your last letter in which you show your interest in the adaptation of my novel *The Secret Agent* for the stage, which has been done by myself in Four Acts, of which the Second is in two Scenes and the Fourth in three, I am sorry to say.[2] By Scenes I mean here what in French is called Tableaux. It was impossible to avoid that, at any rate for me, but one of our most clever producers (Metteurs en scène) assured me that it could be managed without much difficulty. However, the play has been hung up for more than a year now, McKinnel, one of our new actor-managers, having had an option on it for some time. But apparently he was afraid of beginning his career with it. He made three failures with other plays, and I imagine that his funds are now exhausted and that he will never produce it now. His option terminates at the end of this year. This has been a very bad time for theatres and the improvement is not very marked yet.

I am sorry to have no news to give you about our joint undertaking.[3] One copy is in America by now and the other is here of course, but I have not asked Pinker what precisely he is doing and he has volunteered no statement; therefore I beg you to arm yourself

[1] Letter in English.
[2] Originally there were as many as four scenes in the fourth Act. Winawer tried to get round the difficulties of performing the play by planning to divide the stage into two parts: one showing the shop and the other the parlour at the Verlocs' home. Cf. Conrad to Allan Wade, 4 April 1922.
[3] Winawer's comedy *The Book of Job*.

with patience and dismiss for the moment all optimistic thoughts, as I have done. You may, however, be assured that no opportunity will be neglected and no opening untried. You may also be certain that my own play will not be allowed to get in the way. The two things are very different; and, frankly, I don't care very much whether *The Secret Agent* gets on the stage or not. I have lost all interest in it by now and when McKinnel's option expires it will be put into a drawer.

I am, however, having 30 copies[1] of it privately printed for distribution amongst friends, and I will send you one as soon as they are ready. But as to your most kind and flattering proposal to translate it for the Polish stage, I must explain to you the whole situation.

More than a year ago I made over all my copyrights, for translation in Polish and Russian, to my cousin, Miss Angela Zagórska, whose address is: 5 ul. Wilcza, Warsaw. Therefore I must refer you to her for all arrangements, literary and others, connected with the translation and production of that play in Poland. The property of all translation rights in Poland and Russia has been made over to her by legal instrument and she may dispose of them as she thinks fit. All I can venture to say here is that nothing would please me more than to have *The Secret Agent* translated by you and to express an earnest hope that you two will come to a definite understanding on the matter of staging it in Poland.

Would you care to get in communication with her, tell her confidentially of our recent relations, and of course show her this letter? I don't think I will warn her beforehand that she may hear from you because I do not know how you may look at the situation.

She has written to me lately to say she is very anxious to see *The Secret Agent* in its stage form. Therefore I will send her a copy by the same post by which I will send you yours.

Thanks very much for your friendly promise to send me your new fantastic play *FF Rays*.[2] I am looking forward impatiently to its arrival. A fantastic play is a dangerous thing, generally speaking: and I am very curious to see what you have made of it. My warmest wishes for its success with the Cracow public.

With kindest regards
very cordially yours
J. Conrad.

---

[1] Fifty-two copies, according to Jean-Aubry.
[2] *Promienie FF*, staged in Cracow in October 1921 and published in Warsaw 1926.

29 November 1921

72. *To Karola Zagórska*[1]

Oswalds,
29.XI.21

My dear Karolcia,

I have not been at all well this autumn. What torments me more than anything else is the difficulty with which I work—whole days are fruitless! Courage is needed to look into the future with serenity. I should like to know, my dear, if your health has improved. Have you received the book (*Notes on Life and Letters*) which was posted c/o the Consulate?

I am sending you *The Arrow of Gold* in the new edition which is less expensive but looks quite presentable; and *Youth* in a small-size edition—the paper is bad but the print reasonably good. *Typhoon* is at the moment out of print.

With us nothing has changed. Borys is working in London and likes his job very much. John is at school where he does his best and is liked by everybody; he has a formidable appetite which, however, does not make him put on any weight. As to Jessie, she is taking plenty of exercise but it is still impossible for her to claim to be slim. One of my hands (the left one) is done up with a bandage but it doesn't worry me as for the last ten days my work has been getting on better. That is all for the moment, my dear.

Always your affectionate
KONRAD.

73. *To Bruno Winawer*

Oswalds,
Bishopsbourne,
Kent.
9 Dec. 21.

My dear Sir,

Many thanks for the *Monachomachia*.[2] I like the way it is illustrated. C'est tout-à-faitbien. The pattern scheme[3] of these little pictures, their colour and details are most interesting and

---

[1] French translation by Miss Aniela Zagórska, Yale University Library.

[2] An excellent mock-heroic poem (1778) by a distinguished writer, Bishop Ignacy Krasicki (1735–1801). The edition (Cracow 1921) given to Conrad by Winawer was illustrated by Zofia Stryjeńska (born 1894).

[3] Two words in English in the original.

entertaining. I am glad to have this attractive Polish publication; moreover, the quality of the paper and the typography are faultless.

Your favourable opinion of my play[1] pleased me a lot. No doubt, Vous y mettez beaucoup d'indulgence but I cannot really quarrel with you about it. So please accept my cordial handshake—sans phrases.

The division of labour between Aniela and yourself strikes me as an excellent idea.[2] Most likely the first performance will take place on the Polish stage as just a week ago Norman McKinnell returned the MS. to me. I have asked Pinker to put it into a drawer for the time being. I am sorry not to have anything to say about our business.[3]

My best wishes to you for Christmas, for the new year and for many years to come.

Bien à Vous
J. CONRAD.

74. *To Miss Aniela Zagórska*[4]

Oswalds,
14.12.21.

My dear Aniela,

I read with pleasure your letter which reached me two days ago. You can well imagine how glad I am that you have liked my play.[5] It is good to know that the translation of Almayer has already been decided. I feel certain that your translation is excellent. J'ai beaucoup de confiance dans votre tempérament et le tour particulier de votre esprit m'est infiniment sympathique. And I have always felt that you understand me. Your dear letter which you sent after reading my *Notes on Life and Letters* was the best proof of it. It is difficult for me to express the happiness brought to me by your letter.

We still have not thanked you for your portrait. That is the sort of people we are—simply shocking! C'est un très beau dessin— vision d'un artiste; but the resemblance is not very striking. According to my memory you look different. Perhaps after looking at it longer I shall see better what Kamieński wanted to express. Permit

---

1 Dramatic version of *The Secret Agent*.
2 Winawer had proposed to translate in co-operation with Miss Zagórska the dramatic version of *The Secret Agent*.
3 The translation of Winawer's *Księga Hioba*.
4 Miss Zagórska's French translation, Yale University Library.
5 Dramatic version of *The Secret Agent*.

me to kiss you on both cheeks for this gift which, all the same, is precious to me.

I am very pleased that you liked Mr. Winawer. I was not sure as to the outcome of your meeting. I was afraid that something might not be to your liking. Men do not always resemble their works. I think the project of a joint translation is an excellent idea. Be so kind, my dear, as to remember me to Mr. Żeromski and give him my deeply sincere regards. C'est un Maître! The impression left by his personality has remained vivid in my memory. At times I still seem to see and hear him.

We send you our best wishes for Christmas.

Yours with all my heart
KONRAD.

75. *To Miss Aniela Zagórska*[1]

Oswalds,
Bishopsbourne.
Kent.
27th January, 1922.

My dear Anielka,

The reason for my not writing to you was that for about a month I have been in bed with influenza complicated by an attack of gout. C'était charmant. Only today I have come down to my study, where everything somehow looks strange and uninviting.

Thank you for all your letters; vous m'avez réchauffé le cœur; and thank you, my dearest, for all the books you have presented me with, in particular for Fredro,[2] qui m'a donné un plaisir extrême à lire et à regarder les images. You are very good to me, Anielka dear, and I am grateful to you for it although I behave comme un brute.

Nevertheless you must forgive me. I could not work properly the whole of last year—I could not even concentrate my thoughts without a great effort. This makes me worried and fretful. Je ne suis pas très heureux ma chère.

Now there is only one complete edition of my works.[3] Edition de

[1] *Ruch Literacki*, 1927, No. 5.

[2] Aleksander Fredro (1793–1876) was the best Polish writer of comedies. The volume sent by Zagórska was his *Trzy po trzy* ('Tattle prattle'), a beautiful autobiographical book written (between 1844–6) in the vein of Sterne's *A Sentimental Journey*. The action takes place at the end of the Napoleonic wars. Ed. by Henryk Mościcki, Warsaw 1917.

[3] Heinemann, London, 1921.

luxe—750 in England and 750 in America. It was sold out before publication. The price for the 18 volumes was 20 pounds sterling. I can see now in various catalogues that even for £30 it is difficult to get it. The author had six sets (18 vol. each). Of these I have kept two sets—one for each of the boys—the remaining ones were sent as 'politesses' to various personages to whom they were due. That is why, my dear, I could not send you one. C'était tout simplement impossible. However, I can now tell you that this very morning I signed a contract for the publication of a uniform edition, unlimited, of all my works, pour le grand public. I shall send one to you as soon as it starts to come out! But it may possibly take a year's time. Voilà, that is all for today.

Always your most faithful,
KONRAD.

76. *To Bruno Winawer*[1]

Oswalds,
Bishopsbourne,
Kent.
12th Feb. 1922.

Dear Sir,

Thank you for your extremely interesting letter. I very much like your idea of dividing the scene in the 4th Act into two parts.[2]

Would you be so kind as to give to Mrs. Rettinger[3] my friendliest and most respectful regards.

I have suffered a most painful loss in my old friend J. B. Pinker who died five days ago in New York after a very short illness. It's a great sorrow to me. Our friendship lasted for 22 years. He was 6 years younger than myself and I feel quite overpowered by this blow of fate.

This doesn't help our affairs. He was going to try and place the comedy.[4] His son who is taking over after his father has neither his father's experience nor his influential position. Anyway, we shall see.

---

[1] Letter in French; Winawer's copy in Yale University Library.
[2] In the dramatic version of *The Secret Agent*.
[3] Mrs. Otolia Retinger, the first wife of Dr. J. H. Retinger, co-operated with Winawer in translating the dramatic version of *The Secret Agent*. Conrad knew her from his visit to Poland in 1914.
[4] *The Book of Job* by Winawer.

To Bruno Winawer (12 *February* 1922)

Would you kindly give the news to my cousin Angèle? I can't make myself write letters.

Please excuse this short note.

Yours ever
JPH CONRAD.

77. *To Karola Zagórska*[1]

Oswalds,
22.2.1922.

My dear Karola,

I have been in bed for a whole month—it was influenza and gout. Even now I still don't feel well.

Meanwhile, Jessie got suspicious pains in her leg and it appears that one more operation is essential. Tomorrow we are going to London so that Sir Robert Jones may see her and decide.

Mr. Pinker, my agent and friend (did you meet him?), died suddenly a fortnight ago in New York. And so after twenty years all my business affairs have fallen on me. Mr. P.'s son will be in charge of his father's office but it will never be the same.

We kiss you most warmly.

Your affectionate
KONRAD.

P.S. For the last year I've known no peace of mind and cannot work well. You understand what it means. Recently I have begun to feel a slight relaxation. Perhaps it will pass? The boys are well. Think about me.

78. *To Bruno Winawer*[2]

Oswalds
Bishopsbourne
Kent.
12.4.22.

Dear Sir!

I apologize for the delay in replying to your letter of the 14th March. I have been very ill. I found your letter most interesting.

[1] Miss Aniela Zagórska's French translation, in Yale University Library.
[2] *Glos Prawdy*, 1926, No. 114.

Tout ce que vous avez fait est bien fait. However, I must admit to feeling curious as to how it was all done. Could you please send me a copy (typescript) of the text?[1] As to our affairs, I cannot get a definite answer from America and it seems to me it would be best to offer our patient Hiobe to the London Stage Society.[2]

During the London season the Stage Society produces two or three plays pour l'élite de l'intélligence et de la société. They give three performances of each, they pay nothing, but that is the way to get oneself known, as theatre managers attend the performances. I am not a member of the Stage Society but I have friends there. I wrote to the Secretary the day before yesterday. I am only afraid that their programme for the 1922 season has already been fixed. We shall see.

Anyway c'est une distinction to be played by the S.S., and it might lead to a contract. There is now in London an American (I don't remember his name) who is agent for several theatres. Perhaps something could be done with him.

Excuse my scribble. Please be so kind as to tell Miss A. Zagórska that you have had news from me and that I shall soon write to her.

Faites mes amitiés je vous prie à Żeromski pour qui j'ai une vraie affection.

Tout à vous
J. CONRAD.

79. *To Miss Aniela Zagórska*[3]

Oswalds,
19.4.22

My dear Anielcia,

I am answering you immediately although I think that by now you must have received Jessie's letter.

I was in bed for a fortnight and now I am again beginning to work. My financial situation is a bit shaky. Pinker was an optimist. For the last two years my expenses were too big and now I shall have to suffer for it. Enfin. I had nothing to be pleased about and

---

[1] Of Winawer's translation of the dramatic adaptation of *The Secret Agent*. Conrad was particularly interested in Winawer's projects for stage settings. He considered Winawer to be a 'very clever adapter'.

[2] Conrad took great pains to have *The Book of Job* staged. It was Allan Wade who suggested approaching the Stage Society (cf. Conrad's letter to him of 9 April 1922, Jean-Aubry, *Joseph Conrad: Life and Letters*, vol. ii, pp. 269–71). The attempt proved unsuccessful.

[3] Miss Aniela Zagórska's French translation, in Yale University Library.

that is why I did not write. I have just answered Mr. Winawer's letter and asked him to give you my news.

Jessie is well on the whole but still suffering. The treatment did not prove very successful. Borys is working in London and John is on holiday. We embrace you most affectionately.

Forgive me for not writing to you more often. I am still not feeling entirely well and after half a day's work I am terribly tired!

Always your affectionate
KONRAD.

80. *To Bruno Winawer*[1]

Oswalds,
Bishopsbourne,
Kent.
July 19th, 1922.

My dear Sir,

I dictate these few words to thank you most heartily for your letters and especially for your little tale[2] which I have read with absolute delight and appreciation of every point, and greatest sympathy with the mind which conceived it and the literary gift which guided the pen.

During the last few weeks I have been finishing a novel[3] and was too absorbed to write to anybody. You must therefore pardon my long silence.

This moment I receive your letter telling me that the S.A. will be performed in Warsaw.[4] I have been made very happy by hearing this. I hope, my dear Sir, you understand that any part I may have in the proceeds of the royalties has been made over to Miss Angela Zagórska who has the property of my works in Poland and Russia, by a document duly executed here.

I must stop now because I am correcting the MS. of the novel to go at once to America and the time in which to do it is very short.

J. CONRAD.

[1] Letter in English.
[2] Winawer's short novel *Ślepa latarka* ('Dark Lantern'), Warsaw, 1922.
[3] *The Rover*, finished at the end of June.
[4] *The Secret Agent* was never performed in Warsaw, but only in Cracow, in a small theatre, 'Bagatela'.

81. *To Miss Aniela Zagórska*[1]

Oswalds,
8.11.22.

My dear Aniela,

I am asking your forgiveness for dictating this letter. My hand is painful and anyway your English is perfect. I returned from London very tired! It is easier for me to dictate.

As[2] you will know by the telegram I am sending you today, the play[3] has failed notwithstanding a good first night; nearly the whole of the press giving an unfavourable verdict on the ground of defective stagecraft and absence of concentration of effect as a whole. All this in a very friendly and respectful manner.

How it will affect the prospect of the play being produced in Warsaw I cannot tell. I should not be surprised if it stopped it altogether. I would understand it though I would be very sorry.

Please tell Mr. Winawer that of course that will affect the prospects of his play[4] unfavourably. The Dramatic Society has been considering it for the last three weeks, but there is very little chance of them taking it up now. I regret it very much. I hoped that even a half-success for the Agent would have helped to place the *Book of Job*.

Please, my dear, drop me a line about things in general. I am sending you, at Karola's request, a copy of *Victory*. Jessie[5] and the boys send you both their affectionate love.

Always yours
KONRAD.

82. *To Bruno Winawer*[6]

Oswalds,
Bishopsbourne,
Kent.
Nov. 23rd, 1922.

My dear Sir,

Please excuse my writing in English but my hand is painful and I am compelled to dictate—doing so in Polish would mean spelling it out letter by letter.

Thank you very much for your letter received three days ago and for the newspaper page which came by today's post.

[1] Miss Zagórska's copy, with a French translation of the Polish text, in Yale University Library. [2] The English text begins here.
[3] The dramatic version of *The Secret Agent*.
[4] *The Book of Job*, a comedy translated by Conrad.
[5] The rest of the letter is in Polish.
[6] Letter in English, apart from the opening paragraph and the closing words, which

To Bruno Winawer (23 November 1922)

Any failure is disagreeable, but in this case I was not unduly affected and I do not think of it except as a curious and, to me, novel experience.[1] I will also tell you that I anticipated what has happened for reasons which were not exclusively connected with the defects and the difficulties of the play itself. The reading of press-cuttings gave me the impression as of being in a parrot-house. Same tones, same words, same noises. Personally I was treated with great consideration; it is a pity that a little more consideration has not been given to the play. If it had been a criminal act it could not have been more severely condemned. There were, however, a few notable exceptions from the first, and afterwards a certain controversy arose upon the manner in which dramatic critics should exercise their function.

All this is over now. As to the production, I will not enter here upon the subject, except from the practical point of view. The play was presented in Three Acts, the Drawing-room Act becoming the Third Scene of Act Second, and the Fourth Act being then called the Third. That certainly gave a better balance to the composition. I made severe cuts (after the first night) in Scene I (with the Professor), and Scene II (Insp. Heat), and, as to that last, I was very glad to do it, because these two parts were so badly cast that the less those people had to do and say the better, I thought, it would be for the play as a whole. As a matter of fact I wanted to do those cuts during the rehearsals but was not allowed then to have my way. But, upon the whole, I should like you to understand that I have practically nothing to do with the production. I did not go to the première or any other of the ten performances.

I have no remarks or suggestions to offer as to the production in Warsaw. All that will have to come from you; and I am perfectly certain that you will do everything that can be done to make the play acceptable on the stage. But an appeal to a public is like an appeal to the Olympian gods—whose tempers were uncertain and tastes capricious.

I was very much interested in the theatrical announcements and the programme of the Polish Theatre.[2] Your little article on queues as a social function, on the mobility of tastes, on the education of the nouveau riche, and other public matters, made delightful reading.

Warm regards and a handshake

JPH CONRAD.

are in Polish. These Polish fragments are contained in Winawer's letter to Jean-Aubry of 23 Oct. 1924 (in Yale University Library).

[1] The dramatic version of *The Secret Agent* was performed at the Ambassadors Theatre on 2 November and taken off on the 11th.

[2] One of the leading theatres in Warsaw, which was supposed to stage *The Secret Agent*.

83. *To Miss Aniela Zagórska*[1]

Oswalds,
Bishopsbourne,
Kent.
24th November 1922.

My dear Aniela,

I am sending you a photograph which you will be able to use for the publication of the translations.[2] I'm very sorry that you had such difficulties—almost unpleasantnesses—with them; but I am pleased at the news that the edition has already been arranged, and that its publication will begin shortly.

From the time of our return from London three weeks ago, I feel a little better. Jessie also, although from time to time the pain in her leg recurs—which perhaps I feel more than she does. I would be happy if after so many years her suffering ceased.

La controverse in the papers about the fate of *The Secret Agent* has now ceased. We shall see what Warsaw has to say about it! Mr. W.[3] has written to me that la première will be at the end of March. I'm sorry but I have been unable to do anything with his play here. I am beginning to lose hope.

My dearest one! Thank you for *Pożoga*.[4] C'est très, très bien. It seizes hold of and interests one both by its subject and by the way it is written. And also as a documentary it has a great value—for the author knows how to observe and has a soul which is grandement humaine. To say nothing of the style, which reflects so fully her sincerity and her courage—toute la tonalité du récit me charme par la note de simple dignité qui est admirablement soutenue. Jessie embraces you.

Always your loving.
KONRAD.

[1] *Ruch Literacki*, 1927, No. 5.
[2] An edition of *Selected Works* of Conrad was being prepared by Miss Zagórska.
[3] Bruno Winawer; see Conrad's letter to him of 23 Nov. and notes.
[4] Zofia Kossak-Szczucka, *Pożoga: Wspomnienia z Wołynia 1917–19*, Cracow, 1923 (postdated). English translation: *The Blaze: Reminiscences of Volhynia 1917–19*, Allen & Unwin, London, 1935.

84. *To Tadeusz Żuk-Skarszewski*[1]

Oswalds,
Bishopsbourne, Kent
Dec. 29th, 1922.

Dear Sir,

I regret to have to dictate my thanks for your friendly communication of Dec. 18th, relating to some of my family relics now in the possession of Madame Orlikowska.[2]

I should of course be very glad to have them. I regret if it is going to cause any trouble to Madame Orlikowska. I will write to her to the address you mention and I hope that our Legation in Warsaw will consent to take charge of the parcel.

Believe me, my dear Sir, with warm regards to Mrs. Skarszewska and yourself.

Very faithfully yours,
JOSEPH CONRAD.

PS. You will make me happy by sending me your works of which you speak in your letter.[3]

85. *To Miss Aniela Zagórska*[4]

Oswalds,
30.XII.22.

My dear Angela,

I begin by dictating and telling you in English my impression of the translated Almayer, the copy of which reached me two days ago.

I have read it twice with great care and in a thoroughly critical spirit. I am perfectly satisfied and even more than satisfied. As far as I can judge the atmosphere is rendered in a wonderful way and I assure you, my dear, that I am very grateful to you for this faithful interpretation of my work. The appearance of the book, too, pleases me very much and I hope with my whole heart that it will have with the Polish public a success at least as great, as the French translation had in France.[5]

---

[1] L. Krzyżanowski (ed.), *Joseph Conrad: Centennial Essays*, The Polish Institute of Arts and Sciences in America, New York, 1960, p. 133. Tadeusz Żuk-Skarszewski (1858–1933) was a neo-romantic novelist. Letter in English.
[2] Daughter of Dr. Izydor Kopernicki, frequently mentioned in T. Bobrowski's letters to Conrad. [3] The postscript is in Polish in the original.
[4] Miss Zagórska's copy in Yale University Library.
[5] Miss Zagórska says in a note that she has lost the rest of the letter.

86. *To Miss Aniela Zagórska*[1]

Oswalds,
19.1.23.

My dear Aniela,

Thank you for your letter. I am overjoyed that your excellent translation of Almayer has met with such a great success with people whose opinion counts.

I shall be soon writing to Mr. Żeromski—as soon in fact as I complete the third part of my long novel.[2] As to the translation of *Wszystko i nic*[3] by Mr. Żeromski I find the idea of sending the manuscript to our legation[4] utterly absurd! What have they been doing with it for a whole year? I must know all the details before I do something about it myself. Perhaps they've sent the manuscript to various publishers? That would be fatal because it's obvious that it has been turned down. It's bad to go to people with a manuscript which has been rejected. However, I shall try to place it somewhere if only Mr. Żeromski instructs our legation to send me the manuscript avec une petite note. In any case I have to warn you that the 'magazines' don't print translations and the more serious 'reviews' don't accept novels and short stories. At present there is nothing here similar to the *Revue des deux mondes* or *Revue de Paris*.

My hand hurts me now so I must finish. I shall write to you soon.

I kiss you a thousand times and so does Jessie and John. In half an hour I am seeing John off to the station. He is returning to school.

Your faithful,
KONRAD.

87. *To Mrs. Żuk-Skarszewska*[5]

20. I. 1923

Dear Mrs. Skarszewska,

It was very good of you to write. I had no idea I owed the pleasure of receiving those examples of Polish art to your husband.

[1] Miss Zagórska's French translation, in Yale University Library.
[2] *Suspense.*
[3] *All and Nothing* (1919), a long historical story from the times preceding the Polish November Insurrection in 1830.
[4] The Polish legation in London.
[5] L. Krzyżanowski (ed.), *Joseph Conrad: Centennial Essays*, New York, 1960, p. 134. Letter in English.

To Mrs. Żuk-Skarszewska (20 January 1923)

I was intensely delighted. The cover arrived all right by last night's
post.

Many, many thanks.

Will you please give my warm regards to your husband and tell
him I have just finished reading the *Rumak*[1] with the greatest
possible interest. I think it's simply wonderful in its sustained power
and its charm of expression.

I am just now desperately busy with a novel[2] which I must
finish by a given date; and as ill-luck would have it, my secretary is
laid up, so that I must attend myself to that part of my correspondence of which she relieves me generally. I haven't been able as yet
to find time to begin *Pustka*.[3]

Believe me, dear Mrs. Skarszewska, with the greatest regard,

Very faithfully
JOSEPH CONRAD.

88. *To Miss Aniela Zagórska*[4]

Oswalds,
Feb. 12th 1923.

My dearest,

I return you the proof of 'Il Conde'.[5] I dictate this letter because
I want to post it tonight to you. The translation of Mr. L. Piwiń-
ski is really very good. I have made several suggestions as to the
rendering of the English text and proposed a few emendations as to
Polish. As to that last you will have a look and judge of them yourself. I think, my dear, that you can safely let him do the whole of
Set of Six if it is convenient to you.

I have read *Almayer's Folly* with great attention. The only suggestion I can make relates to the very last line where Abdulla
recites the attributes of Allah.

Could it be expressed in Polish with capital letters as below? . . .
szeptem imię Allaha. Łaskawego! Miłosiernego!⁶

My point is that Abdulla recites the well-known formula
mechanically; and if that effect can be conveyed into Polish, too,

---

¹ Tadeusz Żuk-Skarszewski, *Rumak Światowida: karykatura wczorajsza* (*Światowid's
Steed: A Caricature of Yesterday*), a novel, Cracow, 1919.
² *Suspense*, left unfinished.
³ Another Żuk-Skarszewski novel (*Desert*), Cracow, 1918.
⁴ Miss Zagórska's copy in Yale University Library. English in the original.
⁵ For the volume of *A Set of Six*, published in Warsaw in 1924.
⁶ In the original: '. . . breathed out piously the name of Allah! The Merciful! The
Compassionate!'

the impression would be more accurate. But perhaps it may seem to you disagreeable in sight or sound; in which case please leave it as it is. It is quite faithful enough.

Thank you for the press cuttings and the very interesting illustrated paper. I think that the criticisms of the work are intelligent and just and I am very touched by the warmth of appreciation. As to the translation every word in praise of it is *more* than deserved. I admire it immensely and am most grateful to you.[1]

I feel confident that there are people who can appreciate the value of your translation. It is a triumph, my Aniela!—I am carrying on my work with desperate determination.

A thousand kisses
your KONRAD.

89. *To Miss Aniela Zagórska*[2]

Oswalds,
Bishopsbourne,
Kent.
7th March, 1923.

My dear Anielcia,

Thank you for Słowacki's letters.[3] I have not read them yet. I have no time at the moment. My own writing progresses very slowly. I spend all my days sitting at my little table and by the evening I feel so tired that I no longer understand what I am reading.

The beautifully bound copy of *Almayer*[4] has reached me and I send you my warmest embraces for the pleasure it has given me.

Could you, ma chère amie, send me a drawing of the Nałęcz coat of arms? I wish to emboss the crest on the cover of the latest edition of my works. Here, I only have a small seal, from which it is difficult to reproduce a copy. Publication will start in May.

Do any Polish armorials exist smaller and less expensive than Niesiecki?[5] If so, could you possibly buy me a copy, the cost of

---

1 The rest of the letter was in Polish.

2 *Ruch Literacki*, 1927, No. 5.

3 Juliusz Słowacki (1809–49) was, with Mickiewicz, the greatest Polish romantic poet and dramatist. His letters, famous for their style, ran into many editions.

4 *Almayer's Folly*, in Aniela Zagórska's translation, was published as the first volume of Conrad's *Selected Works* in Polish, with an introduction by Stefan Żeromski: *Fantazja Almajera*, Warsaw, 1923.

5 Kacper Niesiecki, *Korona Polska*, Lvov, 1728–43, 4 vols.; many editions and abridged versions; the most extensive Polish armorial.

which I would then repay you. It is important that the drawings should be detailed and clearly reproduced.

I end this letter with a brotherly embrace.

Always yours,
KONRAD.

Sorry for all the trouble I am giving you.

90. *To Stefan Żeromski*[1]

Oswalds,
Bishopsbourne,
Kent.
25th March, 1923.

Dear Sir,

I am sending you my book *Notes on Life and Letters*. I would never have taken the liberty of doing so, had not Aniela Zagórska written to me recently that you wished to have it. The book consists of articles—chiefly contributions to newspapers, written during the course of many years.

Immediately after reading your wonderful preface to *Almayer's Folly* I asked Aniela to convey to you my gratitude for the great favour you have done me. I confess that I cannot find words to describe my profound emotion when I read this appreciation from my country, voiced by you, dear Sir—the greatest master of its literature.

Please accept, dear Sir, my most sincere thanks for the time, thought, and work you have devoted to me and for the sympathetic assessment which disclosed a compatriot in the author.[2]

With all my gratitude, believe me dear Sir, to be always your faithful servant.

J. K. KORZENIOWSKI.

PS. The book will be posted separately tomorrow.

[1] Photocopies in Jean-Aubry and other publications. Stefan Żeromski (1864–1925) was at that time the most respected and most popular Polish man of letters, writing in a strongly romantic and patriotic vein.

[2] Żeromski stressed in his enthusiastic introduction the relevance of Conrad's Polish background. His essay actually had the title 'Author–Compatriot'.

91. *To Bruno Winawer*[1]

Oswalds,
Bishopsbourne,
Kent.
6th April, 1923.

Dear Winawer,

Please accept my (unfortunately!) belated thanks for your letters, newspaper cuttings, and news of our 'Ajent'. Your comedy du Laboratoire[2] is perfect. 'Très chic'—as French painters used to say of their pictures. This formula expressed the highest degree of appreciation. Why are you hesitant about sending me your 'Inżynier'?[3] To tell you the truth for once (a novelist has to lie constantly, from morning till night—and for money at that!) please realize que j'aime beaucoup vos écritures de toutes sortes. You know what?—if you will send it addressed to Curzon Hotel, Curzon Street, London—I shall take it with me to America— comme compagnon de voyage. I shall be in London from the 16th till the 19th. On the 20th I shall leave for Glasgow and sail from there on 21st on the S.S. *Tuscania* whose Captain, David Bone, is an old acquaintance of mine. I shall return on the 10th June. There you have my timetable. As to my programme in the United States—it is going to be a private visit to my publisher, Mr. Doubleday. He has a house at Oyster Bay and I shall stay there with the exception of a few visits I have to pay to people with whom, for many years, I have been in correspondence or to people who came to see us in England. Voilà tout. Even so, I don't feel very much like going.

With a hearty handshake.

Bien à vous
J. CONRAD.

92. *To Miss Aniela Zagórska*[4]

Bishopsbourne,
Kent.
11th April, 1923.

My dearest Aniela,

I know that you are not angry with me, but I also know what a crime it was not to have written to you for so long. But I must tell

---

[1] *Glos Prawdy*, 1926, No. 114.
[2] *Roztwór prof. Pytla* ('Professor Pytel's Solution'), Warsaw, 1921.
[3] R. H., *Inżynier* ('R. H., Engineer'), a comedy, Lvov, 1924 (performed in 1923).
[4] *Pion*, 1934, No. 50.

you that I had a lot of unexpected work, such as, inter alia, the writing of a preface to the biography of my friend Stephen Crane[1] who died young in 1900—some 30,000 words, which for me was a pretty large undertaking. Also I had to revise the English and American texts of my *Rover* (which will be published towards the end of the year), and also the checking and correcting of the first two volumes of the 'uniform edition' of my works, which will be issued in May. Nowadays I easily get tired—and when I am tired I am without conscience and nothing will stir me. A nice cousin you have! I thank you a thousand times for the two volumes of Coats of Arms, which arrived just at the right moment. Jan copied everything that was necessary and now I could send them back if they would be useful. In any case I kiss your hands and thank you for your kindness and the trouble you have taken.

I heard from Mr. Winawer that the *Secret Agent* was performed in Cracow and, I understand, nicely received. I'm afraid that your work (yours and his) has been in vain. That will teach me not to poke my nose where it is not wanted! But I think that that is just what I am doing, going to America. But that is supposed to be for my wife and children's sake—to improve the state of my affairs. I am leaving on the 21st of this month and returning on the 15th June.

We all send you our thanks for the Easter Mass on our behalf—for your unchanging friendship and remembering us. Do not doubt, dearest cousin and friend, our warmest feelings towards you. You are daily in my thoughts and I am always (though old and useless) your true and loving,

KONRAD.

93. *To Miss Aniela Zagórska*[2]

Oswalds,
3.7.23.

Dear Aniela,

Please forgive me, but immediately after my return from America I've begun to suffer from gout in my right arm. I couldn't write and I didn't want to dictate.

. . .

---

[1] Thomas Beer, *Stephen Crane. A study in American letters*, Heinemann, London, 1924. Conrad's preface (about 10,000 words in fact) was later included in his *Last Essays*, edited by Richard Curle in 1926.

[2] Miss Zagórska's French translation, with an omission, in Yale University Library.

Thank you for the copies of the *Nigger*.[1] I like the translation and I am certain that it was a difficult task. But what gives me more pleasure than anything else is your translation of the preface. You did your work admirably—it is a gift of your faithful and true friendship and of your devotion. I kiss your hands and embrace you with real gratitude.

I shall write no more now as it is still difficult for me to write. Jessie sends her love.[2]

Yours with all my heart

KONRAD.

94. *To Bruno Winawer*

Oswalds, Bish. Kent.
9.9.23.

My dear Sir,

I must apologize for my long silence. I have never been a keen letter-writer. It is a special kind of laziness or perhaps a malady of will power and there may be nothing but death to cure me of it!

I am pleased that the Czechs (by the way, I dislike them—I do not know why) are interested in your work. I liked 'Inżynier' very much—very much indeed! Everything: the idea, the exposition, the style. I found there some deep affinities between the two of us—in the mental approach and in the nature of the feelings.

Do you want me to return your MS? My congratulations on your Italian expedition. Obviously it was a success. I prefer not to talk about my voyage.[3] Entre nous, I felt all the time like a man dans un avion, in a mist, in a cloud, in a vapour of idealistic phraseology; I was lost, bewildered, amused—but frightened as well. It was something that could not be caught either by eye or by hand! Obviously some power is hidden behind it—great power undoubtedly—and certainly talkative. Its chatter reminds one of a well-trained parrot. It makes me shiver! Tout cela est confié à Votre discretion as 1° I may be wrong and 2° I have feelings of great friendship towards many people there. Tout le monde a été charmant pour moi là bas. Indeed, one month is not enough to

---

[1] Of the Polish edition of *The Nigger of the 'Narcissus'*; cf. letter to Winawer of 9 September 1923.

[2] Sentence in English in the original.

[3] On an invitation of F. N. Doubleday, his American publisher, Conrad spent a month in the United States (1 May–2 June).

comprehend such a complicated machinery. Perhaps a whole life would not be sufficient.

Your 'chronique' is quite amusing. Thank you for sending it. I agree that the situation is funny although not gay. My warm handshake.

Tout à Vous
JOSEPH CONRAD.

P.S. Nigger's translation épatant.[1] Where did they get this vocabulary from?

95. *To Bruno Winawer*[2]

20 Nov. 23.

Dear Winawer,

All my thanks for your letter and the pamphlet about Einstein[3] which in my opinion is nothing less than a small masterpiece of its kind.

Acceptez, O! Homme versatile, ma poignée de main.

Bien à vous
J. CONRAD.

96. *To Bruno Winawer*[4]

Oswalds,
Bishopsbourne,
Kent.
X'mas Day 1923.

My dear Winawer,

In my thoughts I am with you today. I was unable to write to you in time as for nearly a month I have been in bed and even now I don't feel well. Your letter arrived two days ago. Thank you very much. Please accept my best wishes for the next year and for the whole of your (longest possible) life. Yes, my novel[5] came out

---

[1] A Polish translation, by Jan Lemański, of *The Nigger of the 'Narcissus'* had just appeared in Warsaw as vol. 3 of Conrad's *Selected Works*. The translation was bad, done in an artificially 'poetic', neo-romantic language.

[2] *Glos Prawdy*, 1926, No. 114.

[3] Bruno Winawer, *Jeszcze o Einsteinie: teoria względności z lotu ptaka* ('Again about Einstein: bird's-eye view of the theory of relativity'), Warsaw, 1924.

[4] *Glos Prawdy*, 1926, No. 114.

[5] *The Rover*.

in December. In a few days I shall send you a copy of the American edition.

A hearty handshake,

Bien à vous
J. CONRAD.

97. *To Miss Aniela Zagórska*[1]

Oswalds,
Xmas Day, 1923.

My dear Aniela,

I could not write to you sooner because I was in bed and even now I am not feeling entirely well. My thoughts are with you today—but there is nothing unusual in it. I think of you every day. I wish you all happiness for the coming year and for your whole life and I kiss you paternally.

. . .

In a few days' time I shall send you a copy of the American edition of my novel *The Rover*. We all here send you our affectionate wishes and kisses.

Always yours
KONRAD.

98. *To Bruno Winawer*[2]

Oswalds
Jan. 31st, 1924.

My wrist prevents my using the pen, therefore you must accept this dictated letter.

I am delighted to know that my old *Rover* has appealed to you, I conclude aesthetically as well as emotionally, and that my artistic purpose commends itself to your judgement.

As to its adaptability for the stage, I was at first surprised. But on thinking it over I see the possibility, though of course I do not see the way in which it could be visibly presented and spiritually rendered in spoken words. But it is a fact that the book has got very

---

[1] Miss Zagórska's French translation, with an omission, in Yale University Library.

[2] Letter in English. The copy of this letter, as preserved in Yale University Library, is the only one not made by Winawer himself. The text is not complete and in the last paragraph obviously spoiled. Therefore I have here accepted as a basis the text published by Jean-Aubry in *Joseph Conrad: Life and Letters*, ii, 335, although it too, like the Yale copy, lacks the beginning and the end.

little description, very few disquisitions, and is for the most part in dialogue en forme parlée.

I will tell you at once, however, that if it is to be done you are the man to do it. And I hope with all my heart that you will make the attempt, for Poland at any rate.

That would be a matter of arrangement with Aniela,[1] whom probably you would find more than willing. But being much impressed by what you say as to the drama possibilities, 'Powrótu Korsarza',[2] I am led to think that if done within ten or eleven months there would be a great chance for it in America. The book there is an immense success, and generally J. C. is receiving immense publicity on account of that particular work. Mere curiosity, as to the visual presentation of a novel so much read and talked about, may create a theatrical success; and if you like to try I will do my part in putting the text of your play exactly as you make it, without the slightest change or alteration, back into English; accepting your construction, and whatever spirit your creative instinct will put into it, without discussion. Of course the English will have to be my own.

I put forward this suggestion because I am interested in seeing what you will do. The American prospect may make it worth your while from a practical point of view.

As to England, I admit that my failure with *The Secret Agent* would be very much against a play with which I had anything to do. Mais on ne sait jamais! But I do not think that the Labour Government would forbid the play on the ground that being both Poles we are 'horrid aristocrats' and enemies of the virtuous Bolsheviks.

99. *To Roman Dyboski*[3]

Oswalds,
Bishopsbourne, Kent,
22 Feb. '24.

My dear Sir,

I am sorry I am so late in thanking you for the 2 vols. of Polish Literature[4] which I have read with the highest appreciation—and

---

[1] Zagórska; cf. letter to Winawer of 23 Oct. 1921.

[2] *Return of the Rover* (Polish in the original).

[3] Letter in English. *Czas*, Cracow, 27 March 1927. Roman Dyboski (1883–1945) was an historian of English literature, later a professor of comparative literature at the Jagiellonian University in Cracow.

[4] Roman Dyboski, *Periods of Polish Literary History*, being the Ilchester Lectures for 1923, O.U.P., London, 1923. *Modern Polish Literature*, O.U.P., London, 1924.

for the brochure on the Religious Element in Polish National Life[1] which told me many things I did not know before. I can hardly express my sense of the good and patriotic work you are doing by your publications in English, so attractive in matter and style. People here know very little of Poland—and I am afraid that there is not much general sympathy for the new State. But all this arises from sheer ignorance which only concise and perspicuous exposition of historical truth can gradually dispel. Pray accept my warm and most respectful regards and believe me most sincerely yours,

J. CONRAD.

100. *To Bruno Winawer*[2]

Oswalds,
Bishopsbourne,
Kent.
7th March, 1924.

My dear Sir,

I hope that you have got over your influenza. Although I didn't have it myself I was plagued by my own particular misfortune which always produces an inability to make any mental effort. C'est plus fort que moi. Naturally I should have answered your kind letter long ago. I was moved to see how you had taken my proposal to heart. I am in absolute agreement with your general opinion as to how this work should be done and as to the details of its execution. There is no need for any discussion of it between us. I can also assure you that no one has asked me and probably no one will ask me to dramatize this novel.[3] In any case pour moi vous êtes le seul homme possible.

However, I implore you to approach this work with an easy mind—not thinking about me at all and not feeling bound by any time limit—and with the conviction that should you find this work tedious there will be absolutely nothing on my part against your putting it off either for a certain time—or for ever. You for your part will not hold it against me should I write to you that I feel unable to translate your play[4] into English in a manner worthy of it.

---

[1] Roman Dyboski, 'The Religious Element in Polish National Life', *Sewanee Review*, 1923.
[2] *Glos Prawdy*, 1926, No. 114.
[3] *The Rover* (cf. Conrad's letter to Winawer of 31 January 1924).
[4] *R. H., Inżynier*, mentioned in the postscript.

To Bruno Winawer (7 March 1924)

What do you think about it?
Please forgive my scribble.

A handshake.
J. CONRAD.

PS. Just now I am unable to write more about *Inżynier* except that I read the play with the greatest pleasure. C'est tout à fait bien! Thank you for having sent it.

101. *To Miss Aniela Zagórska*[1]

Oswalds.
16.3.24.

My dear,

. . .

Thank you very much for the newspapers and books. I haven't yet begun the novel. I am very touched by the flattering reaction of the critics to the translation.[2] The article in *Robotnik*[3] is very good and has pleased me a lot.

I kiss you a thousand times

Yours
KONRAD.

102. *To Miss Aniela Zagórska*[4]

Oswalds,
April 28th, 1924.

Ma chère Angèle,

I am obliged to dictate this letter in English as I cannot use my right hand for writing in pen and ink for any length of time. I can just manage to sign my name.

I was very glad to hear from you that you are going to take the holiday on which you have set your heart. I am sorry to tell you that Sir Robert Jones has decided on another operation for Jessie, which he hopes will remove all the causes of those inflammatory

---

[1] Miss Zagórska's French translation, with the beginning omitted, in Yale University Library.
[2] Of the Polish edition of *A Set of Six* (*Sześć opowieści*, Warsaw, 1924).
[3] The daily of the Polish Socialist Party.
[4] Miss Zagórska's copy in Yale University Library.

troubles in the tissues from which she has been suffering so long. This operation will take place in Canterbury towards the end of May, and I hope to be able to transport Jessie back to Oswalds about the middle of June, where of course she will have to remain in bed some time longer.

The period of waiting will not be very pleasant. I will feel it more than Jessie herself who takes everything very quietly as you know. My health has been very wretched for a long time. I do not mean that I have been laid up much, but I have not been able to work, and this gives me considerable anxiety. However, I am feeling a little better just now, though my wrist is still very swollen and very painful.

There can be no question of us going abroad before the end of this year. We will be leaving this house in September, but we have not yet found another and our plans are very unsettled. Of course we will be delighted to have a visit from Miss Rakowska.[1] I remember her mother very well as a charming girl of 20. You do not give us her address in London, or else we might have written suggesting a day, but I hope that she will drop us a line.

Our dear love to you and best wishes for a pleasant journey. You may take it for certain that we will be in this house up to September 1st unless something utterly unexpected happens to call us away.

Your faithful
KONRAD.

103. *To Miss Aniela Zagórska*[2]

2.VI.24.

My dear Aniela,

I have just received your letter and am writing these few words to let you know that the operation[3] will take place on the 13th of this month.

Thank you for your letter and cuttings. I am delighted to know that I am penetrating to the heart and soul and that from the artistic point of view the *Set of Six* is so highly regarded. Here, these short stories weren't successful.

---

[1] Irena Rakowska, daughter of Maria Rakowska, born Ołdakowska (mentioned in Bobrowski's letters to Conrad), visited Oswalds in June.
[2] Miss Zagórska's French translation, Yale University Library.
[3] On Jessie Conrad's knee.

To Miss Aniela Zagórska (2 *June* 1924)

I am not working—I cannot. This rather worries me. But let it remain strictly between us.

Jessie and I kiss you affectionately.

Always yours
KONRAD.

104. *To Stefan Pomarański*[1]

Oswalds,
Bishopsbourne, Kent.
28th June, 1924.

Dear Sir,

Your letter and your 'present'[2] which is so dear to me have arrived and I thank you with all my heart. I shall reply more fully soon, when I have recovered my health which has not been behaving at all well lately. At the moment I am feeling a little better, and I may say that the matter you mention is very much on my conscience. It is not the first time that I have received such reflections from Poland—sometimes from very eminent fellow countrymen. I understand them and appreciate them. *Your letter will not remain unanswered.*[3]

With regard to the matter of electing me an honorary member of the Polish Geographical Society, about which you wrote to me some time ago, I naturally have nothing against it. I am afraid however that my services do not justify your action. I shall shortly send you the note you ask for about my life, my travelling, and activities. I shall also ask for your assistance in becoming a literary member of the Kasa im. Mianowskiego,[4] in regard to which I have received Żeromski's beautiful appeal.

[1] *Ruch Literacki*, 1926, No. 7.
[2] Stefan Pomarański (1893–1944), an historian, sent Conrad a manuscript of Apollo Korzeniowski's poem 'Zgliszcza' (The Cinders) and some other relics.
[3] In the only preserved letter to Conrad (of 22 June 1924, now in Yale University Library), to which the above is apparently the answer, Pomarański wrote 'you seem very foreign to me' and ended with a request: 'I should like this collection to return to Poland some day. . . . For us in Poland it will always be a sacred national relic.' However, 'the matter' mentioned by Conrad was obviously of a more general nature. Pomarański himself explained, when publishing Conrad's letter, that the problem in question—perhaps raised in some other letter of his—was Conrad's return to Poland, and he interpreted the underlined sentence (here italicized) as expressing the writer's wish to do so. There is no other evidence to support this hypothesis, apart from Jessie Conrad's assertion that at the end of his life Conrad frequently talked about going back to Poland and settling there. (*Joseph Conrad and his Circle*, London, 1935, p. 363.)
[4] Józef Mianowski (1804–79) was a well-known physician and pedagogue. In his memory a foundation to support research in science and the humanities was established in 1881.

With regard to the manuscripts of my father you can be at ease. In particular the pencil portrait from those days is very dear to me. I shall try to recompense you one day for that present.

Please accept for the moment a hearty handshake from

KONRAD KORZENIOWSKI.

CONRAD'S POLITICAL
MEMORANDUM
(1914)

[POLITICAL MEMORANDUM]¹

Feeling convinced that all European problems [must be] can be settled only [only by means of a Congress of all the States] after a general armistice by a congress of all the states concerned, my intentions are:

Generally: [At least] To bring up and accustom the public in England to the thought that Poles are entitled to have their *nationality* legally recognized both by the defeated as by the victorious states.

England would have no reason to object to such a recognition, which would have a legal basis, a high moral significance, and practical consequences, and in fact she may be persuaded to support this issue on the grounds of elementary justice.

And particularly: to support and develop goodwill towards Austria (this feeling already existed in July and was expressed by some daily papers). To point out that England is not and never has been engaged in any personal quarrel with Austria; to endeavour to create an atmosphere of favourable public opinion by explaining that the policy of Austria under the strong pressure of Russia was a result of hard necessity and was in no way symptomatic of some unjust ambition of territorial expansion—but nevertheless stressing the point that after many years of patient, cautious, and peaceful policy, Austria would be entitled to be rewarded for her efforts in this war.

It would be my concern to state the last point clearly for the following reason:

I am convinced that during the Congress various coalitions of states will form themselves. It may happen therefore that during the diplomatic negotiations the support of England will be advantageous to Austria. Not so much directed against Russia, of course (although there is no special sentiment for Russia in England) as rather against the pressure of an ally in a matter concerning the partition of a conquered territory, i.e. in particular that of Poland. Public opinion and Parliamentary circles in England may be prepared towards giving Austria such diplomatic support; e.g., the leaders of the Labour Party [as well as the prominent members] and the Conservative Party, and also some prominent members of the Liberal Party, and influential newspapers in both camps.

¹ The manuscript of this memorandum, drafted by Conrad in September 1914, is in the possession of Dr. Teodor Kosch's family in Cracow. Words crossed out by Conrad are given in square brackets.

Conrad's Political Memorandum (1914)

I shall base my argument on two facts: (1) That Germany cannot be defeated now. (2) That England, even if left on her own, will be able to harass Germany [strongly] acutely and for a long time; for there can be no doubt as to England's superiority at sea and the spirit of that country has not changed much since the time of the Napoleonic wars.

Hence, the word of England will always carry some weight in the final settlement of European problems.

Basing myself on these two facts, I intend to point out that although Germany (Prussia) cannot be defeated it may, to some extent, be subdued; and the only way to achieve that is by supporting [of Austria] Austria's claims concerning Polish territories so as to strengthen the anti-German elements in that empire in order to achieve a balance of power against Prussian influence in Europe. In this particular respect, England cannot count on Russia, firstly, because Russia will be defeated and secondly (and mainly!) because Prussia and Russia may, in the near future, be united.

It will be, therefore, in the interest of England to support an Austrian policy towards Poland (even on otherwise unfavourable conditions) and to strengthen the Polish national spirit which is hostile towards the Germans in that Monarchy which in fact can never become dangerous for England, either economically or politically, and as it is one where parliamentary institutions, so highly cherished by the English nation, are [the most] better developed than in any other European country.

STANISŁAW BOBROWSKI, *d.* 1796
m. KATARZYNA BŁAŻOWSKA

MIKOŁAJ, *b.* 1782

JÓZEF, *b.* 1790 *d.* 1850
m. TEOFILA BIBERSTEIN-PILCHOWSKA
(sister of KONSTANCJA KOPROWSKA)

JOHANNA, *b.* 1794

SALOMEA, *b.* 1796

MICHAŁ

STANISŁAW *b.* 1827 *d.* 1859

TADEUSZ *b.* 1829 *d.* 1894
m. JÓZEFA LUBOWIDZKA

KAZIMIERZ *d.* 1868

EWA, *b.* 1833 *d.* 1865
m. APOLLO KORZENIOWSKI

TEOFILA *b.* 1834 *d.* 1851

STEFAN *b.* 1840 *d.* 1863

JÓZEFA, *b.* 1858 *d.* 1870

JÓZEF TEODOR KONRAD KORZENIOWSKI *b.* 1857 *d.* 1924

KAZIMIERZ   MARTA   MARIA   STANISŁAW   TADEUSZ   MICHAŁ   ZUZANNA

305

x

TEODOR KORZENIOWSKI, *d.* 1863
m. JULIA DYAKIEWICZ

ROBERT	HILARY	APOLLO, *b.* 1820
d. 1863	*d.* 1873	*d.* 1863
		m. EWA BOBROWSKA

JÓZEF TEODOR KONRAD
b. 1857
d. 1924
m. JESSIE GEORGE

BORYS   JOHN

BIBLIOGRAPHY

The following selective bibliography contains the books and articles most relevant for a study of Conrad's Polish background. For further bibliographical information see:

KENNETH A. LOHF and EUGENE P. SHEEHY, *Joseph Conrad at Mid-Century*; *Editions and Studies, 1895–1955*, University of Minnesota Press and O.U.P., 1957.

PIOTR GRZEGORCZYK, *Józef Conrad w Polsce* [Joseph Conrad in Poland], Warsaw, 1932.

LUDWIK KRZYŻANOWSKI, 'Joseph Conrad. A Bibliographical Note', in: *Joseph Conrad: Centennial Essays*, ed. L. Krzyżanowski, The Polish Institute of Arts and Sciences in America, New York, 1960.

A good selection of Polish writings on Conrad is edited by Barbara Kocówna: *Studia i wspomnienia o Conradzie* [Conrad: Studies and reminiscences], Warsaw, 1963. Items marked with an asterisk below are contained in this anthology.
Unless otherwise stated, the place of publication of Polish books and periodicals is Warsaw.

BAINES, JOCELYN. *Joseph Conrad: A Critical Biography*, London, 1960.

BLÜTH, RAFAŁ M. 'Dwie rodziny kresowe' [Two borderland families], *Ateneum*, 1939, No. 1.

BOBROWSKI, TADEUSZ. *Pamiętniki* [Memoirs], 2 vols., Lvov, 1900.

BOROWY, WACŁAW. 'J. Conrad sędzią polskiego przekładu swojej noweli "Il Conde"' [J. Conrad as a judge of a Polish translation of his short story "Il Conde"], *Zeszyty Wrocławskie*, Wrocław, 1951, No. 1.

BUSZCZYŃSKI, STEFAN. *Mało znany poeta* [A little known poet (on Apollo Korzeniowski)], Cracow, 1870.

CHWALEWIK, WITOLD. 'Józef Conrad w Kardyfie' [Joseph Conrad at Cardiff], *Ruch Literacki*, 1932, No. 8.

—— 'Conrad and the Literary Tradition', *Kwartalnik Neofilologiczny*, 1958, No. 1/2.

COLEMAN, ARTHUR P., 'Polonisms in the English of Conrad's "Chance"', *Modern Language Notes*, 1931, No. 9.

*CZOSNOWSKI, STEFAN, 'Conradiana', *Epoka*, Cracow, 1929, No. 136 (contains reminiscences of Zygmunt Radzimiński and Tekla Wojakowska).

DĄBROWSKA, MARIA. *Szkice o Conradzie* [Essays on Conrad], 1959.

DĄBROWSKI, MARIAN. 'Rozmowa z J. Conradem' [A talk with J. Conrad], *Tygodnik Illustrowany*, 1914, No. 16.

*DYBOSKI, Roman. 'Z młodości Józefa Conrada' [From J. Conrad's youth'], *Czas*, Cracow, 1927, No. 345 (reminiscences of Jadwiga Kałuska).

*—— 'Spotkanie z Conradem' [Meeting Conrad], *Czas*, Cracow, 1932, No. 71.

—— 'Pierwiastki angielskie a pierwiastki polskie w umysłowości Conrada' [English and Polish elements in Conrad's mentality], *Księga pamiątkowa ku czci Mariana Zdziechowskiego*, Cracow, 1933.

GILLON, ADAM. *The Eternal Solitary*, New York, 1960.

GOMULICKI, WIKTOR. 'Polak czy Anglik?' [A Pole or an Englishman?], *Życie i Sztuka*, Petersburg, 1905, No. 1.

HERLING-GRUDZIŃSKI, GUSTAW. 'W oczach Conrada' [In Conrad's eyes], *Kultura*, Paris, 1957, No. 10.

JABŁKOWSKA, RÓŻA. *Joseph Conrad*. Wrocław, 1961.

Bibliography

JASIENICA, PAWEŁ. *Biały front* [The White front (on Stefan Bobrowski and the 1863 insurrection)], 1954.

JEAN-AUBRY, C. *Joseph Conrad: Life and Letters*, 2 vols., London, 1927.

KLEINER, JULIUSZ. 'Oddźwięk ballady mickiewiczowskiej w opowieści Conrada' [Echoes of Mickiewicz's ballad in a tale by Conrad], *Dziennik Literacki*, Cracow, 1949, No. 19.

*KOCÓWNA, BARBARA. 'Żywa tradycja Conradowska' [The living Conrad tradition], *Przegląd Humanistyczny*, 1961, No. 1.

KRZYŻANOWSKI, JULIAN. 'U źródeł publicystyki Conrada' [On the sources of Conrad's political journalism], *Ruch Literacki*, 1932, No. 8.

KRZYŻANOWSKI, LUDWIK. 'Joseph Conrad's "Prince Roman": Fact and Fiction', in: *Joseph Conrad: Centennial Essays*.

—— 'Joseph Conrad: Some Polish Documents', ibid.

MIŁOSZ, CZESŁAW. 'Conrad in Polish Eyes', *Atlantic Monthly*, Dec. 1957.

NAJDER, ZDZISŁAW. 'Polskie lata Conrada' [Conrad's Polish years], *Twórczość*, 1956, No. 11.

—— 'Conrad Under Polish Eyes', *Polish Perspectives*, Warsaw, 1958, No. 1.

*PERŁOWSKI, JAN. 'O Conradzie i Kiplingu' [On Conrad and Kipling], *Przegląd Współczesny*, 1937, No. 4.

PETERKIEWICZ, JERZY. 'Patriotic Irritability', *Twentieth Century*, Dec. 1957.

RACZYŃSKI, EDWARD. 'Spotkanie w poselstwie w Londynie' [A meeting in the London legation], *Wiadomości*, London, 1949, No. 33/4.

RAKOWSKA-ŁUNIEWSKA, IRENA. 'U Konrada Korzeniowskiego' [At Konrad Korzeniowski's home], *Pion*, 1934, No. 50.

RETINGER, JÓZEF HIERONIM. *Conrad and his Contemporaries*, New York, 1943.

TABORSKI, ROMAN. *Apollo Korzeniowski*. Wrocław, 1957.

TARNAWSKI, WIT (ed.). *Conrad żywy* [The living Conrad], London, 1957 (particularly essays by Paweł Hostowiec, Czesław Miłosz, and Tymon Terlecki).

UJEJSKI, JÓZEF. *O Konradzie Korzeniowskim*, 1936; French trans., *Joseph Conrad*, Paris, 1939.

WOHLFAHRT, PAUL. 'War Joseph Conrad ein englischer Dichter ?', *Germanoslavica*, 1936, No. 4.

ZAGÓRSKA, ANIELA. 'Conrad a literatura polska' [Conrad and Polish literature], *Wiadomości Literackie*, 1924, No. 33.

—— 'Conrad a Polska' [Conrad and Poland], *Wiadomości Literackie*, 1924, No. 36.

*—— 'Kilka wspomnień o Conradzie' [A few reminiscences on Conrad], *Wiadomości Literackie*, 1929, No. 51.

ZAGÓRSKA, KAROLA. 'Pod dachem Konrada Korzeniowskiego' [Under Konrad Korzeniowski's roof], *Kultura*, 1932, Nos. 2, 3.

ZUBRZYCKA, T. [pseud. of Mrs. Otolia Retinger]. 'Syn dwu ojczyzn. Ze wspomnień o Józefie Conradzie-Korzeniowskim' [Son of two fatherlands. Some reminiscences on Joseph Conrad-Korzeniowski], *Iskry*, 1931, Nos. 8–10.

*ŻEROMSKI, STEFAN. 'Joseph Conrad.' Introduction to: J. Conrad, *Pisma wybrane*, Warsaw, 1923.

Z. S. (TADEUSZ ŻUK-SKARSZEWSKI). 'Conradiana', *Poland*, Chicago, 1926, Nos. 8–11; 1927, Nos. 1, 8.

The only attempt at a synthesis should be mentioned separately: G. MORF's erratic and by now almost entirely obsolete study, *The Polish Heritage of Joseph Conrad*, London, 1930.

INDEX OF NAMES AND TITLES

(Conrad's writings are indexed under the entry for Conrad.)

Index of Names and Titles

Index of Names and Titles

Index of Names and Titles

PRINTED IN GREAT BRITAIN
AT THE UNIVERSITY PRESS, OXFORD
BY VIVIAN RIDLER
PRINTER TO THE UNIVERSITY